AQA Spanish
Higher

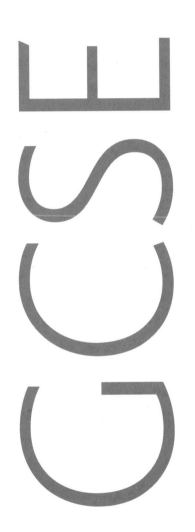

Jackie Coe
Christine Dalton
Vincent Everett
John Halksworth
Abigail Hardwick
Ana Kolkowska
María Candelaria Rodríguez Lorenzo
Samantha Lunn
María Dolores Giménez Martínez
Libby Mitchell
Fiona Wilson

Nelson Thornes

First edition published in 2009 by Nelson Thornes Ltd

This edition published in 2013 by:
Nelson Thornes Ltd
Delta Place
27 Bath Road
CHELTENHAM
GL53 7TH
United Kingdom

13 14 15 16 17 / 10 9 8 7 6 5 4 3 2 1

A catalogue record for this book is available from the British Library

ISBN 978 1 4085 2182 3

Cover photograph: Carmen Martínez Banús / iStockphoto
Illustrations by Kathy Baxendale, Mark Draisey, Dylan Gibson, Celia Hart, Abel Ippolito
and Dave Russell
Page make-up by Hart McLeod, Cambridge
Printed and bound in Spain by GraphyCems

Contents

4   Contents

Context – Home and environment, Topic 5 – Home and local area
5.1 Home 5.2 Local area and region 5.3 Life at home and special occasions

Context – Home and environment, Topic 6 – Environment
6.1 Current problems facing the planet 6.2 Local issues and action

Reading

Learning vocabulary

Writing

Getting ready for the exam

Building grammar knowledge

Listening

Developing exam strategies

Speaking

Understanding how the exam works

The AQA GCSE Spanish exam is divided into four main subject areas, called **Contexts**. This book is divided up in the same way, with colour coding to help you know where you are. Each Context is divided into two **Topics**, making a total of eight Topics to study during the course.

| Lifestyle | Leisure | Home and environment | Work and education |

The exam is divided up according to the four **Language Skills**: Listening, Speaking, Reading and Writing. Each one of these has its own separate exam, either in the form of an end-of-course paper or as a Controlled Assessment.

Writing (30%) (Controlled Assessment)

Listening (20%) (Exam)

Speaking (30%) (Controlled Assessment)

Reading (20%) (Exam)

AQA GCSE Spanish

📖 Reading

The Student Book contains plenty of Spanish reading material on the kind of subjects that come up in the GCSE exam. A headphones icon means the texts are also recorded so that you can compare the spoken and written word. The activities that follow the reading passages are similar to the types of questions you'll encounter in the exam.

🎧 Listening

Some activities only have a headphones icon. This means they're for developing listening skills and you won't see the words written down. The recordings are available from the Kerboodle book – just click on the icon next to the activity. A few of these recordings also exist as video, to help to bring the Spanish language alive.

🗨 Speaking

Your ability to speak in Spanish accounts for 30% of your final mark. In every Topic there are activities that are designed to build up the skills you need for your Speaking Controlled Assessment while using the language you have just learnt.

✏️ Writing

Many students think that Writing is the hardest part of the exam, but it doesn't have to be if you are properly prepared. Each Topic contains carefully structured tasks that will help you to develop the skills you need to maximise your grade.

Ⓥ Learning vocabulary

You can't get away from the fact that vocabulary has to be learnt in order to do well in the exam, so we are giving you help with this in various different ways.

- Vocabulary lists – For each section where new language is introduced there is a list of up to 20 useful words that come up in the tasks. There are also recordings to help you learn to pronounce each word correctly. Why not start by learning these?
- Vocabulary tasks – Every Foundation spread starts with a vocabulary activity. You might work

on these together as a class, or you can use them for practice and revision at home.

- Context lists – AQA have made lists of words that come up in their exams, one for each of the four subject areas or Contexts. We have put these lists in Kerboodle and added English translations.
- Interactive activities – If you learn well by getting instant feedback, why not try out the vocabulary builder in Kerboodle?

Ⓖ Building grammar knowledge

Understanding grammar is the key to building your own phrases. AQA GCSE Spanish helps you to consolidate your grammar knowledge in a logical way.

- Grammar boxes outline the grammar points you need to know for the exam.
- Activities next to the boxes provide instant practice, before you have had time to forget what you have just read.
- Interactive grammar activities in Kerboodle give you more practice.
- There is a Grammar section with verb tables at the back of the Student Book, to refer to whenever you need to.

Desde hace

Use *desde hace* + present tense to say how long you have been doing something.

Estoy casado desde hace dos años. – I have been married for two years.

Gramática pág

Language structure boxes

These tables provide the scaffolding you need to construct different sentences for Speaking and Writing. On Kerboodle you will find editable versions matched to most of the Student Book Topics, allowing you to get creative by adding your own ideas and vocabulary items.

Me Mi		nombre	llamo es	Carla
Tengo	un dos	hermano/a(s) tío/a(s) primo/a(s) perro(s) gato(s)	que se llama ... que se llaman ...	y pero

 **Enlace** **Accessing Groundwork Student Book pages**

Where you see this link icon in your book, this means you can access Groundwork pages, offering more basic activities and grammar practice for revision or catch-up work, directly from your Higher Kerboodle Book.

Developing exam strategies

Getting a good grade at GCSE Spanish is not just about how much you know; it is also about how you apply this knowledge in the exam. Throughout the book you will find strategy boxes that are linked to exam-type activities. Read them carefully and use the suggestions to help you improve your grade.

Use pictures to help you focus

The pictures in questions 1 and 2 tell you whereabouts in the advert to focus. The fact that for both questions there is a (3) means that each time there is only one item that is not mentioned. Make sure you write down three letters each time.

Estrategia 1a

Getting ready for the exam

At the end of each Context, you will find an Exam Practice section. There are four of these in the book. They give you:

- further practice in the sort of Reading and Listening questions you will meet in the exam
- recaps on Reading and Listening strategies, plus a few new ones
- some sample tasks for Speaking and Writing Controlled Assessments, with example answers
- exam technique advice to explain everything you need to know about AQA Controlled Assessments
- some Grade boosters to tell you what you need to do to push up your grade.

Grade booster

To reach grade A, you need to ...

- Write 40 to 50 words per bullet point, conveying a lot of relevant information clearly, e.g. bullet point 1. You could give a lot of details here. Limit yourself to 40–50 words and focus on quality of communication.
- Be generally accurate in your attempts at complex sentences and verb tenses.

Kerboodle offers an innovative, blended range of products to help engage teachers and students alike. It can be purchased as a whole learning solution or in parts, depending on the needs of each school, college, department and learner.

Kerboodle for AQA GCSE Spanish includes differentiated resources focused on developing key grammar, vocab, listening, reading and writing skills. These engaging and varied resources include videos of native speakers, self-marking tests, listening activities with downloadable transcripts, interactive vocabulary builders, practice questions with study tips and comprehensive teacher support.

Our AQA GCSE Spanish Kerboodle resources are accompanied by online interactive versions of the Student Books. All your Kerboodle resources are embedded to open directly from the book page.

Where appropriate there are links to support Groundwork and Higher activities.

Find out more at www.kerboodle.com

Log into Kerboodle at live.kerboodle.com

How old you are, where you live

1 📖🎧 Match up each sentence 1–6 with the correct photo A–F.

1 Tengo quince años.
2 Tengo veinte años.
3 Tengo tres años.
4 Tengo ocho años.
5 Tengo cuarenta y cinco años.
6 Tiene once meses.

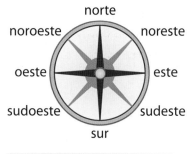

0	cero	11	once
1	uno	12	doce
2	dos	13	trece
3	tres	14	catorce
4	cuatro	15	quince
5	cinco	16	dieciséis
6	seis	17	diecisiete
7	siete	18	dieciocho
8	ocho	19	diecinueve
9	nueve	20	veinte
10	diez		

2 ✏️ Look at the map of Spain, then copy the sentences and fill in the gaps with the correct point of the compass.

Ejemplo: Mérida está en el <u>oeste</u> de España.

1 Vivo en Málaga. Está en el _____ de España.
2 Soy de Bilbao, una ciudad grande en el _____ de España.
3 La capital de España, Madrid, está en el _____ del país.
4 Sevilla, en el _____ de España, es una ciudad muy histórica.
5 La arquitectura de Barcelona, en el _____ de España, es muy conocida.
6 ¿Conoces Alicante? Es una ciudad muy turística en el _____ de España.

norte
noroeste · noreste
oeste · este
sudoeste · sudeste
sur

| en el sur | in the south |
| en el centro | in the centre |

Months, days, dates and times

Fechas y celebraciones en Gran Bretaña

El primero de **enero** es un día festivo y una oportunidad para celebrar con la familia.

El catorce de **febrero** es el Día de San Valentín para los novios y parejas enamoradas.

Un domingo en **marzo** es el Día de la Madre.

El primero de **abril** es el Día de los Inocentes.

El primero de **mayo** es el Día del Trabajo.

En **junio** hay el Día del Padre.

En **julio** y **agosto** hay vacaciones escolares.

El cinco de **noviembre** hay fuegos artificiales y una fogata.

Los niños reciben sus regalos de Navidad el veinticinco de **diciembre**.

La hora

las doce

menos cinco		y cinco
menos diez		y diez
menos cuarto		y cuarto
menos veinte		y veinte
menos veinticinco		y veinticinco
y media		

son las (doce) = it is (12) o'clock

a las (doce) = at (12) o'clock

BUT *es la* una = it is 1 o'clock

a la una = at 1 o'clock

24-hour times

13.10 = *a las trece diez*

18.20 = *a las dieciocho veinte*

20.15 = *a las veinte quince*

1 📖 🎧 Read the calendar of dates. Which special days that we celebrate in the UK are mentioned?

2 ✏️ Write a list of birthdays that are important to you. You can write the numbers in figures.

Ejemplo: *Mi cumpleaños es el 22 de abril.*
My birthday is on the 22nd of April.

El cumpleaños de mi (madre) es el uno / primero de septiembre.
My (mother)'s birthday is on the 1st of September.

3 ✏️ Put the days of the week into the correct order, starting with Monday.

miércoles   sábado   lunes
jueves   domingo   viernes   martes

4 📖 Match up each time mentioned with the correct clock face.

1 Nos vemos <u>a las cinco</u>.

2 La película empieza <u>a la una y media</u>.

3 ¿Qué hora es? <u>Son las seis y cuarto</u>.

4 ¡Rápido! <u>Son las ocho menos cuarto</u>.

5 El tren sale <u>a las diecisiete diez</u>.

6 Nos encontramos <u>a las tres y cinco</u>.

A   B   C   D   E   F   G   H   I

Classroom equipment, colours

1a ✏️ Copy the sentences and fill in the gaps with *el, la, los* or *las*.

1 Cierra _____ puerta, por favor.
2 Abrid el libro y mirad _____ páginas 12 y 13.
3 Primero hay que leer _____ texto.
4 No os olvidéis de hacer _____ deberes.

1b ✏️ Match up the Spanish sentences 1–4 in Activity 1a with their English translations below.

a First you have to read the text.
b Open the book and look at pages 12 and 13.
c Don't forget to do your homework.
d Close the door, please.

2 📖🎧 Match up each sentence with the correct picture.

1 ¿Puedo ir al lavabo?
2 Siento llegar tarde.
   Perdí el autobús.
3 No entiendo la pregunta.
   ¿Podría repetirla, por favor?

3 📖 Look at the pictures. Which box, A or B, does each item 1–8 appear in?

Ejemplo: 1 B

1 un bolígrafo rojo
2 un sacapuntas rojo
3 un estuche negro y rojo
4 una goma verde
5 un estuche amarillo
6 una goma blanca y azul
7 unos lápices grises
8 una regla amarilla

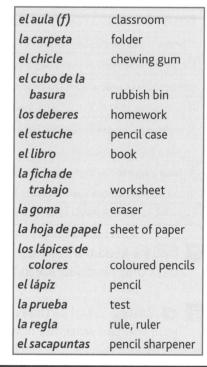

el aula (f)	classroom
la carpeta	folder
el chicle	chewing gum
el cubo de la basura	rubbish bin
los deberes	homework
el estuche	pencil case
el libro	book
la ficha de trabajo	worksheet
la goma	eraser
la hoja de papel	sheet of paper
los lápices de colores	coloured pencils
el lápiz	pencil
la prueba	test
la regla	rule, ruler
el sacapuntas	pencil sharpener

Gramática · página 174

Articles: *el, la, los, las*

The Spanish word for 'the' agrees with the noun that follows:

el libro – the book   *los libros* – the books
la pizarra – the board   *las pizarras* – the boards

Articles: *un, una, unos, unas*

The words for 'a / an' (singular) and 'some' (plural) also agree with the noun that follows:

un libro – a book   *unos libros* – some books
una pizarra – a board   *unas pizarras* – some boards

Gramática · página 174

Colours and agreement of adjectives

Colours are adjectives. They agree with the word they describe: *un estuche amarillo, unos bolígrafos azules, una carpeta negra.*

All numbers, dates

1 👄✏️ Work with a partner. Partner A writes down six numbers and reads them out. Partner B writes them down. Check the numbers together, then swap roles.

2 📖🎧 Match up the dates.

1 1/11   2 20/8   3 31/12

a   el veinte de agosto
b   el treinta y uno de diciembre
c   el primero de noviembre

3 📖🎧 Read the speech bubbles and answer the questions in English.

1   a   When is Sebastián's birthday?
    b   When is Carlota's birthday?
2   a   What date is the village festival this year?
    b   What date was the village festival last year?
3   a   What date does the new school term start?
    b   When does José Carlos get back from holiday?

> Mi hermano Sebastián y yo somos gemelos. Yo nací primero, a las 23h52 el siete de julio y él nació a las 00h06 del día siguiente, el día ocho.

> El último día de curso es el 24 de junio. Las clases no empezarán otra vez hasta el tres de septiembre. Me voy de viaje casi todo el mes de agosto, desde el día dos hasta el veintinueve.

Carlota   **Gerardo**   **José Carlos**

> La fiesta de mi pueblo se celebra el primer domingo del mes de agosto. Este año cae el día dos pero el año pasado cayó el día uno.

20	veinte
21	veintiuno (veintiuna)
30	treinta
31	treinta y uno (treinta y una)
40	cuarenta
50	cincuenta
60	sesenta
70	setenta
80	ochenta
90	noventa
100	cien, ciento
101	ciento uno (ciento una)
200	doscientos (doscientas)
300	trescientos/as
400	cuatrocientos/as
500	quinientos/as
600	seiscientos/as
700	setecientos/as
800	ochocientos/as
900	novecientos/as
1000	mil
1002	mil dos
2000	dos mil
5000	cinco mil
10,000	diez mil
1,000,000	un millón
2,000,000	dos millones

4 ✏️ Look at the following pictures and dates. Use the words under each picture to write a description of what happens on each date.

Ejemplo: El 22 de septiembre es el cumpleaños de María. Lo celebramos con una tarta.

22/9 celebrar – cumpleaños – tarta

8/4 restaurante – abrir – cena

17/8 vacaciones – avión – Mallorca

Numbers

Numbers 16 to 29 are written as one word, e.g. *diecisiete*.

For compounds of *ciento* note the spelling of *quinientos*, *setecientos* and *novecientos*.

y is used between the tens and unit digits: 146 *ciento cuarenta y seis*.

The word *mil* is never pluralised in a specific number and is never preceded by *un*: 2012 *dos mil doce*.

But: *Había miles de personas en la plaza de toros.*

The word *millón* is pluralised and is used with *un* in the singular: *un millón*, *cinco millones*.

Dates

el primero / uno *de* agosto	1st August
el dos *de* abril *del* dos mil quince	2nd April 2015

Gramática   *página 188*

Spanish pronunciation

🎧 It is not hard to produce the correct sounds for a good Spanish accent.

The most important thing to remember is that all Spanish vowels are short:

a	as in *casa*	o	as in *como*
e	as in *tengo*	u	as in *su*
i	as in *si*		

🎧 Then there are some patterns of letters which make these sounds:

ca co cu	hard 'c' (before 'a', 'o' or 'u') sounds like the English 'k' e.g. *caro, costumbre, cultivar*
ce ci z	soft 'c' (before 'e' or 'i') and the letter 'z' sound like 'th' e.g. *doce* (do**th**eh); *cinco* (**th**inkoh); *diez* (die**th**)

NB In Latin America these are pronounced like an 's'.

ch	sounds like English 'ch' in 'chop' e.g. *chica*
ga go gu	hard 'g' (before 'a', 'o' or 'u') sounds like English 'g' in 'got' e.g. *gato, gordo, gusto*
ge gi j	soft 'g' (before 'e' or 'i') and the letter 'j' sound like an 'h' produced from the back of the throat e.g. *geografía, gimnasia, jamón*
h	the letter 'h' is always silent in Spanish e.g. *¡Hola!*
ll	the double consonant 'll' sounds like 'y' e.g. *me llamo* (meh yamo)
ñ	accented 'ñ' sounds like 'ny' e.g. *España*
qu	always sounds like 'k' and never like 'kw' in Spanish e.g. *¿Qué tal?*
r	within a word always pronounced more strongly than in English, try to 'roll' or 'growl' it slightly e.g. *enero*
r	at the beginning of a word, *rr* within a word should be rolled quite strongly if you can e.g. *Roberto, perro*
v	at the beginning of a word sounds like 'b' e.g. *veinte*

1 Now try saying these well-known Spanish-speaking places with the correct accent:

Barcelona   Argentina   Lanzarote
Venezuela   Mallorca

🎧 **The alphabet sounds**

A	ah	B	beh	C	theh
CH	cheh	D	deh	E	eh
F	efeh	G	jeh (back of your throat)	H	atcheh
I	ee	J	jota	K	kah
L	eleh	LL	eyeh	M	emeh
N	eneh	Ñ	enyeh	O	oh
P	peh	Q	koo	R	erreh
RR	erreh dobleh	S	eseh	T	teh
U	oo	V	ooveh	W	ooveh dobleh
X	ehkees	Y	eh greeyega	Z	thetah

Typing Spanish accents and punctuation

When typing in Spanish make sure you change the language by clicking on:

Tools > Language > Set language > Spanish (Spain – Traditional Sort)

The punctuation for *¿* and *¡* should then appear automatically.

The easiest way to get the accents on vowels is by pressing the Ctrl and @ keys at the same time, then remove your fingers from the keys and press the letter you want: *á; é; í; ó; ú*. To get the *ñ* you have to click on: Insert > symbol > then find *ñ*.

In addition to short cuts given for *á, é, í, ó* and *ú, ñ* can be produced by pressing Ctrl / Shift / @ then 'n'; *¿* can be produced by pressing Ctrl / Shift / ALT / '?'; and *¡* can be produced by pressing Ctrl / Shift / ALT / '!'.

Alternatively, to type accents you can hold down the ALT key and type the appropriate number on the number pad. Make sure that the Number Lock is on. You can't do this on laptops.

160 = á	130 = é	161 = í	162 = ó
163 = ú	164 = ñ	168 = ¿	173 = ¡

Using a dictionary

Stress

Stress when pronouncing a language does not have the same meaning as 'being stressed out'. Stress is where you put the emphasis on a word, e.g. in English we say 'com**pu**ter' not '**com**puter'.

In Spanish the stress rules are:

- if a word ends in a vowel, an *n* or *s*: stress the second to last syllable.

  e.g. Bar / ce / **lo** / na   ex / **am** / en   **chi** / cos

- for words ending in the other consonants: stress the last syllable.

  e.g. pa / **pel**   pro / fe / **sor**   co / **mer**

- **BUT** some words don't follow these rules, so there is an accent to show you where to put the emphasis.

  e.g. ma / te / **má** / ti / cas   es / ta / **ción**
  jó / ven / es (but *joven* – no accent needed)

Note that all words ending in *-ón* and *-ión* need an accent on the *o*.

■ Using a dictionary

Spanish > English

- Make sure that you find the meaning that makes sense for the particular sentence you are translating. Many Spanish words have more than one meaning, e.g. *el tiempo* = time **and** weather. Some words mean different things in different Spanish-speaking countries as well.

- If you are trying to work out the meaning of a verb, you will have to find the infinitive in the dictionary (ending in *-ar*, *-er* or *-ir*) and then look at the verb ending to work out the person and tense of the verb.

  e.g. *grabaron* > *grabar* = to record

English > Spanish

- Make sure you know whether the word you need is a noun (a person, place or thing), a verb (usually an action) or an adjective (describes a noun).

- Sometimes the word in English can be the same.

Example of dictionary layout

Ignore the words in [ ]. They are to show Spanish speakers how to pronounce the English word.

light [laÎt] n. *luz* f.

English word | n. = noun | the Spanish noun 'light' | f. = feminine (you will need *la luz* for 'the light' and *una luz* for 'a light')

light [laÎt] adj. *ligero* (not heavy); *claro* (colour)

adj. = adjective | the Spanish adjectives for 'light' (two meanings)

light [laÎt] vt. *encender*

vt. = verb | the Spanish verb 'to light' (i.e. 'to light a candle')

- It is very important to understand that a dictionary will help you to find individual words but you have to use your knowledge of how the Spanish language works in order to put a sentence together. Very often the way a phrase is said is completely different from the English, e.g. *Me gusta el chocolate* literally means 'the chocolate pleases me', but we would say 'I like chocolate'.

- The most common mistake people make when using a dictionary is thinking that they can translate something literally word for word, without realising if the Spanish they have looked up is a noun, verb or adjective. The result can be quite funny for an English speaker who knows Spanish, but a Spanish speaker won't understand anything.

1 See if you can work out what the student wanted to say, then try to produce the correct version:

Yo lata la obra de teatro fútbol.

- *Yo* ('I') – not usually used with the verb
- *lata* ('can') – noun, e.g. a can of drink
- *la obra de teatro* ('play') – noun, e.g. a play at the theatre
- *fútbol* (football) – noun
  Correct version: *puedo jugar al fútbol.*
  puedo ('I can' – irregular verb, present tense);
  jugar (infinitive of verb 'to play'); *al fútbol* (*al* needed after *jugar* with a sport).

1.1 F La dieta

1 **V** Decide whether the following items of food are healthy or unhealthy.

el agua	las hamburguesas	el arroz	el atún
las patatas fritas	la fruta	el pastel	los guisantes
el salchichón	la pasta	la naranjada	el pescado
la cerveza	el perrito caliente	la ensalada

sana (*healthy*)	malsana (*unhealthy*)
el agua	

2a 📖 🎧 Read the article. Then read the following sentences and find the three that are true.

1 Fátima no bebe té.
2 A Ángel le encanta la sopa.
3 Eli come mucha fruta y chocolate.
4 Marga come mucha comida sana.
5 La comida favorita de Javier es la comida basura.
6 A Fátima le gusta mucho la ensalada.

Estrategia 2a–2b

Picking out key words when reading

Watch out for words which can change the meaning of a sentence, like: *poco* – not very; *demasiado* – too (much).

El chocolate es poco saludable. – Chocolate is **not very** healthy.

La comida basura es demasiado barata. – Junk food is **too** cheap.

Bebo bastante agua con el almuerzo. – I drink **quite a lot of** water with my lunch.

Me gustan mucho los mariscos. – I like seafood **very much**.

Para el desayuno como mucha fruta y cereales. También bebo bastante agua, pero no bebo demasiado zumo. No como pasteles, pero me gusta mucho comer chocolate para el almuerzo.
Eli 16 años

Para el almuerzo me encanta tomar verdura y pollo. No me gusta nada la comida basura. Para la cena mi comida favorita es la sopa.
Ángel 13 años

Soy vegetariano, detesto la comida basura. Me encantan las verduras, la fruta y beber mucho té. La comida sana me encanta
Javier 15 años

No como verduras, sopa o fruta. No me gustan nada. La comida rápida no es sana, pero me encantan los perritos calientes y las patatas fritas. Para el almuerzo como un poco de pollo y bebo mucha agua con gas.
Marga 14 años

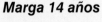

No soy vegetariana, pero no como carne de cerdo. Soy musulmana. Me encantan las patatas, la carne de cordero y la ensalada. Para la cena no me gusta comer pescado. Bebo mucho té y zumo de fruta.
Fátima 15 años

2b 📖 🗨 Now tell your partner four facts about your own eating habits including things you like and don't like.

Ejemplo:

> No como carne pero no soy vegetariana. Me gusta mucho comer pescado. Me encantan también las verduras. No bebo té o café. Bebo zumo de fruta, de naranja o de manzana.

3 🄶 Copy the sentences and fill in the gaps with the appropriate adjective and ending from the list below.

1 El pescado es _____.
2 Los cereales son _____ para el desayuno.
3 El chorizo es _____, pero tiene mucha grasa.
4 Las patatas fritas son muy _____ para la salud.
5 En México hay muchos platos _____, como el chile con carne.
6 La sangría es una bebida muy _____ de España.

delicioso	ideales	típica	sano
picantes	deliciosas	sanas	malas

4a 🎧 Listen to five people talking about their diet. Decide if they eat a healthy diet (**H**), an unhealthy diet (**U**) or a mixture of the two (**H + U**).

1 Ana   **2** Carolina   **3** Juan   **4** María   **5** José

4b 🎧 Listen again and write notes in English to back up your answer. The first one has been done to help you.

Ejemplo: Ana = U because loves fast food. Goes to pizza / hamburger places a lot.

5 ✏ Write a paragraph similar to those in the article opposite, but about yourself.

- Say what you like to eat and drink.
- Give information about your diet, saying whether it is healthy / unhealthy or a mixture.
- Mention something you don't like or don't eat.

Me gusta / Me encanta	comer	la comida rápida / el pescado / las verduras / la fruta / el chocolate.
	beber	el café / el té / el zumo de fruta.
Mi dieta	(no) es (bastante / muy)	sana / saludable.
Soy / No soy	vegetariano/a.	
(No) Como	la carne de cerdo / los mariscos / los productos lácteos.	
(No) Bebo	las bebidas alcohólicas / el café.	

Gramática *página 174*

Making adjectives agree

Adjectives ending in *-o*:

el pescado es sano (masculine)

los cereales son sanos (masculine plural)

la fruta es sana (feminine)

las verduras son sanas (feminine plural)

Other adjectives stay the same for the singular and add *-s* or *-es* for the plural.

Some adjectives are irregular, e.g. nationalities. See page 175

Also learn how to form *-er* verbs, like *beber* and *comer*, in the present tense.

See page 28

 **Enlace**

1.1 Groundwork is available in the Foundation book.

1.1 H Dietas diferentes

Objetivos

Comparing different diets

Using the verb *ser* (to be)

Picking out key words when listening

A Normalmente como hamburguesas, perritos calientes, patatas fritas y pizza todos los días. Me gusta mucho la comida rápida. Mi dieta no es muy sana, pero es barata y deliciosa. También es muy fácil de seguir. Detesto la ensalada, las verduras y todo tipo de fruta. En mi opinión, los vegetarianos son muy raros.

B Mi dieta es muy sana. Como mucho pescado normalmente porque soy vegetariana. El pescado es importante en mi dieta porque contiene proteínas. España es ideal, porque el pescado es muy bueno y hay muchos mariscos. Los mariscos son deliciosos, pero muy caros. Como muchas verduras también – ¡son muy ricas y baratas!

C Mi dieta es limitada porque no hay supermercados en la selva. Como mucho pescado y mucha fruta. Claro, ¡el pescado y la fruta son muy frescos! Mi plato favorito es el plátano frito y es muy típico aquí. También bebo 'chicha'. La chicha es una bebida alcohólica preparada con yuca (un tipo de patata) y saliva. Para los turistas, la idea es horrible. En mi opinión, es una bebida deliciosa.

D Mi nueva dieta es muy difícil para mí. Para el desayuno tomo cereales con fruta y bebo un zumo de naranja. Para el almuerzo como pescado o pollo con ensalada porque no contienen mucha grasa y son saludables. Bebo agua mineral. Finalmente, para la cena tomo sopa y un yogur. La dieta es aburrida y no me gusta nada. Prefiero comer chorizo, tortilla y tapas, pero contienen mucha grasa y no son saludables.

Elena

Antonio

Javier

Luisa

1a 📖🎧 Match up each speech bubble with the correct name. Write A, B, C, D and the name of the person.

1b 📖🎧 Write the name of the person who …

1 eats salad.
2 eats cheap, unhealthy food.
3 drinks something strange.
4 loves seafood.
5 doesn't like their diet.
6 catches their own fish.
7 likes typical Spanish, non-vegetarian food.

2 🄶 Translate the following sentences into English.

Ejemplo: La fruta es deliciosa. – *Fruit is delicious.*
(Note that in Spanish you say: '<u>The</u> fruit is delicious'.)

1 Soy inglés.
2 Mi dieta es sana.
3 ¿Eres español?
4 Los perritos calientes son horribles.
5 Somos vegetarianos.
6 Mis amigos son divertidos.
7 Usted es muy inteligente.

Using the verb *ser* (to be)

SINGULAR	PLURAL
soy – I am	*somos* – we are
eres – you are	*sois* – you (plural) are
(*¿eres?* – are you?)	(*¿sois?* – are you?)
es – he / she / it is	*son* – they are
mi padre es – my father is	*mis amigos son* – my friends are
Also: *usted es* – you (formal) are	*ustedes son* – you (formal, plural) are

There are two verbs meaning 'to be' in Spanish: *ser* and *estar*.

For more information about *estar*, see page 187.

Ser describes a person, place or thing that is permanent and does not change from day to day:

Soy inglés. – I am English.

Also learn how to form regular and irregular adjectives. *See page 29*

Gramática *página 187*

3 🎧 Listen to Carlos, a marathon runner, talking about what he normally does before a race. Listen carefully to the details and answer the following questions in English.

1   What does Carlos eat and drink just before a run?
2   What does he do after breakfast?
3   Why does Carlos need to rest after breakfast?
4   Why do runners have to eat or drink during a run?
5   When does Carlos eat chocolate? How much chocolate does he have? (2)
6   What kind of fish does he normally eat?
7   What does he never eat or drink? (2)

> **Picking out key words when listening**
>
> When there are questions in English at Higher level, you need to listen carefully because there are sure to be some details in there that you are expected to notice. Also check whether some questions have a number after them. This indicates that you need to give more than one piece of information.

Estrategia 3

4 💬 Work with a partner. Take turns to be A and B. It is healthy-eating week at school.

Change the underlined parts to fit the pictures and try to add reasons as to why what is eaten is healthy. Award up to 10 points for being healthy.

A Para el desayuno tomo <u>cereales</u>.

B Los <u>cereales</u> son sanos. ¡Muy bien! ¡Ocho puntos!

A Para la cena como <u>pollo y patatas fritas</u>. No como <u>fruta</u>.

B Las <u>patatas fritas</u> son malas. ¡Un desastre! ¡Tres puntos!

(No) Como	cereales / tostadas / huevos / pollo / pescado / sopa / verduras / patatas fritas	para	el desayuno / el almuerzo / la cena.
(No) Bebo	café / té / leche / agua		
El pollo / El pescado La fruta / La sopa	es		sano / rico / picante / ideal. sana / rica / picante / ideal.
	contiene / tiene		mucha grasa / mucha proteína / mucho azúcar.
Los cereales / Los huevos Las hamburguesas / Las patatas fritas / Las verduras	son		sanos / ricos / picantes / ideales. sanas / ricas / picantes / ideales.
	contienen / tienen		muchas proteínas / muchas vitaminas.

1.2 F — Buenos y malos hábitos

1 ⓥ Choose which statement you agree with most and write down **a**, **b** or **c**.

		a	b	c
1	Prefiero comer	fruta.	pasteles.	chocolate.
2	Detesto beber	gaseosas.	agua.	café.
3	Prefiero acostarme	antes de las 10.	después de medianoche.	antes de las 11.
4	Es necesario evitar	el tabaco.	el ejercicio.	la comida basura.
5	Es importante	estar en forma.	comer mucho.	relajarme.
6	Me gusta más	hacer ciclismo.	ir al cine.	ir a la discoteca.

Si la a es tu respuesta favorita, eres como Gabriela:

Para mí es importante comer y beber cosas sanas y quiero mantenerme en forma. Me gusta dormir bien, pero no demasiado porque así es posible estar aún más cansada. Odio los malos hábitos como el tabaco.

Conclusión: ¡Enhorabuena! La alimentación buena es necesaria. Sabes lo que es bueno y malo para tu cuerpo. Quieres llevar una vida sana y activa.

Si la b es tu respuesta favorita, eres como Marta:

Me encanta comer y tomo bastante comida rápida y gaseosas. Soy joven y necesito energía, ¿no? No soy muy deportista y creo que hacer ejercicio es realmente aburrido y difícil. Prefiero salir con mis amigos o jugar en el ordenador hasta medianoche.

Conclusión: ¿Quieres morir joven? Tu rutina es un desastre para el cuerpo. Tienes que comer más sano y dormir más. Otra cosa: el ejercicio es necesario para tener energía – las gaseosas, no. Se pueden hacer muchos deportes divertidos con tus amigos. Es importante cambiar tus hábitos AHORA.

Si la c es tu respuesta favorita, eres como Juan:

Quiero llevar una vida sana, pero es difícil. No tengo hábitos muy malos como el fumar. Tengo que estudiar mucho y no tengo tiempo para practicar deportes. Además el chocolate es necesario para motivarme.

Conclusión: Tienes buenas intenciones, pero es necesario hacer más para estar en forma. Se pueden hacer muchas actividades activas como parte de tu rutina normal. Comer un poco de chocolate no es un problema, pero es importante también comer frutas y verduras. ¡Tienes que hacer un esfuerzo, hombre!

2a 📖 🎧 Read the key to the magazine quiz. Then read the following statements and find the four that are true.

1 Gabriela eats a healthy diet.
2 Gabriela is a heavy smoker.
3 Marta needs more sleep.
4 Marta needs to do more exercise.
5 Marta is a very energetic person.
6 Juan has stopped smoking.
7 Juan doesn't have much time to study because he practises sport.
8 Juan doesn't have enough time to exercise.

Using cognates to help you work out meaning

One way to help you work out the meaning of a text is to look for words that are similar in English and Spanish. Although the meaning might not be exactly the same, it is likely to be similar. These words are called **cognates**, e.g. *rápida* (rapid, quick), *chocolate* (chocolate), *practicar* (to practise).

Estrategia 2a–2b

2b 📖 🎧 What three pieces of advice are given to Marta and Juan?

3a Ⓖ Read the key to the magazine quiz again and make two lists of infinitives, one of normal infinitives and another of reflexive infinitives.

> *Ejemplo:*   *comer* (normal infinitive)
> *mantenerme en forma* (*mantenerse en forma*)
> (reflexive infinitive)

3b Ⓖ Match up these key Spanish verbs with their English equivalent.

1 Odio / Detesto …	a You can …
2 Me gusta …	b I want …
3 Quiero …	c I like …
4 Tengo que …	d I hate …
5 Se puede …	e I have to …

3c Ⓖ Translate these sentences into Spanish.

1 I hate eating fruit, but I like drinking water.
2 It's important to sleep well and to have a healthy diet.
3 I have to do more sport.
4 You can avoid bad habits.

4a 🎧 People call *el médico Miguel* on his radio show. What are they worried about? Choose one option from this list for each of the four people.

sleeping	drinking	diet	smoking

not being fit	feeling ill	feeling stressed

4b 🎧 Listen again. What advice does Miguel give to each person?

5a 📖 Pick a team: the 'Superfits' or the 'Sofa Slobs'.

'Superfits' team:
- Write a list of things you do to lead a healthy lifestyle.
- Now write some negative comments about the 'Sofa Slobs' team and also write some advice for them.

'Sofa Slobs' team:
- Write a list of things you do to lead an unhealthy lifestyle.
- Now write some negative comments about the 'Superfits' team and give them some advice.

5b 🗨 Use your lists to argue with the other team and prove that your lifestyle is the best. You can do this with a partner or in groups.

Gramática · página 186

Using verbs with the infinitive

The first verb shows who is doing the action:

quiero (I want)
prefiero (I prefer)
tienes que (you have to)
¿quieres …? (do you want?)

The second verb goes in the infinitive (ending in -ar, -er or -ir):

jugar (to play / playing)
comer (to eat / eating)
hacer (to do / doing)
dormir (to sleep / sleeping)

Reflexive verbs end in -*se*:

e.g. *Es importante mantenerse en forma.*

But if you talk about yourself:

Quiero mantenerme en forma.

For more on using reflexive verbs in the infinitive, see page 28.

 **Enlace**

1.2 Groundwork is available in the Foundation book.

1.2 H ¿Te mantienes en forma?

Objetivos
Keeping fit
Using *tener* in different ways
Listening for negative expressions

1a 📖 🎧 Read the advert and find the Spanish equivalents of these words and phrases. Look at the glossary at the back of the book when you have finished, to check you have got them right.

1 (you) can enjoy
2 best place
3 (we) help you look after
4 daily
5 on the seafront
6 (you) cannot miss
7 Moreover
8 Soon

1b 📖 🎧 Four different people think they might like to visit the spa at Playa Caleta. Decide which paragraph from the advert would convince them to go to there. Match up each person 1–4 with the correct paragraph A–D.

1 My husband and I practise sports daily. We need to keep fit since we have heart problems.

2 My doctor says I need to change my diet. In order to do that, I need to learn more about what makes up a healthy diet.

3 I am a doctor and I probably work too hard. I need to relax and switch off.

4 I hate going to the gym! I find them quite claustrophobic, with tiny windows and always crowded.

Spa en Playa Caleta

A ¿Tienes mucho trabajo? ¿Necesitas un masaje? Entonces visita nuestro spa. Aquí puedes disfrutar de una estupenda piscina, un gimnasio y un restaurante donde preparan magníficos platos internacionales. Nuestro spa es el mejor lugar para relajarse y olvidar los problemas. Además, se adapta a las necesidades de los clientes.

B Te ayudamos a cuidar tu cuerpo y mantenerte en forma a través del agua. ¡Ven a nuestra piscina, aprende y practica con nuestros profesores! Haciendo ejercicio diariamente puedes evitar, por ejemplo, ataques cardíacos. También puedes disfrutar de un buen masaje antes de ir a casa.

C Si prefieres entrenar y realizar ejercicios de más esfuerzo, visita el gimnasio de nuestras instalaciones, ¡en primera línea de mar! Practicar deporte, ver la playa desde las enormes ventanas y poder respirar el aire del mar. ¡Es una experiencia que no te puedes perder!

D Y si tu alimentación no es bastante sana o simplemente quieres disfrutar de una comida exquisita, ven a nuestro magnífico restaurante. ¡Cuídate y olvida la comida basura! Aquí tenemos todo lo que puedes desear. Además, tu cuerpo necesita una buena alimentación para estar sano y ser feliz. Así que, si lo deseas, te enseñamos a llevar una dieta sana en nuestros estupendos cursos todos los fines de semana.

¡Esperamos tu visita muy pronto!

2a 🄶 Copy the sentences and fill in the gaps using the verb *tener*. In order to conjugate the verb correctly you must think about the number of people involved in the action.

Ejemplo: María y yo (nosotros) tenemos frío.

1 Los deportistas _____ mucha hambre después de hacer ejercicio.

2 ¿_____ (tú) calor? ¡Claro, es verano!

3 Corro diez kilómetros cada mañana, salgo muy temprano y _____ frío. Siempre llevo un jersey.

4 Ese chico practica el baloncesto desde hace mucho tiempo. Ahora _____ 20 años.

5 Después de hacer ejercicio por la tarde, nos relajamos y _____ sueño.

2b **G** Copy and complete the sentences with words from the grammar box. They are all expressions that you can use with *tener*.

1 Tengo mucha ____. ¿Tienes un poco de agua, por favor?
2 Pedro tiene mucha _____ y es muy buen jugador. Siempre gana al ajedrez.
3 ¡Lo siento, no podemos hablar ahora contigo! Marcos y yo tenemos ____.
4 La nueva película de Tarantino tiene bastante _____.
5 No me gusta estar solo en casa. Tengo mucho _____.

3 🎧 Listen to three people saying why they go to health spas, what they do and don't do there, and how they feel after their visits. Then read the statements below and find the five that are true.

Speaker 1
1 I can only visit the spa once a month.
2 I forget all my problems when I am swimming; I like the feeling of the water around me.
3 I don't like having a massage.

Speaker 2
4 I go to the spa to relax, but I also do quite a bit of exercise in the gym.
5 I have to make a great effort to go to the swimming pool.
6 I feel good when I get back home from the spa.

Speaker 3
7 I don't like going to the spa very much, but it is good for my health.
8 Someone helps me do some exercises in the swimming pool.
9 I love swimming because it helps me relax my arms and legs.
10 Doing exercise in the gym is dangerous for my back.

4 🖉 Imagine you are a very well-known sports personality (you choose the sport). You have been asked to contribute to a health magazine. Include in your article:

■ the things you do to keep fit
■ the things you eat to keep fit
■ your reasons for these choices
■ things that you don't do or eat
■ your reasons for these choices.

Gramática *página 187*

Using *tener* in different ways

First check that you can conjugate *tener* by looking at page 194 of the verb tables. *Tener* can have different meanings when used in certain expressions:

tener (15) años	to be (15) years old
tener calor	to be hot
tener frío	to be cold
tener hambre	to be hungry
tener sed	to be thirsty
tener miedo	to be frightened
tener sueño	to be tired
tener prisa	to be in a hurry
tener éxito	to be successful
tener suerte	to be lucky
tener dolor de (cabeza / estómago, etc.)	to have a (head)ache / (stomach)ache, etc.

Also learn about making a sentence negative.
See page 29

Estrategia 3

Listening for negative expressions

Listen carefully for negative words in Spanish. They change the meaning of the sentence and therefore can catch you out.

***Nunca** practico deporte.* – I never practise sports.

*No me gusta **mucho** el pescado.* – I don't like fish very much.

*No me gusta **nada** la comida basura.* – I don't like junk food at all.

1.3 F Tu opinión es muy importante

Objetivos

Opinions about tobacco, alcohol and drugs

Using comparative adjectives

Expressing your opinion in different ways

1 ⓥ Work with a partner. Take turns to read the following statements from a web debate. Decide if you agree or not.

1 El alcohol es más adictivo que las drogas.
2 El tabaco es menos adictivo que la droga dura.
3 La rehabilitación es mejor para los drogadictos que la cárcel.
4 El cannabis es peor para la salud que el alcohol.
5 La droga blanda es tan peligrosa como la droga dura.
6 El tabaco causa tantas enfermedades como el alcohol.
7 La cocaína causa más problemas que los cigarrillos.
8 Las drogas causan más problemas sociales que el alcohol.

Ana

En España hay más fumadores que en toda Europa (a excepción de Grecia). Tradicionalmente el tabaco forma una parte importante de la vida social en los bares y cafeterías. Los adolescentes observan a los adultos y quieren imitarles.

Pero ahora existe mucha más información sobre los peligros del tabaco. Además, es más difícil fumar con las restricciones de la Ley Anti-Tabaco porque no se puede fumar en los sitios públicos.

Los jóvenes dan su opinión sobre el tabaquismo:

No fumo y no me gusta el tabaco. Creo que es un hábito muy malo y el olor es asqueroso. Los cigarrillos causan muchos problemas de salud: cáncer, enfermedades cardíacas y problemas respiratorios. Además el fumar pasivo nos afecta a todos. Es muy preocupante.

Javier

Mi padre fuma 20 cigarrillos al día. Sé que es difícil dejar de fumar y en mi opinión el tabaco es demasiado barato.

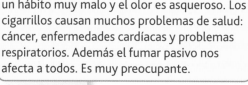

En el instituto mis profesores hablan mucho del tabaco y las consecuencias para el corazón y los pulmones. No es saludable, claro, pero mis amigas fuman en la discoteca y quiero hacer lo mismo. Sólo fumamos dos o tres cigarrillos los sábados por la noche. No causan mucho daño.

Nuria

2 📖 🎧 Match up each person with the correct statement. Write **A** (Ana), **J** (Javier) or **N** (Nuria).

1 'It's a worrying health issue.'
2 'I want to be the same as the others.'
3 'The price should be increased.'
4 'We are given plenty of information about smoking.'
5 'Giving up smoking is not easy.'

Using comparative adjectives

When making comparisons you can use:

más + adjective or noun + *que* – more … than
menos + adjective or noun + *que* – less … than
mejor que – better than
peor que – worse than
tan + adjective + *como* – as … as
tanto(a) + singular noun + *como* – as much … as
tantos(as) + plural noun + *como* – as many … as
e.g. *El zumo de fruta es más sano que la cerveza.* – Fruit juice is more healthy / healthier than beer.

Also learn how to form *-ar* verbs in the present tense. *See page 28*

Gramática *página 175*

3 **G** Copy the sentences and fill in the gaps with *más*, *menos*, *mejor*, *peor*, *tan*, *tanto(s)* or *tanta(s)*.

1 El alcohol es _____ caro en Inglaterra que en España.
2 La droga blanda es _____ adictiva que la droga dura.
3 Las drogas causan _____ problemas para la sociedad como para el individuo.
4 El agua es _____ que el alcohol para la salud.
5 El alcohol es _____ peligroso como el tabaco.
6 La violencia por drogas en Colombia es _____ que en España.

4a 🎧 You are going to hear four parts (a–d) of a TV debate about drugs and alcohol. Match up each part with one of the summaries (1–6).

1 Drug rehabilitation isn't working.
2 Alcohol abuse is getting worse.
3 Soft drugs should be legalised.
4 A lot of crime is drug-related.
5 Alcohol abuse can cause depression.
6 Drugs are too easily available.

4b 🎧 Listen again and answer the following questions in English.

1 Why does the woman think there are more problems with alcohol nowadays?
2 Why is the man more worried about drugs and drug addicts? (2)
3 Why does the man think that drug rehabilitation is useless?
4 What is the man's opinion about where drug addicts should be?

5 🖊 You are taking part in a web debate. In groups, write some threads of conversation from a forum on smoking, alcohol and drugs. Include:

- your opinion
- some facts about alcohol, smoking and drugs
- comparisons between dangers of drugs, alcohol and tobacco
- some questions.

El alcohol El tabaco	(no) es	más menos tan	adictivo/a peligroso/a	como que	el alcohol. la droga.
La rehabilitación	es	menos más	útil cara	que	la cárcel.
Las drogas Los borrachos	(no) causan	más menos	problemas accidentes	que	los fumadores.
Los fumadores Las drogas		tanto(s) tanta(s)	problemas	como	los borrachos. los drogadictos.

Expressing your opinion in different ways

Estrategia 5

Try to add some of these to your dialogue:

- *Creo que / Pienso que / Opino que / Me parece* – I think that
- *En mi opinión* – In my opinion
- *Me da igual* – I don't care
- *Estoy de acuerdo* – I agree
- *Estoy a favor (de)* – I am in favour (of)
- *Estoy en contra (de)* – I am against

 **Enlace**

1.3 Groundwork is available in the Foundation book.

1.3 H ¡Elige unos hábitos correctos!

1a 📖 🎧 Read the blogs from two young people living in Spain and Peru. Then find the Spanish equivalents of these words and phrases in the text.

1 nowadays
2 to get drunk
3 more expensive … than
4 … are there so many …
5 I know
6 … pays better than …

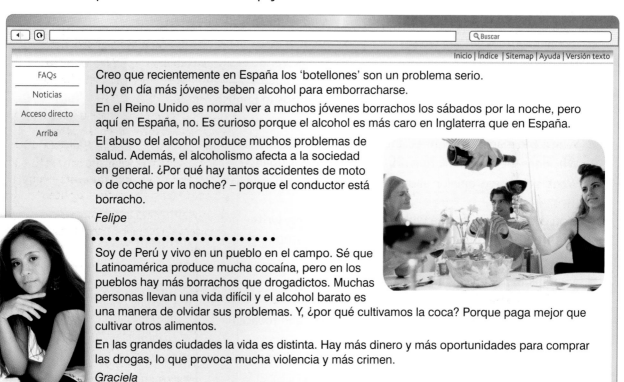

Inicio | Índice | Sitemap | Ayuda | Versión texto

🔍 Buscar

FAQs
Noticias
Acceso directo
Arriba

Creo que recientemente en España los 'botellones' son un problema serio.
Hoy en día más jóvenes beben alcohol para emborracharse.

En el Reino Unido es normal ver a muchos jóvenes borrachos los sábados por la noche, pero aquí en España, no. Es curioso porque el alcohol es más caro en Inglaterra que en España.

El abuso del alcohol produce muchos problemas de salud. Además, el alcoholismo afecta a la sociedad en general. ¿Por qué hay tantos accidentes de moto o de coche por la noche? – porque el conductor está borracho.

Felipe

Soy de Perú y vivo en un pueblo en el campo. Sé que Latinoamérica produce mucha cocaína, pero en los pueblos hay más borrachos que drogadictos. Muchas personas llevan una vida difícil y el alcohol barato es una manera de olvidar sus problemas. Y, ¿por qué cultivamos la coca? Porque paga mejor que cultivar otros alimentos.

En las grandes ciudades la vida es distinta. Hay más dinero y más oportunidades para comprar las drogas, lo que provoca mucha violencia y más crimen.

Graciela

1b 📖 🎧 Read the blogs again and decide if the following statements are true (**T**), false (**F**) or not mentioned in the text (**?**).

Felipe says that …
1 now more young people get drunk in Spain.
2 there are strict laws about under-age drinking.
3 alcohol is more expensive in Spain than in the UK.

Graciela thinks that …
4 there is a serious drug problem in her town.
5 drugs cause violence and crime.

2 **G** Copy the sentences and fill in the gaps with the correct form of the verb in brackets. If you think it might be irregular, check to see if it is listed on pages 191–194. If it isn't listed, assume it is regular.

1 Carmen _____ una dieta sana. (llevar)
2 Mi hermana y yo _____ cada día al gimnasio. (ir)
3 Mis amigos _____ que fumar droga es muy peligroso. (decir)
4 La droga no _____ tan importante en España como en Colombia. (ser)
5 Mis padres nunca _____ alcohol. (beber)
6 Mi amigo Pedro _____ dos cigarrillos al día. No es un gran fumador. (fumar)

3a 🎧 Listen to three people giving their opinions on the smoking ban in public places. For each speaker, decide whether their comments on the subject are positive (**P**), negative (**N**) or positive and negative (**P + N**).

1 Carmen   2 Ricardo   3 Yolanda

3b 🎧 Listen again and answer the following questions in English.

1 Why does Carmen think the smoking ban is not fair for smokers? (2)
2 Is Ricardo a smoker? How do we know this?
3 How does Ricardo think the smoking ban could be made fairer for smokers?
4 Does Yolanda go out more or less with her friends than she used to? How do we know this? (2)
5 In what way does Yolanda think the smoking ban could be improved?
6 Why does she think the smoking ban may be positive for smokers?

4 🗨 You are conducting a survey with sixth-form students from your Spanish-speaking link school in a video-conference. Work with a partner: Partner A asks the questions and Partner B takes on the role of the student answering them.

A ¿Fumas?   **B** No, no fumo.

A ¿Fuma alguien en tu familia?   **B** Mis amigos no fuman, pero mi padre fuma veinte cigarrillos al día.

A ¿Cuál es tu opinión sobre el tabaco?   **B** Creo que es horrible porque los cigarrillos causan muchos problemas de salud.

Gramática *página 180*

Present tense verbs – regular and irregular

There are three groups of regular verbs in Spanish: *-ar*, *-er* and *-ir*. The endings of the present tense regular verbs are given at the very beginning of the verb tables on page 190. The verbs given there are *hablar*, *comer* and *vivir*, but you can transfer their endings onto any regular verbs.

e.g. *Él nada en la piscina todos los días.* – He swims in the swimming pool every day.

Ramón bebe un zumo de naranja. – Ramón is drinking an orange juice.

Este restaurante prohíbe fumar en su terraza. – This restaurant forbids smoking on its terrace.

To find the present tense of irregular verbs, look them up on the other pages of the verb tables (pages 191–194). Remember that you can't take your verb tables into the exam – you need to learn the endings by heart!

Also learn more about common patterns in regular present tense verbs. *See page 29*

Estrategia 3b

Inferring meaning when listening

For the Higher listening, when there are English questions, you are sometimes expected to infer meaning (work something out) rather than just find the right piece of information and translate it into English. Here is an example from Activity 3b:

4 Does Yolanda go out more or less with her friends than she used to? How do we know this? (2)

She says that because of the smoking ban she now goes out with her friends every weekend. This implies that before the smoking ban, she did not go out as often as this, so you can work out that she now goes out more often.

You will find one more example of this type of question in Activity 3b.

(G) Health

1 Copy out the following message and fill in the gaps with the correct part of the *-er* verbs in brackets.

Me llamo Javier. _____ (comer) mucha fruta y _____ (beber) mucha agua. Mi amigo, Felipe _____ (comer) demasiadas patatas fritas y mis amigos Juan y Pepe _____ (beber) mucha Coca-Cola, que no es bueno para la salud.

Y tú, ¿qué _____ (comer) y _____ (beber) normalmente?

(G)ramática página 180

Regular -er verbs

To find the present tense endings, look at the regular verb tables on page 190. The order given is always the same: I, you, he /she, we, you (pl.), they.

come – he / she eats
mi padre bebe – my father drinks

2 For each sentence, work out and write down the appropriate infinitive from the options below. Don't forget to change the *-se* to *-me* or *-te* if necessary.

1 Es necesario _____ por la dieta.
2 Es importante _____ después de hacer ejercicio.
3 Prefiero _____ temprano.
4 Tengo que _____ a las 7 todos los días para ir a trabajar.
5 ¿Quieres _____? ¡Ve al gimnasio!

preocuparse (*to worry*)

dormirse (*to go to sleep*)

relajarse (*to relax*)

mantenerse en forma (*to keep fit*)

levantarse (*to get up*)

(G)ramática página 185

Infinitives of reflexive verbs

Reflexive verbs have *-se* on the end, e.g. *mantenerse en forma* (to keep fit).

If you are talking about yourself, this changes to *-me*:

Quiero relajarme. – I want to relax.

For talking to someone, use *-te*.

Debes acostarte temprano. – You should go to bed early.

3 Choose the appropriate verb form to complete these sentences.

Ejemplo: **1** No fumo.

1 No fuma / fumas / fumo porque no me gusta el olor. (*I*)
2 ¿Fumamos / Fumas / Fuma? – Yo, no. (*You singular*)
3 El tabaco afecta / afecto / afectan a muchas personas. (*Smoking*)
4 Los cigarrillos causáis / causan / causa cáncer. (*Cigarettes*)
5 Necesito / Necesitan / Necesitamos una prohibición total. (*We*)
6 ¿Evito / Evitamos / Evitáis todos los cigarrillos? ¡Muy bien! (*You plural*)

(G)ramática página 180

Regular -ar verbs

To find out the present tense endings, look at the regular verb tables on page 190.

Fumar, causar, necesitar and all other regular *-ar* verbs follow the same pattern as *hablar*.

No fumamos regularmente. – We do not smoke regularly.

4 Make up some sentences using these adjectives: *frito, sano, picante, asado, salado, dulce, sabroso, vegetariano, azul, nacional, español.*

> **ⓖramática** *página 174*
>
> **Regular and irregular adjectives**
>
> Remember that regular adjectives end in -*o* (m), -*a* (f) or -*e* (m and f). All of these have an -*s* on the end for plural nouns.
>
> Some adjectives ending in -*l (azul, nacional)* are the same with masculine and feminine nouns.
>
> Nationality nouns ending in -*l (español)* have a feminine form with an -*a (española).*
>
> Both types have -*es* when describing plural nouns.
>
> *La tortilla española es un plato nacional famoso.* – Spanish omelette is a famous national dish.

5 Copy the sentences below and fill in the gaps with *no, nunca* or *nada.* Use the English words in brackets to help you. Then translate the sentences into English.

1 _____ voy a la piscina. _____ me gusta porque siempre hay mucha gente. (*never, don't*)

2 Mi dieta _____ es muy sana. Como demasiada grasa. (*not*)

3 '¿Te gusta beber alcohol los fines de semana?' '_____ me gusta _____. Detesto el alcohol.' (*not at all*)

4 _____ como comida basura porque tengo que mantenerme en forma. (*never*)

5 _____ me gusta _____ ir al gimnasio. ¡Es aburrido! (*not at all*)

6 _____ fumo. _____ me gusta el olor del tabaco. (*never, don't*)

> **ⓖramática** *página 186*
>
> **Using different negative forms**
>
> Make sure you use the correct negative form: *no* (not), *nunca* (never), *nada* (not at all, nothing). Sometimes you need to use two in Spanish, where you would only use one in English.
>
> *No como carne nunca.* – I never eat meat.
>
> If you start the sentence with *nunca*, you don't need the *no*.
>
> *Nunco como carne.*

6 Copy the sentences and fill in the gaps with the correct form of the verb in brackets.

1 Mi madre y yo _____ dejar de fumar. (querer)

2 Hoy en día muchos jóvenes _____ los fines de semana. (beber)

3 Mis amigos nunca _____ droga. (consumir)

4 Carlos solo _____ tres o cuatro cigarrillos a la semana. (fumar)

5 _____ demasiada cerveza. Sabes que no es muy bueno para tu salud. (tomar)

6 (Yo) _____ cada día en un cuaderno los ejercicios que hago en el gimnasio. (escribir)

> **ⓖramática** *página 180*
>
> **Present tense verbs – common patterns**
>
> Learn the endings for the regular -*ar* verbs like *fumar* and *hablar* by heart:
>
> -*o*, -*as*, -*a,*- *amos*, -*áis*, -*an*
>
> Remember to take the -*ar* off before adding the endings.
>
> Also learn the endings for regular -*er* verbs, like *comer* and *beber*:
>
> -*o*, -*es*, -*e*, -*emos*, -*éis*, -*en*

Health

Topic 1.1 You are what you eat

1.1 F La dieta ➡ *pages 16–17*

el	arroz	rice
el	atún	tuna
la	cerveza	beer
el	chocolate	chocolate
la	comida basura	junk food
la	ensalada	salad
los	guisantes	peas
la	hamburguesa	hamburger
la	manzana	apple
los	mariscos	seafood
la	naranja	orange
el	pastel	cake
las	patatas fritas	chips / crisps
el	perrito caliente	hot dog
el	plátano	banana
el	pollo	chicken
el	salchichón	salami-style sausage
	sano/a	healthy
el	té	tea
	vegetariano/a	vegetarian

1.1 H Dietas diferentes ➡ *pages 18–19*

el	alcohol	alcohol
la	alimentación	food
el	azúcar	sugar
la	barra (de pan)	loaf of bread
la	bebida	drink
la	carne	meat
los	calamares	squid
el	chorizo	spicy sausage
la	comida	meal / food / lunch
la	comida rápida	fast food
	delicioso/a	delicious
	fresco/a	fresh
	glotón / glotona	greedy

Learning new vocabulary

As you work through Topic 1, refer to these vocabulary pages to help you find out what new words mean. There is one list for each sub-topic. To help you to learn the words, try covering the English words and testing yourself, or asking a friend to test you. You might like to download the audio file to help you with pronunciation. Find ways of learning that work for you, such as spotting connections with English: *la fruta* is like 'fruit'. How many other connections can you find?

la	grasa	fat
el	jamón (de york)	(cooked) ham
el	jamón serrano	cured ham
la	merluza	hake
	sabroso/a	tasty
las	tapas	snacks / tapas
la	zanahoria	carrot

Topic 1.2 How healthy are you?

1.2 F Buenos y malos hábitos ➡ *pages 20–21*

	activo/a	active / energetic
la	bebida con gas	fizzy drink
	bueno/a	good
	cansado/a	tired
el	deporte	sport
	deportista	sporty
	dormir	to sleep
el	ejercicio	exercise
	estar en forma	to be fit
	evitar	to avoid
	fumar	to smoke
	malo/a	bad
el	(gran) fumador	(heavy) smoker
	necesario/a	necessary
	odiar	to hate
	practicar	to practise / do
	preferir	to prefer
	relajarse	to relax
la	rutina	routine
el	tabaco	tobacco

1.2 H ¿Te mantienes en forma? ➡ *pages 22–23*

	aprender	to learn
el	*ataque cardíaco*	heart attack
el	*cigarrillo*	cigarette
el	*corazón*	heart
	correr	to run
	cuidar	to look after / take care
	enérgico/a	energetic
	entrenar(se)	to train
el	*esfuerzo*	effort
	estar estresado/a	to be stressed
	estupendo/a	wonderful
el	*gimnasio*	gym
	hacer aerobic	to do aerobics
	lograr	to achieve / get / manage
	mantenerse en forma	to keep fit
el	*masaje*	massage
	necesitar	to need
	peligroso/a	dangerous
	poco/a	a little / few
el	*trabajo*	work

Topic 1.3 Tobacco, alcohol and drugs

1.3 F Tu opinión es muy importante
➡ *pages 24–25*

el	*accidente*	accident
	barato/a	cheap
	caro/a	expensive
	dañar	to damage / harm
el	*daño*	damage / harm
	dejar de + inf.	to stop
la	*depresión*	depression
la	*droga dura / blanda*	hard / soft drug
los	*lugares públicos*	public places
	morir	to die
	muerto/a	dead
	negativo/a	negative
	positivo/a	positive

	prohibido/a	prohibited / forbidden
	prohibir	to prohibit / forbid
	recomendar	to recommend
	robar	to steal
la	*salud*	health
	útil	useful
	violento/a	violent

1.3 H ¡Elige unos hábitos correctos!
➡ *pages 26–27*

	adecuado/a	appropriate / suitable
	aumentar	to increase
el	*cáncer*	cancer
el	*consumidor*	consumer
	consumir	to take / consume
el	*consumo*	consumption
la (una)	*copa*	(a) drink / cup / trophy
los	*derechos*	rights
el	*drogadicto*	drug addict
el	*fumador pasivo*	passive smoker
los	*jóvenes*	young people
el	*olor*	smell
	olvidar	to forget
el	*peligro*	danger
el	*porro*	joint / spliff
	respiratorio/a	respiratory
el	*riesgo*	risk
el	*síndrome de abstinencia*	withdrawal symptoms
la	*sustancia química*	chemical substance
el	*tabaquismo*	smoking

2.1 F   Me llevo muy bien con mi familia

1a 🅥 Read the following adjectives. Copy them out, sorting them into two separate lists: 'appearance' and 'character'.

| amable | calvo | delgada | fuerte | feliz | pelirroja | triste |

| rizado | aburrida | alegre | egoísta | azul | hablador | corto |

| orgulloso | castaño | perezoso | tímida | gorda | largo |

1b 🅥 Read the adjectives again. Say whether each one is masculine (**M**), feminine (**F**) or could be either (**M / F**).

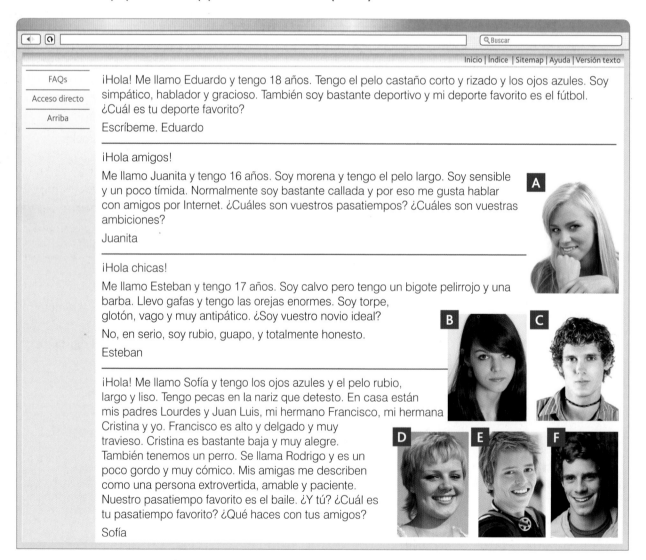

🔍 Buscar

Inicio | Índice | Sitemap | Ayuda | Versión texto

FAQs

Acceso directo

Arriba

¡Hola! Me llamo Eduardo y tengo 18 años. Tengo el pelo castaño corto y rizado y los ojos azules. Soy simpático, hablador y gracioso. También soy bastante deportivo y mi deporte favorito es el fútbol. ¿Cuál es tu deporte favorito?

Escríbeme. Eduardo

¡Hola amigos!

Me llamo Juanita y tengo 16 años. Soy morena y tengo el pelo largo. Soy sensible y un poco tímida. Normalmente soy bastante callada y por eso me gusta hablar con amigos por Internet. ¿Cuáles son vuestros pasatiempos? ¿Cuáles son vuestras ambiciones?

Juanita

¡Hola chicas!

Me llamo Esteban y tengo 17 años. Soy calvo pero tengo un bigote pelirrojo y una barba. Llevo gafas y tengo las orejas enormes. Soy torpe, glotón, vago y muy antipático. ¿Soy vuestro novio ideal?

No, en serio, soy rubio, guapo, y totalmente honesto.

Esteban

¡Hola! Me llamo Sofía y tengo los ojos azules y el pelo rubio, largo y liso. Tengo pecas en la nariz que detesto. En casa están mis padres Lourdes y Juan Luis, mi hermano Francisco, mi hermana Cristina y yo. Francisco es alto y delgado y muy travieso. Cristina es bastante baja y muy alegre. También tenemos un perro. Se llama Rodrigo y es un poco gordo y muy cómico. Mis amigas me describen como una persona extrovertida, amable y paciente. Nuestro pasatiempo favorito es el baile. ¿Y tú? ¿Cuál es tu pasatiempo favorito? ¿Qué haces con tus amigos?

Sofía

2a 📖 🎧 Read the webpage and match up each description with the correct photo. Write Eduardo, Juanita, Esteban, Sofía and the correct letter.

2b 📖 🎧 Summarise in English the information Sofía gives about her family. Mention at least eight things.

3 Ⓖ Copy the sentences and fill in the gaps with the correct reflexive pronoun: *me / te / se / nos / os.*

1 ___ llevo bien con mi padre.
2 Hay muchos problemas entre mi hermano y mi hermana. Siempre ___ pelean mucho.
3 Estamos muy contentos. No ___ quejamos.
4 ¿ ___ llevas bien con tus primos?
5 ¿ ___ marcháis ahora?
6 Mi amiga Rosa ___ pone roja cuando habla con mi hermano.

4a 🎧 Listen to Ángel, Flora, Lola and Alberto talking about themselves, family members and friends. Match up each person with the correct category below.

a Self   b Family   c Friends

4b 🎧 Listen again. How do the speakers describe family, friends or themselves? Copy and complete the sentences with the missing words.

1 Ángel says Marta has got _____ and _____.
2 Marta is an _____, very _____ and gets on well with everybody.
3 Flora and Juan _____, but they sometimes argue when they have problems.
4 Lola's family says that she is a bit _____ but very _____.
5 Lola says she is (physically) _____ and _____. But her family says she is _____.
6 Esteban's hair is _____, like Alberto's hair. And in character, he is _____ and _____, but he sometimes looks sad.

5 🗨 Imagine you are taking part in a speed-dating event. Talk for 30–60 seconds about yourself and your family.

- Give personal details (name, age).
- Talk about your family / friends.
- Describe yourself (hair, eyes, height).
- Describe your personality.
- Add any other relevant information.

Estrategia 2a–2b

Recognising false friends

Looking for words that are similar to English does not always work. There are some 'false friends': words that look like a word in English, but actually mean something different in Spanish.

What English words do these Spanish ones remind you of?

simpático sensible largo vago sensato embarazada pariente soportar

Now find out their proper meaning.

Ⓖ Gramática *página 185*

Using reflexive verbs

Remember, reflexive verbs end in -*se: quejarse* (to complain), *llevarse bien /mal* (to get on well /badly).

To use a reflexive verb in the present tense, you drop -*se* and write the correct reflexive pronoun before the verb. You add the normal endings as shown below.

SINGULAR | PLURAL
me llevo (I get on) | *nos llevamos* (we get on)
te llevas (you get on) | *os lleváis* (you get on)
se lleva (he /she gets on) | *se llevan* (they get on)

Also learn the plural forms of possessive adjectives.

See page 44

Enlace

2.1 Groundwork is available in the Foundation book.

2.1 H ¡Qué comprensivo es mi novio!

Objetivos

Describing relationships in detail

Possessive adjectives (singular and plural)

Linking phrases with connectives

Me llamo María y salgo con Antonio, mi novio, desde hace seis meses. En general somos una pareja feliz y normalmente Antonio es un chico cariñoso, comprensivo y honrado. Sin embargo recientemente no nos llevamos muy bien. Antonio tiene un nuevo amigo que se llama Enrique. Creo que es importante salir con tus amigos y no sólo con tu novia pero, en mi opinión, la influencia de Enrique no es muy positiva. Después de estar con Enrique, Antonio se pone impaciente y se enfada conmigo. Su temperamento cambia totalmente. Al final nos peleamos cuando, en realidad, no hay problema entre nosotros. ¿Qué puedo hacer?

María

Ahora mi abuela vive con nosotros porque mi abuelo está muerto y no quiere vivir sola. El problema es que mi hermana mayor, Teresa, no se lleva bien con mi abuela y siempre hay discusiones horribles en casa. Mi abuela critica mucho a los adolescentes: la ropa, los novios, los estudios y las notas del colegio, la dieta, las horas de salir, el dinero ... vamos, todo. Entonces, Teresa se enfada y luego Teresa y mi abuela se pelean. No lo aguanto. Claro que la barrera generacional puede ser difícil. Mi abuela tiene ideas de una generación diferente aunque también pienso que es un poco intolerante. Por otro lado, mi hermana tiene que relacionarse mejor con mi abuela y ser menos egoísta. ¿Cómo puedo ayudar?

Borja

1a 📖 🎧 Read the emails. Find the Spanish equivalents of the following phrases.

1 six months ago
2 he gets angry
3 doesn't get on well with ...
4 less selfish
5 (I want to) marry her
6 to convince her

Elena es mi novia y estoy muy enamorado de ella. Nos llevamos muy bien, tenemos mucho en común y por eso quiero casarme con ella. Desafortunadamente Elena piensa que el matrimonio sólo causa problemas. Además, tiene una imagen del hombre ideal y, claro, no soy perfecto. Todos tenemos defectos, ¿no? En mi opinión, Elena es cobarde y debe tener más confianza en mí.

¿Qué puedo hacer para convencerla?

Luis

1b 📖 🎧 Read the emails again and answer the following questions in English.

1 What is the relationship between the following people:

	Relationship
María and Antonio	
Antonio and Enrique	
Borja and Teresa	
Luis and Elena	

2 What is the main problem for the following people?

a María   b Borja   c Luis

Choose from: different opinions about marriage / age gap / arguments between family members / money / changes of mood / not having friends.

3 Do you think María likes Enrique? Give two reasons.

4 Do you think Borja's grandmother is a positive influence on the family? Give two reasons.

5 Do you think Elena wants to get married? Give a reason for your answer.

2 **G** Copy the sentences and fill in the gaps with the correct form of the possessive adjectives given in brackets.

1 _____ madre está muy enferma. (*our*)

2 _____ padres se llevan muy mal con mi tío Juan. (*my*)

3 Éstas son _____ primas Carmela y Ana. (*their*)

4 ¿Cuándo vienen _____ amigos? (*your, plural informal*)

5 Quiero conocer a _____ hermanas porque son muy guapas. (*your, singular informal*)

6 ¿Dónde viven _____ hermanastras? (*your, plural informal*)

3 📹 Watch the video clip and answer the following questions.

1 Which problem with Javier does his mother mention first?
   a bad marks at school   b staying out late   c not talking

2 Note three things that Javier says his mother criticises him for.

3 What does Javier want his mother to stop doing?
   a treating him like a little boy
   b being too fussy about tidying the house
   c worrying about him

4 What problem does Javier have with his father?
   a won't give him freedom   c always argues with his mother
   b too busy at work

5 How would you best describe Elisa's comment?
   a insensitive   b helpful   c rude

4 ✎ Make up your own email to a problem page. Use connectives to improve your writing.

■ Explain what the problem is.
■ Give an example of something to illustrate this problem.
■ Say what the consequences are.
■ Ask for help.

En general Desafortunadamente Afortunadamente	me llevo bien / mal mi hermano se pelea	con	mi amigo. mi hermano. mis padres.
	mis amigos se relacionan bien / mal		
Por eso Pero También Así que	(no) hay	problemas con discusiones sobre	los estudios. la ropa / el dinero. los amigos / novios. las horas de salir.

Possessive adjectives (singular and plural)

Gramática   página 176

You already know how to use *mi*, *tu*, *su* followed by singular and plural nouns.

Mi prima > **mis** primas

Note that possessive adjectives also have forms for more than one person. They must agree with the noun that follows in number (singular and plural) and gender (masculine and feminine).

nuestro(s) / nuestra(s) – our

vuestro(s) / vuestra(s) – your (informal, i.e. for friends and people of your own age)

su(s) – their / your (*ustedes*) (formal, i.e. for strangers and adults you don't know well)

Nuestra prima no es egoísta. – Our cousin isn't selfish.

Vuestros padres se llevan bien con mi tío. – Your parents get on well with my uncle.

Also learn about subject pronouns.

See page 45

Linking phrases with connectives

Estrategia 4

Use connectives such as *también* (also, too), and *por eso* (that's why, because of that) to improve your writing and extend your sentences.

Tengo problemas con mi padre y también con mi madre. – I have problems with my dad and with my mum, too.

Me llevo mal con mi hermano y por eso nunca lo llamo. – I don't get on well with my brother and that's why I never call him.

2.2 F — Somos muy felices

1a **V** In pairs, read the adjectives below. Sort them into two separate lists: 'desirable' or 'not desirable' qualities for a future partner.

> aburrido   borracho   comprensiva   contenta   divertido
> divorciada   guapa   loco   rica   soltero

1b **V** Read the adjectives again. Say whether each one is masculine (**M**) or feminine (**F**).

2a 📖 🎧 Read the article and write the name of the person who …

1 is married to Don Marcos.
2 is 16 years old.
3 is Lucía's son.
4 used to be married to Lucía.
5 doesn't want to get married.
6 is a single mother.

Personajes de La Calle de Intriga: una telenovela latinoamericana.

Lucía está casada con Don Marcos desde hace seis meses. Don Marcos es su quinto marido y tienen 12 hijos entre los dos. Lucía es rica, pero no está contenta porque es un matrimonio aburrido y sin amor. Quiere tener más aventuras en la vida, pero no quiere estar separada ni divorciada por quinta vez.

Lucía

Hugo es el hijo mayor de Lucía. Vive con su madre y su padrastro porque no tiene trabajo. Está en el paro desde hace dos años y no quiere trabajar. Prefiere dormir, salir en moto y estar con chicas guapas. Su madre, Lucía, busca a una esposa rica para Hugo, pero él no quiere casarse. Prefiere ser soltero. Hay muchos problemas y conflictos entre Hugo, su padrastro y sus hermanastros, pero Hugo no está preocupado por nada. Sólo quiere pasarlo bien.

Hugo

Mariela es la asistenta de la casa de Don Marcos. Trabaja y vive en la casa desde hace 18 años. Es madre soltera y cuida a su hija sola. Su hija se llama Yolanda y tiene 16 años. Yolanda quiere descubrir quién es su padre. Además, Yolanda está enamorada de Hugo. Es un secreto y sufre mucho porque Hugo no la trata bien.

Mariela y Yolanda

Ramón es el ex-marido de Lucía aunque todavía está enamorado de ella. Vive en la casa de enfrente desde hace tres meses. Está jubilado y ahora que ya no trabaja, puede concentrarse en su obsesión: Lucía. Es muy celoso y está un poco loco. Le gusta espiar a Lucía y a Don Marcos por el telescopio. Tiene una pistola y quiere usarla.

Ramón

Los Señores Menéndez son los vecinos de Don Marcos. Tienen dos niñas de tres años que son gemelas. Parece la familia perfecta. Un día llega Paulina, la nueva niñera y la situación cambia de una manera desastrosa.

La familia Menéndez

Estrategia 2a–2b

2b 📖 🎧 Read the article again and answer the following questions in English.

1 Why is Lucía unhappy?
2 What is Hugo's job?
3 What is Yolanda's secret?
4 What does Ramón like doing?
5 Who is Paulina?
6 Who seems to be the most relaxed character? Why?

3a Ⓖ 🗨 Work with a partner. Partner B pretends to be one of the characters from the article on page 36. Partner A has to work out who it is by asking questions using *estar*. Partner B answers in full sentences. Then swap roles.

Ejemplo: **A** ¿Estás casado/a?   **B** No estoy casado/a …

3b Ⓖ 🗨 Now describe a character or pair of characters to the rest of the class for them to guess.

4a 🎧 Listen to the conversations Paulina has with three people (Víctor, Rosa and Juan) she meets on the street. Note down their marital status, the number of children they have and how long they have lived in the street.

4b 🎧 Listen again and answer the following questions.

1 What does Paulina say about herself during the three conversations?

2 What is Rosa's reaction towards Paulina?
   a friendly
   b suspicious
   c scared

3 What is Juan's behaviour towards Paulina like?
   a helpful
   b shy
   c flirtatious

5 ✏ Work in groups. Write a cast list of an imaginary family in a soap opera. Write the description of this imaginary family. You might like to search online to find some photos to add.

Estoy / Está ¿Estás?	casado/a divorciado/a separado/a enamorado/a jubilado/a	desde hace dos meses / tres años.
Soy / Es ¿Eres?	soltero/a guapo/a inglés / inglesa	

Working out meanings when reading

When you come across a new word see if you can work out the meaning from other words and phrases you do understand.

e.g. The phrase *estar en el paro* comes between two pieces of information about Hugo not having a job (*no tiene trabajo*) and not wanting to work (*no quiere trabajar*). It seems that this state that he has been in for two years must have something to do with not having a job, and in fact it means 'to be unemployed'.

Using *estar* + past participle

Use *estar* (to be) with the past participle to explain a situation someone or something is in. Past participles usually end in *-ado* or *-ido* and they work like adjectives, agreeing with the person they are describing in number (singular or plural) and gender (male or female).

estás casado – you are married
están enfadadas – they are angry

With adjectives, you usually use *ser* (also meaning 'to be').

soy joven – I am young

Also learn how to use *desde hace* (since) + present.

See page 44

Ⓖramática   página 187

🔗 **Enlace**

2.2 Groundwork is available in the Foundation book.

2.2 H ¡El futuro será maravilloso!

A los 20 años voy a casarme. Tengo una novia que se llama Rosario y estamos muy enamorados. Para mí el matrimonio será muy importante. Me gustaría tener un niño o dos, pero no quiero una familia muy numerosa. Tengo tres hermanos y cuatro hermanas y es mucho trabajo para mi madre. Además, tienes que considerar el futuro del planeta en general. ¿Habrá suficiente comida para todos? Entonces a los 65 años, ¿qué vamos a hacer Rosario y yo? Pues, no sé exactamente, pero me gustaría estar bien de salud para jugar con mis nietos. **Raúl**

El año que viene voy a ir a la universidad y por eso a los 20 años voy a vivir con mi familia como ahora. Es demasiado caro vivir sola. Después de la universidad, me gustaría trabajar en Nueva York y será fantástico. Quiero casarme y mi marido ideal sería guapo, inteligente y gracioso. Sin embargo, no tengo mucha paciencia con los bebés. Prefiero ser independiente y por eso no voy a tener niños. ¿Y a los 65 años? Claro, voy a jubilarme, voy a ser rica y voy a aprovechar todas las oportunidades que tengo. Lo importante es pasarlo bien. **Chelo**

En el futuro quiero ser médico y me gustaría trabajar en Amazonas en América Latina. Hay muchas familias y niños que necesitan ayuda allí. Será necesario dedicarme a la medicina y entonces los pacientes van a ser las personas más importantes para mí. Desafortunadamente creo que no voy a poder casarme porque en la selva la vida sería difícil para una esposa. Es una pena porque me gustaría tener niños. A los 65 años voy a continuar trabajando. Finalmente me imagino que una residencia de ancianos será mi única opción, que me preocupa un poco, pero no quiero ser demasiado pesimista. **Roberto**

1a 📖 🎧 Read the article in which three students are imagining what their life will be like when they are 20, 35 and 65 years old. Find the Spanish equivalents of the words and phrases below.

1 … am going to marry
2 large family
3 to be healthy
4 Next year
5 too expensive
6 … am going to retire
7 (it) will be necessary
8 It's a shame

1b 📖 🎧 Read the article again. Who …

1 is going to get married when they are 20?
2 is still going to live with their parents in their 20s?
3 is going to be a doctor?
4 doesn't want to have children?
5 doesn't think they will get married?
6 says they will have a comfortable retirement?
7 is a bit worried about old age?
8 wants to spend time with grandchildren?

2 **G** Choose the appropriate verb form for the person named in brackets and copy out the correct sentences.

Ejemplo: No van / voy / va a salir (*they*). No <u>van</u> a salir.

1 Voy / Vas / Va a casarme el año próximo. (*I*)
2 Mi hermana van / va / vamos a trabajar en Australia. (*my sister*)
3 Oye, Cristina, ¿vais / va / vas a tener niños en el futuro? (*you, singular informal*)
4 Mi novio y yo vamos / voy / van a ir a la universidad. (*we*)
5 ¿Van / Vais / Vamos a casaros por la iglesia? (*you, plural informal*)
6 Voy / Vais /Vamos a casarme en la playa. ¡Después será / habrá / vamos una gran fiesta! (*I*)

3a 🎧 Listen to Habibi, Juan and Paula talking about future plans. Match up each person with the correct category 1–5 below.

1 definitely won't get married
2 will possibly get married
3 will live with a partner but not get married
4 will definitely get married
5 probably won't get married

3b 🎧 Listen again and answer the following questions in English.

1 Does Habibi want to be a doctor? How do we know this?
2 What would Habibi like to do? (2)
3 Is Juan going to have children? How do we know this?
4 Does Juan live with Leticia at present? How do we know this?
5 Would Paula like to share her life with somebody now? How do we know this?
6 What are the positive aspects of living with somebody for Paula? (2)

4 🗨 Predict what you will be doing at the ages of 20, 35 and 65. Work with a partner, asking and answering the following questions.

■ ¿Qué vas a hacer a los 20 años?
■ ¿Dónde vas a vivir?
■ ¿Dónde vas a trabajar?
■ ¿Vas a casarte? ¿Por qué?
■ ¿Cómo sería tu pareja ideal?
■ ¿Te gustaría tener niños? ¿Por qué? / ¿Por qué no?
■ ¿Qué te gustaría hacer después de jubilarte?

G **Gramática** *página 183*

Using the immediate future tense

To say what you are going to do, use *ir + a + infinitive*.

Voy a vivir sola. – I am going to live on my own.

You can also use *habrá* and *será* to talk about the future.

Present – *hay* (there is, there are)
Future – *habrá* (there will be)

Present – *es* (he / she / it is)
Future – *será* (he / she / it will be)

Habrá problemas graves. – There will be serious problems.

Éste es Pablo. Será mi marido dentro de dos meses. – This is Pablo. He will be my husband in two months.

Also learn how to talk about future using *gustaría* (would like), *sería* (would be).

See page 45

Estrategia 4

Using conversation fillers

If you want to keep the conversation going and sound fluent in Spanish, use conversation fillers:

bueno, bien, pues, veamos … – well …

vamos a ver … – let's see …

Sabes … – You know …

Entonces … – Then …

These words help you create pauses in a natural way and also give you time to think.

2.3 F Se necesita más igualdad para las mujeres

1 Ⓥ Read the lists below and find the odd one out in each one (the one that is not a social issue).

1 la pobreza   la discriminación contra las mujeres   la salud   la violencia
2 el alcoholismo   los sin hogar   los inmigrantes ilegales   la política
3 los derechos de los niños   el medio ambiente   los drogadictos   el racismo

◄ | ⟳ | 🔍 Buscar

Inicio | Índice | Sitemap | Ayuda | Versión texto

FAQs

Noticias

Acceso directo

Arriba

El día 8 de marzo se celebra La Noche de la Mujer en Bogotá, Colombia. Los hombres tienen que estar en casa y las mujeres tienen que salir. La mayoría de las mujeres que participan son estudiantes o trabajadoras entre 18 y 25 años. Es interesante porque todos los años durante La Noche de la Mujer hay menos violencia y menos crimen. Según una encuesta, más del 80% de las mujeres piensan que es una buena idea.

Pero, ¿cuál es tu opinión?

Estoy de acuerdo con La Noche de la Mujer porque así se pueden considerar los derechos de las mujeres. Se habla de la igualdad, pero hay mucha discriminación todavía y creo que es necesario hacer más para ayudar.

Marcelo

Estoy en contra de esta idea porque se necesita un programa de acción política y educación más serio. En Colombia la igualdad no existe ni en casa ni en el lugar de trabajo. Y la situación es horrorosa en otros países donde se puede maltratar y matar a las mujeres legalmente. Nunca voy a estar a favor de una noche de diversión cuando hay tantas mujeres que son víctimas de la violencia.

Pilar

2 📖 🎧 Read the blogs about Women's Night in Bogotá and decide whether the following statements are true (**T**), false (**F**) or not mentioned (**?**).

1 On 8th March in Bogotá, Colombian women have to stay at home.
2 Most of the people who go out are over 40.
3 Most women think it is a good idea.
4 Originally it was the President's wife who thought of the idea.
5 Marcelo thinks women's rights are important.
6 Pilar thinks that the event helps to promote women's equality.
7 Pilar suffers from domestic violence.

3 Ⓖ Put the words in these phrases into the correct order.

1 más tolerancia necesita se
2 a la educar puede gente se
3 violencia mucho se doméstica no la habla de
4 racismo que España se hay en dice

4 🎧 Listen to the opinions about gender and race issues (1–6). Which of the following options (a–f) does each person refer to?

a Accepting differences
b Changing attitudes through education
c Physical abuse in the home
d Discrimination against gay people
e Immigrant workers
f Women in politics

5 ✏ Write a short speech in Spanish about how to tackle gender and race discrimination. Mention:

■ what is said about the issues (facts / details / statistics)
■ if you agree or disagree with the situation / issue
■ what is needed to help
■ what people can do to help
■ what people must do.

(No) Hay	muchos problemas para	las mujeres.
Se dice que hay	mucha discriminación /	los inmigrantes.
Se habla de	violencia contra	los extranjeros.
	(la) igualdad para	los gitanos.
	(la) desigualdad para	
Se necesita (más)	comprensión / educación / tolerancia / trabajo / acción política.	
Se puede(n)	educar a la gente / hacer más para ayudar / cambiar las	
Se debe(n)	actitudes.	

Using reflexive phrases

Ⓖ **Gramática** *página 185*

In English the passive form is often used, e.g. 'various possibilities can be considered', 'more understanding is needed'. In Spanish an active sentence is used instead. A reflexive form of the verb is used, so you need to remember to put *se* at the beginning.

Se puede considerar varias posibilidades. – Various possibilities **can be considered**.

Se necesita más comprensión. – More understanding **is needed**.

This reflexive form is also used for sentences in English that would start with 'people', 'one' or 'you'.

Se habla de la igualdad. – **People talk** about equality.

Se debe pensar en los vecinos. – **You should** think about your neighbours.

Also learn about making phrases negative.

See page 44

Checking your pronunciation

Estrategia 5

It is important to revise pronunciation rules, especially when the written word is similar to the English. There is a summary of Spanish pronunciation rules on page 170.

In English, vowels change their sounds when you add an 'e' to the end of a word (known as a split digraph), e.g. pin, pine. In Spanish, vowels always have the same sounds. The one that can catch you out most easily is the 'i' sound, which is pronounced 'ee'; e.g. *crimen* is pronounced *cree-men*, and *sin* (meaning 'without') is pronounced *seen*.

🔗 *Enlace*

2.3 Groundwork is available in the Foundation book.

2.3 H   Debemos ayudar a los pobres

Objetivos

Giving opinions on social issues and equality

Using *hay que, tener que, deber* + infinitive

Recognising positive and negative opinions

1a 📖 🎧 Read the article about charity work in Peru. Find the Spanish equivalents of the words and phrases below.

1 suburbs
2 The sad thing is …
3 don't understand
4 On the other hand …
5 very proud of
6 well paid

Una visita a un pueblo joven

Mi destino es Lima, ciudad capital de Perú. Tiene una población de más de 9 millones y aproximadamente el 50% de los habitantes viven en un pueblo joven. Un 'pueblo joven' es un barrio pobre en las afueras de la ciudad donde las casas son muy básicas y a veces no hay agua corriente ni electricidad.

Las expectativas y la realidad

Muchas personas abandonan sus pueblos en el campo y vienen a los pueblos jóvenes porque buscan colegios mejores para sus niños o trabajo para los adultos. Lo triste es que sus expectativas no son realistas. En muchos pueblos jóvenes las condiciones de vida no son muy sanitarias, por ejemplo no hay agua limpia y hay muchas enfermedades como el cólera. Lo horroroso es que la diarrea causa la mayoría de las muertes entre los niños porque los padres no comprenden o no pueden pagar el tratamiento.

Optimismo y desarrollo

Por otro lado no hay que ser demasiado pesimista. La pobreza no tiene que arruinarles la vida. El nombre 'pueblo joven' es más optimista que los nombres 'shanty town' o 'slums' en inglés. El pueblo es 'joven', es nuevo, es básico, pero en el futuro va a ser mejor. Existe la posibilidad de desarrollo.

Las casas y la comunidad

Al principio las casas están hechas de cartón o de metal, pero, poco a poco, los habitantes pueden construir las casas con piedra o ladrillos, y al final tienen un techo y ventanas de cristal. Lo bueno es que hay una sensación de comunidad. Los habitantes tienen que participar juntos en obras como la construcción de carreteras y alcantarillas. Después, la comunidad puede tener agua limpia y electricidad. Todos están muy orgullosos de los progresos en el pueblo joven.

Los pobres y los ricos

Lo malo es que todavía es difícil para los pobres tener un trabajo bien pagado porque hay muchos prejuicios. El 5% de la población es muy rico y tiene el 95% de la riqueza de Perú. Es una situación muy injusta. Hay ONGs como la Asociación SOLAC para ayudar a los pobres, pero los ricos, los gerentes de la industria y los políticos deben dar más oportunidades de educación, de salud y de trabajo a los pobres.

1b 📖 🎧 Read the article again and answer these questions. Try to work out the meanings of words you don't know before looking them up.

1 Lima is a **a** capital city. **b** country. **c** village.

2 A *pueblo joven* is a **a** country village. **b** shanty town.
c youth centre.

3 According to the article, in Peru 5% of the population is
a very poor. **b** very sick. **c** very rich.

4 Why do people leave their village and move to a
pueblo joven?

5 Note down three positive things mentioned about
Peru and the *pueblos jóvenes*.

6 Note down three negative things mentioned.

2 🄖 Match up the two halves of these sentences, then translate them into English.

1 Para evitar el cólera
hay …

2 El gobierno …

3 Los pobres deben …

4 Tenemos que …

a participar en el proceso político.

b considerar el futuro de nuestros
niños.

c que tener agua limpia.

d debe crear más oportunidades
de educación.

3 🎧 Listen to three people saying whether they agree with the government which states that their city has improved a lot recently. Decide whether each person's opinion is positive (**P**), negative (**N**) or positive and negative (**P + N**).

Martín   Zuleima   Alfredo

4 ✏️ Write about your own or an imaginary city. Include the following information:

- some positive things about it
- the problems that exist
- a few things that ought to be done to improve the situation.

En mi / esta ciudad En mi / esta región	(no) hay (mucha, poco/a)	pobreza discriminación hacia las mujeres droga	sin embargo pero y tampoco	(no) hay	violencia. problemas de alcoholismo.
Hay que …	mejorar	soluciones prácticas.			
Tenemos que …	ayudar	dinero a los que lo necesitan.			
Debemos …	buscar	la educación.			
Se debe …	dar	a los sin hogar.			

Gramática *página 186*

Using *hay que, tener que, deber* + infinitive

- Saying 'have to':

Hay que + infinitive   you / people have to …

Hay que never has a change of ending.

Tener que + infinitive   to have to …

Change *tener* to the correct part of the verb.

Tengo que ayudar. – I have to help.

Tenemos que mejorar – We have to improve.

- Saying 'must':

Deber + infinitive

Deber is a regular -er verb like *comer*.

Los políticos deben crear trabajos. – The politicians must create jobs.

Also learn more about how to use *lo* + adjective.

See page 45

Recognising positive and negative opinions

Estrategia 3

It is not just *no* that indicates a negative sentence. Listen out for words like *pero* (but), *por otro lado* (on the other hand), *sin embargo* (however), *nada* (nothing), *nunca* (never), *tampoco* (neither). These words give you hints that the person talking is giving you an opposite opinion to the one they have just given.

Using language you know

Estrategia 4

If you don't have much information about the subject you have to write about, you don't have to stick to the truth – say things you know how to say in Spanish!

(G) Relationships and choices

1 Read the following singular sentences and make them plural. Be careful with possessive adjectives and remember to use the correct form of the verb.

1 Mi tío tiene dos hijas.
2 Su padre vive en Barcelona.
3 Tu hermano no se lleva bien con mi hermana.
4 ¿Tu hermanastro discute con tu madre?
5 Mi amiga es bastante simpática.
6 ¡Ésta es su tía!

> **Gramática** *página 176*
>
> **Possessive adjectives**
> Remember, possessive adjectives come before the person or thing they are referring to. Note that in Spanish they must agree with the noun that follows in number (singular and plural).
> *mi > mis, tu > tus, su > sus*
> *Mi prima vive en Sevilla.* – My cousin lives in Seville.
> *Mis primas viven en Sevilla.* – My cousins live in Seville.

2 Imagine that you are a character in a soap opera. Write about how long you have done or been the things listed below. Don't forget to use connectives in your writing, e.g. *desde hace, sin embargo, porque, así que* or *pero*.

estoy ... casado/a / divorciado/a / separado/a / enamorado/a

soy soltero/a

soy feliz / triste

estoy preocupado/a / loco/a / en el paro

> **Gramática** *página 187*
>
> **Desde hace**
> Use *desde hace* + present tense to say how long you have been doing something.
> *Estoy casado desde hace dos años.* – I have been married for two years.

3 Write the following sentences in the negative form.

1 Es español.
2 En mi ciudad hay violencia.
3 Siempre soy paciente.
4 Tenemos muchas oportunidades.
5 Mi amigo tiene todo.
6 Las chicas son inteligentes y divertidas.

siempre (*always*)

todo (*everything*)

> **Gramática** *página 186*
>
> **Forming the negative**
> ■ To make a sentence negative put *no* in front of the verb:
> *No tengo hermanos.*
> ■ You can also use the following negative expressions:
> *nunca / jamás* – never
> *nadie* – no one
> *nada* – nothing
> *ni ... ni* – neither ... nor
> *no ... ningún(o/a)* – no / not any
> ■ There are two ways of using *nunca / nadie / nada*:
> 1 Put it at the start of the sentence:
> *Nunca voy a Madrid.* – I never go to Madrid.
> 2 Put *no* before the verb, with *nunca / nadie / nada* after the verb:
> *No voy nunca a Madrid.*

4 Copy the sentences and fill in the gaps with the correct subject pronouns.

1 _____ voy al cine y _____ vas al supermercado.

2 _____ es muy simpático, pero _____ es mal educada.

3 _____ tenemos 16 años. ¿Y _____ ? (*you, plural informal*)

4 Es _____ muy amable. (*you, singular formal*)

5 ¿Son _____ ingleses? (*you, plural formal*)

6 Mi madre y _____ tenemos muy buena relación.

> ### Subject pronouns
> In English subject pronouns are always needed. In Spanish, they are usually left out because the verb indicates who is doing the action. They are used for the following:
> - to emphasise the 'I', 'you', etc.
> - to make it clear who is speaking
> - to ask questions: *¿Y tú?*
>
> The subject pronouns are listed on page 178.
>
> *¡No te preocupes! ¡Yo hablaré con mi padre!* – Don't worry! I'll talk to my father!
>
> *Ella se lleva bien con su familia.* – She gets on well with her family.
>
> **Gramática** *página 178*

5 Choose the appropriate verb form in each sentence and write out the sentence correctly.

1 Mi novia ideal me gustaría / sería / le gustaría muy inteligente.

2 Me gustaría / Sería / Serías tener muchos niños en el futuro.

3 ¿Serías / Nos gustaría / Te gustaría salir conmigo?

4 Tú gustaría / sería / serías mi pareja perfecta.

5 Mis padres viven en un piso, pero en el futuro les gustaría / le gustaría / serían vivir en una casa.

6 Ana y yo nos gustaría / seríamos / sería muy felices compartiendo nuestras vidas.

> ### Saying 'would like' and 'would be'
> Use the conditional tense to say 'would like' or 'would be'. It can be followed by an infinitive or by an adjective.
>
> *Me gustaría tener muchos hijos* – I would like to have many children.
>
> *Sería muy feliz viviendo sola.* – I would be very happy living on my own.
>
> **Gramática** *página 184*

6 Look at the diagram about Mexico. Write some sentences giving your reaction to the information, using the examples in the box below. Try to extend your sentences with more details.

Lo	bueno	Lo	importante
	malo		necesario
	mejor (*best thing*)		difícil
	peor (*worst thing*)		interesante

> ### Lo + adjective
> - If you put *lo* in front of an adjective it means 'the ... thing':
>
> *lo importante* – the important thing
>
> - You can use it with *es que*:
>
> *Lo bueno es que hay agua limpia.* – The good thing is that there is clean water.
>
> - You can also use it followed by an infinitive:
>
> *Lo importante es educar a la gente.* – The important thing is to educate the public.
>
> **Gramática** *página 174*

Relationships and choices

Topic 2.1 Relationships with family and friends

2.1 F Me llevo muy bien con mi familia
➡ *pages 32–33*

aburrido/a	boring
alegre	happy / cheerful
alto/a	tall
amable	nice / pleasant
calvo/a	bald
corto/a	short (hair)
delgado/a	thin
egoísta	selfish
feliz	happy
fuerte	strong
gordo/a	fat
gracioso/a	funny
hablador(a)	chatty / talkative
llevarse bien / mal con	to get on well / badly with
orgulloso/a	proud
las pecas	freckles
pelirrojo/a	red-haired
perezoso/a	lazy
rizado/a	curly
tímido/a	shy

2.1 H ¡Qué comprensivo es mi novio!
➡ *pages 34–35*

la	barrera generacional	generation gap
	cambiar	to change
	cariñoso/a	loving / affectionate
	comprensivo/a	understanding
la	confianza	trust
	confiar	to trust somebody
la	discusión	argument
	discutir	to argue
	enamorarse	to fall in love

	enfadarse	to get angry
	honrado/a	honest / honourable
el	marido	husband
la	mujer	wife / woman
la	novia	girlfriend
el	novio	boyfriend
la	pareja	partner / couple
	pelearse	to fight / fall out
la	relación	relationship
	relacionarse	to relate to / get to know
	salir (con)	to go out (with)

Topic 2.2 Marriage, partnership and future plans

2.2 F Somos muy felices ➡ *pages 36–37*

	borracho/a	drunk
	casado/a	married
	contento/a	happy
	cuidar	to look after
	decepcionado/a	disappointed
	decepcionar	to disappoint
	desagradable	unpleasant
	desastroso/a	disastrous
	divertido/a	fun
	estar enamorado/a	to be in love
	guapo/a	good-looking
	jubilado/a	retired
	loco/a	mad
el	padrastro	stepfather
	pasarlo bien / mal	to have a good / bad time
	preocupar(se)	to worry
	rico/a	rich / tasty
	separado/a	separated
	separarse	to separate
	una vez	once

2.2 H ¡El futuro será maravilloso!
➡ *pages 38–39*

la	carrera	profession / race
	creer	to believe
	dejar (el hogar)	*to leave (home)*
	elegir	to choose
	estar bien (de salud)	to be healthy
el	futuro	the future
	interesante	exciting / interesting
	jubilarse	to retire
	libre	free / available
	llegar a ser	to become
la	madre soltera	single mother
la	mascota	pet
	numeroso/a	*large / numerous*
	paciente	patient
	pasado /a (de moda)	*old-fashioned*
	pesimista	pessimistic
la	responsabilidad	responsibility
	sentir(se)	to feel
	tener suerte	to be lucky
	tomar un año libre / sabático	to have a gap year

Topic 2.3 Social issues and equality

2.3 F Se necesita más igualdad para las mujeres ➡ *pages 40-41*

	agresivo/a	aggressive
	alojarse	to stay
	ayudar	to help
la	campaña	campaign
la	*comprensión*	*understanding*
	confiar	*to trust*
el	crimen	crime
	educar	to educate
	estar a favor	to be in favour
	estar de acuerdo	to agree
	estar en contra	to be against
el	extranjero	foreigner / abroad

	físico/a	physical
	horroroso/a	horrific
	maltratar	to abuse
el	maltrato	abuse
	matar	to kill
	quedarse	to stay
	quejarse	to complain
	tolerante	tolerant
la	víctima	victim

2.3 H Debemos ayudar a los pobres
➡ *pages 42-43*

	acoger	to welcome / accept
las	afueras	outskirts / suburbs
	buscar	to look for
	construir	to build
	dar	to give
	dar de comer	to feed
	deber	must / to owe
	duro/a	hard
	enfermo/a	ill
el	habitante	inhabitant
	hacer falta	to need / be needed
	intentar	*to try*
	mismo/a	same
la	*obra benéfica*	*charitable work*
	ocuparse de	*to look after*
	poder	to be able to
	tener que	to have to
	triste	sad
la	vivienda	home / housing
la	zona	area

Higher – Exam practice

info

These pages give you the chance to try GCSE-style practice exam questions at grades B–A*, based on the AQA Context of Lifestyle.

Enlace

Foundation practice exam questions (grades D–C) are available at the end of this Context in the Foundation book.

Reportero: ¿Desde cuándo vives en Madrid, María?

María: Vivo aquí desde hace nueve meses. Vengo originalmente de Guatemala. Ahora mi hermano y yo vivimos con nuestros tíos. En casa también vive nuestro primo y el abuelo.

Reportero: Y, ¿qué haces aquí?

María: Soy estudiante en la universidad. Estudio inglés y francés.

Reportero: ¿Por qué quieres estudiar aquí y no en tu país de origen?

María: Bueno, mis tíos me invitaron y es una oportunidad para visitar Europa y conocer culturas diferentes. Voy a viajar a Inglaterra y a Francia en agosto. También se puede hacer nuevos amigos.

Reportero: ¿Y piensas que hay muchas diferencias entre los jóvenes españoles y los jóvenes de Guatemala?

María: Creo que depende de la personalidad de cada uno. No hay que pensar en estereotipos. Por ejemplo, mi mejor amiga en Guatemala se llama Elisa y es muy extrovertida. En cambio, Eduardo, otro amigo, es bastante tímido. Tengo dos amigas españolas, Laura y Juanita. Laura es muy divertida y nos hace reír. Por otra parte, Juanita es más formal con todos, pero me llevo bien con las dos.

Reportero: Y, ¿tienes amigos de otras nacionalidades?

María: Sí. Yusuf es de Marruecos. Es inmigrante y trabaja en España desde hace tres años. Después del colegio, era muy difícil encontrar trabajo en Marruecos y hay más posibilidades aquí. Debe ser duro estar separado de su familia, pero es una persona muy independiente y madura. Para él, lo más importante es ganar suficiente dinero y así ayuda a sus padres y hermanos en Marruecos porque son pobres. En el futuro le gustaría volver a Marruecos para crear un negocio y así dar trabajo a otros jóvenes marroquíes. Es una buena idea. Le admiro mucho.

Reportero: Entonces, ¿los inmigrantes deben volver a su propio país, en tu opinión?

María: No. No digo eso. La tasa de nacimientos en España es muy baja y hay que acoger a los extranjeros para hacer todos los trabajos necesarios. Los inmigrantes son necesarios para la economía. Contribuyen con ocho billones de euros en impuestos.

Reportero: Estoy de acuerdo.

1a 📖 Read the interview. Match up each of María's friends with the correct description. Copy the grid and fill in the correct number for each.

Elisa	*Ejemplo:* 3
Eduardo	
Juanita	
Laura	
Yusuf	

1 funny
2 chatty
3 outgoing
4 intelligent
5 shy
6 independent
7 polite

Total = 4 marks

1b 📖 Read the interview again. Decide whether the following statements are true (**T**), false (**F**) or not mentioned (**?**).

1 María is from Guatemala.
2 María is studying at a university in Spain.
3 Yusuf works in a school.
4 Yusuf helps his family financially.
5 In the future Yusuf would like to stay in Spain.
6 María believes that Spain needs people from abroad to come and work there.

Total = 6 marks

2 🎧 Listen to the interview with María about her relationships and choose the correct answer from the options given.

1 María's relationship with her parents is …
a loving.
b really bad.
c up and down.

2 María believes that a true friend must be …
a forgiving.
b ready to listen.
c honest.

3 In the future María would like to …
a work with children.
b have children.
c be a nanny in Spain.

4 María thinks that people should …
a help each other more.
b be responsible for helping themselves.
c demand more help from the government.

Total = 4 marks

3a 🎧 Listen to Luis, Nuria and Yolanda giving their opinions of the situation of women in their country. Decide whether each person's opinion is positive (**P**), negative (**N**) or positive and negative (**P + N**).

Total = 3 marks

3b 🎧 Listen again and answer the following questions in English.

1 What does Luis think about the possibility of establishing equal rights for women in his country?
2 He says that women don't help themselves. Why does he think this is the case? (2)
3 Nuria talks about two factors that make the situation unfavourable for the women in her country. What are these? (2)
4 What positive initiative does she mention?
5 What is the main aim of the organisation Yolanda volunteers for?
6 In her opinion, in which two areas do things need to change for this aim to begin to be realised? (2)

Total = 9 marks

Total for Reading and Listening = 26 marks

Estrategia 1b

Linking statements with the text

When you have an exam question where you have to link a number of statements with the text, you will find that the statements go in roughly the same order as the text, rather than jumping about. However, as you are working at Higher level, don't expect it to be completely straightforward. When you have found that María is at a university, you have to go back to the beginning to check whether it is in Spain or not.

Estrategia 2

Predict the language you might hear

In the Listening exam use the five minutes' reading time at the beginning to try to predict the kind of vocabulary and structures you might need to understand. Read the introduction to each question, as it summarises the topic you are going to hear. Don't leave blank answers – write something!

Estrategia 3a

Listen for negative constructions

When you see the question type where you are asked to spot positive and negative opinions, you need to listen for negative clue words. The easiest one is *no*, which makes a sentence negative. Don't forget that you can make a sentence negative using *nunca* (never) or *nadie* (nobody).

Higher – Speaking

La vida sana

Your Spanish exchange partner asks you some questions from a survey about healthy living. You have to:

1 say if your lifestyle is generally healthy or not
2 talk about your diet now and when you were younger
3 describe healthy activities
4 give your opinion about smoking
5 talk about alcohol in the UK
6 say what you will do to be more healthy in future.
7 !

! Remember you will have to respond to something that you have not yet prepared.

1 **Say if your lifestyle is generally healthy or not.**
 – are you healthier now than when younger?
 – say if your diet is good or bad for your health
 – what would you like to do about your level of fitness?
 – say why you continue with any bad habits

Estrategia
Start your plan. Remember that the maximum number of words allowed in your plan is 40. Write a maximum of six words for each bullet point. See Exam technique S2.
Here are some suggested words for bullet point 1:
sano/a, salud, estar en forma, hábito.
For the first bullet point use the imperfect and the present tenses to compare the past and the present, e.g.
Cuando era pequeño …
hacía mucho deporte / veía la televisión todo el día …
pero ahora …
no hago mucho deporte / soy mucho más activo …
porque es importante para mí estar en forma.

2 **Talk about your diet now and when you were younger.**
 – describe your meals now and when you were younger
 – say which foods are healthy and why
 – are people more or less healthy now than 50 years ago, and why
 – give your opinion of healthy eating

Estrategia
Suggested words for your notes:
desayuno, contener, verduras, grasa, proteína, odiar.
To extend the language in the first sub-division use, e.g. *Ayer comí / bebí* (preterite); *era / estaba …* (imperfect).
For the third sub-division use the imperfect tense to describe how people used to eat, e.g. *Creo que la comida era más sana en el pasado porque no había tanta comida precocinada.*

3 **Describe healthy activities.**
 – say what, if any, sport you like doing
 – does your daily routine help you be healthy or not?
 – what activities have you done recently and which would you like to do?
 – say if you are stressed / relaxed and why

Estrategia
Suggested words for your notes: *hacer ejercicio, dormir, estresado/a, necesario*; add two more of your own.
You can use the infinitive of the verb after *me gusta, se puede, es necesario, hace falta*, etc.
Always try to add extra details (e.g. where, who with, when …).
When saying what you would like to do in the future you can use *cuando sea mayor …*

4 Give your opinion about smoking.

- say if you, your family or friends smoke and why
- talk about the dangers of smoking
- give some facts about smoking (in the UK or a Spanish-speaking country)
- say if you agree with the Spanish smoking law and why

> *Estrategia*
>
> Suggested words for your notes: *pulmones, causar, prohibido/a*; add three more of your own.
>
> Check that the verb ending agrees with the person you are talking about (I, my mother, my friends, etc.). See page 180 to revise verb endings.

5 Talk about alcohol in the UK.

- talk about how much alcohol young people typically drink
- explain the reasons people drink alcohol, and why they drink to excess
- mention what kinds of problems alcohol causes in the UK, and the possible impact on the future
- compare the dangers of alcohol with smoking

> *Estrategia*
>
> Suggested words for your notes: *adictivo/a, violencia*; add four more of your own
>
> Link the ideas in the first sub-division with a pronoun, e.g. *Mis amigos y yo bebemos alcohol a veces, por ejemplo en una fiesta. Lo hacemos porque todo el mundo lo hace y porque nos preocupa mucho lo que piensan los otros.*
>
> Always check the pronunciation guide (page 14) when preparing the Speaking assessment, especially for more complex vocabulary.

6 Say what you will do to be more healthy in future.

- say which food or drink you will eat or avoid and why
- say what activities you would like to do, and when you plan on doing them
- mention any habits you should change, and how you will try to do that
- explain why you want to be more healthy

> *Estrategia*
>
> Write down six words on this subject for your notes. Use pages 30–31 to help you.
>
> Make sure that you use a wide variety of language structures and refer to the past, present and future wherever possible. The simplest ways to refer to the future are using *voy a* + infinitive (I am going to …); *me gustaría* + infinitive (I would like …); *se debería* + infinitive (you / people should…)
>
> If possible, include the simple future, future and conditional. See page 183 to revise the future.

7 **!** At this point, you may be asked …

- if school helps you to be fit and healthy, and how
- your opinion about drugs
- to compare the dangers of drugs, cigarettes and / or alcohol
- why it is important to be healthy.

> *Estrategia*
>
> Even if the question is a complete surprise, you will have learnt enough relevant vocabulary and phrases to say something. Remember to use conversation fillers to keep your conversation going.

> *Enlace*
>
> Foundation sample assessment tasks for this Context can be found in the Foundation book.

Higher – Writing

Mi familia, mis amigos y yo

You are writing about yourself on the internet to a Spanish friend, Juan. You could write as yourself or imagine you are a celebrity or a character in a TV programme.

Write about yourself, your family and friends, your opinions and concerns.

1 Say your age and what you look like.

2 Describe your personality and interests now and when you were younger.

3 Talk about your family.

4 Say if you get on with members of your family and why / why not.

5 Describe your friends.

6 Say what you want to do in the future.

7 Talk about a social problem you feel strongly about.

> ### info
> **Important information:**
> This sample task is for practice purposes only and should not be used as an actual assessment task. Study it to find out how to plan your Controlled Assessment efficiently to gain maximum marks and / or work through it as a mock exam task before the actual Controlled Assessment.

1 Say your age and what you look like.

- say how old you are, when you were born, and when your birthday is
- describe your hair and eyes, and say if anything has changed since you were younger
- describe your height and build
- give extra physical details (glasses / freckles, etc.)

> **Estrategia**
> Start your plan. Remember that the maximum number of words allowed in your plan is 40. Write a maximum of six words for each bullet point. Here are some suggested words for bullet point 1: *moreno*, *castaño*, *de tamaño medio*, *pecas*, *rizado*.
> You could compare your present and past appearance:
> *Antes tenía … era …* (Before, I had … I was …) *pero ahora tengo … soy…* (but now I have … am …). See page 182 for more information about the imperfect tense.
> See also Exam technique W2.

2 Describe your personality and interests now and when you were younger.

- describe what you are like as a person, both good and less good attributes
- compare your personality with those of your family and / or friends
- say what your main hobbies are, and why you like them
- say what you used to do when you were younger and how you have changed

> **Estrategia**
> Suggested words for your notes: *simpático/a*, *gracioso/a*, *pasatiempo*, *extrovertido/a*, *vago/a*; add one more of your own.
> Try to avoid a long list of adjectives after *soy* or *mi amigo es* … Use *bastante*, *muy*, *un poco*, *demasiado* in front of adjectives to vary the language, or use adverbs such as *a veces*, *mucho*.

3 Talk about your family.

- describe the different people in your family
- say who is married / divorced / single and for how long
- mention something you have done recently with your family, e.g. a special occasion or celebration
- ask a question about Juan's family

> **Estrategia**
> Suggested words for your notes: *casado/a*, *desde hace*, *soltero/a*, *abuelo/a*; add two more of your own.
> You can mention your extended family as well.
> To talk about what you have done use the preterite or perfect tense. See pages 181–182 for more information.

3 **G** Copy these sentences and fill in the gaps with the correct verb. Then translate them into English.

1   El sábado _____ en la piscina.
2   Montse _____ la trompeta por la mañana.
3   El fin de semana Guillermo _____ al tenis.
4   ¿_____ con tus amigos?

tocó	nadé	saliste	jugó

4 🎧 Copy the table, then listen to the conversations and tick the boxes to show what each person did at the weekend.

	Alberto	Carla	José Luis
Helped at home			
Listened to music			
Played a sport			
Played a video game			
Played a musical instrument			
Took the dog for a walk			
Watched TV			

5 🗨 Work with a partner. Use the language structure box to keep talking and talking about what you did at the weekend. While you talk, your partner will 'scribble-time' you. This means that when you talk, they keep colouring in a box. If you pause, they will stop colouring until you carry on. Use the connectives and time words to keep giving more detail.

El fin de semana El sábado El domingo Primero Luego Después Por la mañana Por la tarde	fui	al cine a la playa a la ciudad	con un amigo. con mis amigos. con mi familia.
	vi	un programa una película un partido	con mi hermano. con mi hermana. con mi perro.
	jugué al tenis salí ____é ____í	en … en … un campeonato en … la piscina en … la playa	y pero porque sin embargo

Reading strategies – exam technique

For this type of activity, at first glance, it may look as if the answer is both people in every case. You need to read closer and look for the detail:

■ negatives (things they don't do)
■ other people (but not them)
■ time frame (they might be going to do it, but they haven't yet)
■ different ways of saying the same thing (synonyms)

Estrategia 2

Using the preterite tense

Use the preterite tense to talk about what you did or what happened in the past.

nadar
nadé – I swam
nadaste – you swam
nadó – he / she / it swam

comer
comí – I ate
comiste – you ate
comió – he / she / it ate

salir
salí – I went out
saliste – you went out
salió – he / she / it went out

Have you spotted irregular verbs like these on this page: *vi, fui, hice*?
See page 68

Gramática   página 181

Using time words

As well as time expressions such as *anoche, ayer, por la tarde*, you can use:

primero – first
después – afterwards
entonces – then
enseguida – straightaway
finalmente – finally

Estrategia 5

Enlace

3.1 Groundwork is available in the Foundation book.

3.1 H ¿Qué hicisteis?

El diario de una joven madrileña

sábado, 15 de enero

Por la mañana me despertó un ruido tremendo en casa. Mi hermano empezó a tocar la batería, mi hermana pequeña lloró porque mi padre apagó la tele y justo en el mismo momento, mi madre decidió pasar la aspiradora. ¡Qué jaleo! Invité a mi hermanita a ver dibujos animados en mi ordenador portátil, cerré bien la puerta de mi dormitorio y escuché música en mi MP3. ¡Pura tranquilidad!

Después leí las noticias en el portátil y escribí un correo electrónico. Llamé a unas amigas del insti y hablé un rato con ellas. Luego jugué al ping-pong con mi hermano y gané el partido. Pero luego jugamos un videojuego y ganó él.

Por la tarde recibí un mensaje de mi amiga Alba. Me invitó a ver una película en su casa. Menos mal porque en aquel momento mis hermanos y mis padres se pelearon porque todos querían ver un programa diferente en la tele. A mi hermano le gusta Gran Hermano, a mi madre una telenovela o un documental y a mi padre las noticias o el deporte.

Alba y yo elegimos una película de acción porque no nos gustan nada las películas románticas ni las comedias. Comimos palomitas y bebimos Coca-Cola. Volví a casa a eso de las nueve. Luego cené, leí un rato y me acosté.

Gabriela

1a 📖🎧 Read Gabriela's diary, then put the pictures into the correct order.

1b 📖🎧 Read the diary again and choose the correct answer to complete the sentences.

1 She was woken up by …   a her family.   b her brother.   c her alarm clock.
2 She got some peace and quiet by …   a shutting her brother's door.   b playing on her computer.
   c listening to music.
3 When she played games against her brother …   a they both won.   b he won.   c she won.
4 Her friend sent her a message …   a but she wanted to watch TV.
   b which saved her from a family argument.   c which caused an argument.
5 She went to bed …   a at about 9 o'clock.   b before 9 o'clock.   c after 9 o'clock.

Gramática página 182

Estrategia 2

2 **G** Match up the English and Spanish verbs. Pay attention to the person of each one.

1 I swam
2 I listened
3 he called
4 she swam
5 they listened
6 I called
7 we swam
8 they went out
9 we went out

escucharon	escuché	llamó
llamé	nadó	nadé
nadamos	salimos	salieron

All persons of the preterite tense

Regular verbs have the following endings in the preterite:

-ar	-er	-ir
escuchar	comer	escribir
escuché	comí	escribí
escuchaste	comiste	escribiste
escuchó	comió	escribió
escuchamos	comimos	escribimos
escuchasteis	comisteis	escribisteis
escucharon	comieron	escribieron

Have you spotted any of these verb forms: *jugué, toqué, saqué, practiqué?*

For more on regular verbs with spelling changes in the preterite, see page 69.

3 🎧 Listen to the conversations and answer the questions in English.

1 What event did Laura go to and where did it take place?
2 What event did Pablo take part in and what was the outcome?
3 Why do you think Pablo is still feeling fed up?
4 Why was it a special weekend for Noelia?
5 How would you describe Noelia's mood now?
6 Where did Raúl go for the weekend and who did he go with?
7 Why do you think the radio presenter asks Raúl if he has won the lottery?
8 What is Raúl's answer?

Laura

Learning verbs

There is no shortcut to learning verbs. Make sure you understand the order of the persons, so you know which ending to use. Practise chanting the verbs, then get a friend to test you. Start with the three model verbs *escuchar*, *comer* and *escribir*, then try other regular verbs. Pay close attention to getting the endings exactly right, including the accents. Try making a verb poster or cards with the endings colour coded. Knowing your verbs is key to being able to express yourself in Spanish.

Pablo

Noelia

Raúl

4 🖋 Write a series of 'Good News, Bad News' statements in Spanish. You can use Gabriela's letter for inspiration.

Ejemplo:

'I listened to music ... My brother played the drums!'
'I played ping-pong ... My brother won!'
'I started to watch TV ... My dad turned off the TV!'

3.2 F ¿Te gusta estar de moda?

1 **V** When you go shopping for clothes, what do you look for?
Put these qualities in order of importance for you.

- Quiero algo **diferente**.
- Sólo compro ropa **de marca**.
- A veces compro **de segunda mano**.
- Me gusta la ropa **cara**.
- Busco el precio más **barato**.

- Necesito algo **cómodo**.
- Tiene que ser **de buena calidad**.
- Compro ropa **elegante**.
- Siempre sé qué está **de moda**.
- Prefiero la ropa **deportiva**.

Mateo

Creo que cada uno debe tener su propia imagen y su propio estilo. Es aburrido si todo el mundo lleva los mismos colores y los mismos estilos simplemente para ir a la moda. Nunca compro ropa de marca porque es muy cara y no vale la pena. Me gusta vestirme de manera original y muy diferente a los demás.

Juan

Alba

No compro mucha ropa pero la que tengo es de buena calidad. Prefiero llevar estilos clásicos. Nunca compro ropa en Internet – la compro en los grandes almacenes o en tiendas de ropa porque es importante que esté bien hecha.

Nicolá

Eso de la moda no me interesa nada. Además, odio ir de compras. Para mí, es más importante la comodidad. Con una camiseta, unos vaqueros y zapatillas de deporte tengo suficiente. Prefiero gastar dinero en disfrutar de mi tiempo libre que en ropa y complementos.

Voy de compras todos los fines de semana y leo muchas revistas porque creo que, para estar de moda, tengo que ver lo que hay en las tiendas de ropa, cuáles son las tendencias del momento y qué colores se usan. Todo eso me encanta. Adoro la ropa y los complementos. También son super importantes para mí el peinado y el maquillaje.

2a 📖 🎧 Read the accounts of personal fashion preference, and find who says that:

1 there are more important things than shopping.
2 it's not worth buying designer clothes.

3 he / she has to keep up with trends.
4 it's important to buy well-made clothes.

2b 📖 🎧 Read the accounts again and match up each person with one of the following descriptions, giving reasons for your choices.

1 The most fashion-conscious person.
2 The least fashion-conscious person.
3 Someone who likes to be different.

4 The person least likely to buy clothes in a sale.
5 The person whose attitude to fashion is similar to yours.

3a 📹 First just listen to the video soundtrack, without seeing the images and answer the following questions. Then watch the video and check your answers.

1 The girl wants to try on …
   a a jacket.
   b a skirt.
   c a dress.

2 How many items does she decide to buy?
   a one
   b two
   c four

3 How does she pay?
   a cash
   b cheque
   c card

4 What did the boy buy?
   a a T-shirt and some socks
   b a shirt and a hat
   c a shirt and some shoes

3b 📹 Watch again and say what the following expressions mean.

1 Quisiera probar aquel vestido que está en el escaparate.
2 ¿Qué talla lleva usted?
3 Los probadores están al fondo.
4 ¿Cómo le van?

4 🅖 Act out the following dialogues, using actions to show you understand exactly what the different demonstrative pronouns mean.

> – Quiero comprar unos pantalones negros, talla grande.
> – Tengo éstos o ésos.
> – No, prefiero aquéllos.

> – Necesito una camiseta blanca pero no me gusta ésa.
> – También tengo ésta.
> – Gracias. ¿Puedo probármela?

> – Me gustan las camisas. ¿Qué talla es ésta?
> – Ésa es grande.
> – ¿Tiene pequeñas?
> – Aquéllas son pequeñas.

5 ✏ Read the four accounts of personal style in Activity 2 again. Write a similar paragraph about your own fashion preferences.

Gramática — página 179

Demonstrative pronouns

A demonstrative pronoun is a word like 'this', 'that', 'these' or 'those'. Use them instead of a noun to avoid repeating it. They change according to the gender and number of the noun they are referring to.

¿Te gustan ésos? No, me gustan éstos. – Do you like those? No, I like these.

éste means 'this one' (near me). It can change to *ésta / éstos / éstas.*

ése means 'that one' (near you). It can change to *ésa / ésos / ésas.*

aquél means 'that one' (somewhere else). It can change to *aquélla / aquéllos / aquéllas.*

The neuter forms *eso*, *esto* and *aquello* represent an idea rather than replacing a specific noun.

Eso no me interesa. – That doesn't interest me.

Also learn how *aquí*, *allí* and *allá* follow a similar pattern.

See page 68

Estrategia 5

Be expressive about your likes, dislikes and preferences

Adoro la ropa y los complementos.

Me gusta leer revistas de moda.

Me encanta ir de compras.

Odio el color verde.

Adapting a model

Using a model can work at different levels:

■ Selecting whole sentences that apply to you.

■ Adapting part of a sentence and changing the example.

■ Covering the same ideas in your own words.

■ Improving your work by picking up new words.

 **Enlace**

> 3.2 Groundwork is available in the Foundation book.

3.2 H   ¿En qué gastas tu dinero?

El consumismo y los jóvenes

- Los chicos son más consumistas que las chicas, pero ellas gastan la mitad de su dinero en ropa.

- Los chicos se dejan influir más por cuestiones como la moda, las marcas o la publicidad que las chicas.

- Los jóvenes españoles de entre 14 y 24 años gastan alrededor de 120 euros al mes (unos 30 euros a la semana).

- El ocio es lo que importa. Los jóvenes disfrutan más del tiempo libre que los mayores. Gastan el dinero en salir con los amigos y en comer fuera de casa.

- Los jóvenes que trabajan ahorran más y valoran mucho más el dinero que los que siguen recibiendo la paga.

- La paga semanal media de los españoles de 16 y 17 años es algo más de 11.50 euros. Sin embargo, la mayoría dice que siempre hay que ir pidiendo más 'pasta'.

- El 15% de los jóvenes tienen adicción al consumo (son adictos a las compras). Según los psicólogos, compran para mejorar su autoestima y para ser admirados.

1a 📖 🎧 Read the article. Find the Spanish equivalents of these words and phrases.

1	they spend	7	carry on getting
2	half	8	pocket money
3	brands	9	average
4	around	10	'dosh'
5	leisure	11	self-esteem
6	they save		

Learn real language

Make your Spanish more authentic by reading real texts from magazines, newspapers and the internet. Notice the useful expressions and try to include them in your writing and speaking.

Estrategia 1a

1b 📖 🎧 Read the article again and answer the following questions in English.

1 According to the survey, who spends more, girls or boys?
2 What do girls spend half their money on?
3 What are boys more influenced by than girls?
4 How much, on average, do young people in Spain spend per week?
5 What is more important to young people than to older people?
6 Who saves more and has a better sense of the value of money?
7 What is the average weekly allowance for Spanish 16- to 17-year-olds?
8 According to the experts, why do people become addicted to shopping?

'More / Less / Stay the same' exam questions

Make yourself a word shape poster for these key expressions, e.g.

| más | menos | igual |
| mismo | seguir | cambiar |

Estrategia 1b

2 🎧 Listen to a Spanish teenager being interviewed for a market research survey. Note his responses to the survey by answering these questions.

1 What does the boy usually spend his money on? (Mention three things.)

2 Where does his money come from? (Mention two sources.)

3 What does the boy say about saving money? (Mention two details.)

4 From what the boy says, do you think his parents are:

    1 understanding / generous?

    2 strict?

    3 unfair?

Gramática · *página 176*

Indefinite adjectives

Alguno/a, cada, mismo/a, otro/a, todo/a

These agree with the word they describe and usually appear before the word:

todos los precios, todas las tiendas

el mismo estilo, la misma tienda, los mismos colores

otro día, otra camisa, otros colores

algunas camisetas, algunos calcetines

cada always stays the same: *cada semana, cada año*

Also learn about comparative and superlative adverbs, e.g. 'more frequently', 'most responsibly'.

See page 69

---

3 🄖 🗩 Work with a partner. Read the dialogue aloud, completing it with the correct forms of the indefinite adjectives.

Cliente: Hola. Quisiera comprar (**1**) _____ botas. (unos / unas)

Dependienta: (**2**) _____ las botas que tenemos están aquí. (Todos / Todas)

Cliente: Me gustan aquellas botas marrones. ¿Tienen el (**3**) _____ modelo en negro? (mismo / misma)

Dependienta: No, pero a lo mejor las tendremos la semana que viene.

Cliente: Muy bien. Suelo venir aquí al centro comercial (**4**) _____ (todos / todas) las semanas, así que pasaré (**5**) _____ (otro / otra) día. Adiós.

Dependienta: Adiós. Hasta luego.

---

4 🗩 Work with a partner. Use the language structure box to ask and answer questions. Include ways to extend, personalise and vary your answers.

- ¿De dónde recibes tu dinero?
- ¿En qué lo gastas?
- ¿Cuánto dinero gastas y cuánto dinero ahorras?

¿De dónde recibes tu dinero?		
Lo recibo de	mis padres	cada semana.
	mis abuelos	por mi cumpleaños.
Lo gano porque trabajo	los sábados	en una tienda.
	los domingos	en un restaurante.
	durante las vacaciones	
Lo gasto en	salir con los amigos.	
	comprar ropa.	
	los deportes.	
Generalmente	gasto … libras	a la semana.
Normalmente	ahorro … libras	al mes.

3.3 F Los medios y la comunicación

Objetivos

Comparing different media and technologies

Using *fue* meaning 'was'

Predicting what you are going to hear

1 **V** Read these sentences about different kinds of media. Decide if they are digital (**D**), non-digital (**N**) or both (**D + N**).

1 Me gusta ver películas en DVD.
2 Leo el periódico gratis en el tren por la mañana.
3 Siempre estoy en contacto con mis amigos en una red social.
4 Cuando era pequeño, compraba tebeos.
5 Escucho música en mi reproductor de MP3.
6 Envío mensajes a mis amigos con el móvil.
7 Leo una revista porque me gustan las fotos.

2a 📖 🎧 Read what Luisa has to say about different media. In each case decide if her opinion is positive (**P**), negative (**N**) or positive and negative (**P + N**).

1 Newspapers and magazines
2 Watching TV
3 A website
4 Social network sites

Luisa

A Mi padre siempre recomienda leer el periódico, pero no lo leo nunca porque parece muy aburrido para los jóvenes. Además, no entiendo mucho de lo que dicen. Y la única vez que leí una revista, fue en la sala de espera del dentista. ¡Qué pena! No compro revistas porque hay otras cosas mejores y más relevantes. En Internet, por ejemplo, encontré información sobre el festival de música de Benicàssim. Fue muy fácil encontrar exactamente lo que necesitaba.

B No hay nada peor que ver un documental sobre jardines con mi madre. ¿Te imaginas? Pues ya no tengo que hacerlo, porque puedo ver los programas que quiero en mi portátil. Y los veo en línea a la hora que yo quiero. Simplemente vas a la página web del canal de televisión, y allí encuentras tus programas favoritos.

C ¿No puedes hacer los deberes? ¿No encuentras la información necesaria? Yo tenía ese problema, pero encontré un sitio web donde los alumnos comparten ideas sobre las tareas. Te das cuenta de que no estás solo. Fue muy útil, y hay secciones para las diferentes asignaturas. No podría recomendarlo más.

D En España la red social 'T' es más popular que la 'F'. ¿Pero cuál es mejor? La primera vez que entré en 'F', fue una experiencia muy confusa. Hay tantas opciones, vínculos, amigos potenciales … En comparación, 'T' es más básico. Posiblemente demasiado básico. Por tanto, depende de lo que tú quieres. Si simplemente quieres comunicarte con tus amigos reales, 'T' es para ti. Si quieres comunicarte con el mundo entero, quizás 'F' es mejor.

Estrategia 2a

Spotting positives / negatives

Watch out for:

False negatives: *No tiene nada malo.* (positive)

Questions: *¿Es malo? ¡No!* (positive)

'Too': *Es tranquilo → Es demasiado tranquilo.* (negative)

Distractors: irrelevant positives / negatives about something else or other people's opinions.

Time frame: *Todo iba bien, antes de la invención de …* (false positive – used to be)

Exclamations: *¡Genial!, ¡Qué lástima!*

2b 📖 🎧 Give details from what Luisa says to explain your answers to Activity 2a. Answer in English.

3 **G** Practise making your own sentences with *fue* by joining the halves below.

Vi un programa de humor ...   ... fue aburrido/a.
Vi un documental sobre animales ...   ... fue fascinante.
Vi una telenovela australiana ...   ... fue ridículo/a.
Vi un programa de deporte ...   ... fue impresionante.
Vi un programa de noticias ...   ... fue muy divertido/a.

4a 🎧 Listen to three people being interviewed about communication technology. Write down which of the following items each interviewee mentions.

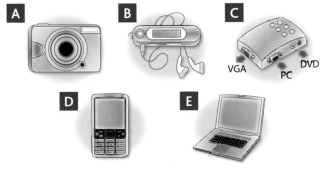

4b 🎧 Listen again. Make a list of the uses mentioned for each item, e.g. keeping in touch with friends, for security reasons, etc.

5 💬 Answer these questions on different forms of technology and media. The language structure box will remind you of some of the words you can use to extend your answer.

1   ¿Te gusta leer revistas o periódicos?
2   ¿Ves mucho la televisión?
3   ¿Pasas mucho tiempo en Internet?
4   ¿Qué opinas de las redes sociales?

Verb + infinitive	Present tense	Preterite tense	Fue ...
Me gusta ...	Leo	Leí	... útil
Prefiero ...	Escucho	Escuché	... fácil
Puedes ...	Veo	Vi	... divertido
Tienes que ...	Compro	Compré	... aburrido
No ...	Hablo	Hablé	... fascinante
... leer ... escuchar			
... ver ... comprar			
... hablar ... utilizar			

Gramática *página 182*

Using *fue* meaning 'was'
The preterite tense of *ser* (to be) is the same as *ir* (to go).
fui – I was
fuiste – you were
fue – he / she / it was
fuimos – we were
fuisteis – you were
fueron – they were
Also learn about *mejor* and *peor*.
See page 68

Estrategia 4b

Predicting what you are going to hear

Remember, in the exam you only hear each item twice. So it is important to be prepared. Think through what words you are likely to hear and what the logical answers would be, before you listen.

Enlace
3.3 Groundwork is available in the Foundation book.

3.3 H La tecnología y las diferentes generaciones

Encuesta: la tecnología y tú

Adoro mi móvil. Mis padres me lo regalaron por mi cumpleaños. Tiene cámara de fotos y de vídeo. Más que nada, lo uso para comunicarme con mis amigos. Mando muchos mensajes porque salen más económicos que las llamadas. Sin embargo mis padres me pagan los gastos del móvil. Dicen que se sienten más tranquilos al tener el móvil porque puedo llamarles para decirles con quién y dónde estoy y a qué hora llegaré a casa. ¿Y las desventajas? Veo muy pocas: que son bastante caros los móviles y son fáciles de robar.

Sara, 15 años

¿Cuáles de los siguientes aparatos son más importantes para ti?
- el teléfono móvil
- el ordenador portátil
- el MP3
- la cámara digital
- la videoconsola
- el equipo de música
- la televisión plana o de plasma

¿Cuáles son, en tu opinión, las ventajas de la nueva tecnología?

¿Cuáles son las desventajas?

Tengo un móvil y un ordenador pero lo que más me gusta últimamente es mi videoconsola. Es nueva. No me la regalaron mis padres. La compré con el dinero que gano trabajando los fines de semana. No tengo muchos juegos todavía pero a lo mejor me van a regalar algunos en Navidad o en Reyes. Mis padres a veces se quejan porque paso mucho tiempo jugando en la videoconsola. Pero yo lo paso estupendamente. Es muy entretenido y nunca estoy aburrido. Además, dicen que algunos videojuegos te mejoran la concentración, la coordinación y las reacciones. ¡Vaya excusa para seguir jugando!

Jorge, 16 años

Para mí es imprescindible el portátil. El que tengo no es el último modelo porque antes era de mi hermano. Me lo pasó a mí cuando él compró uno nuevo. Sin embargo es muy útil y tiene muchas ventajas. Por ejemplo, como tenemos banda ancha en casa, puedo conectarme fácilmente a Internet. Navegar en la red es entretenido e incluso educativo. No tengo que ir a la biblioteca o a la librería a buscar datos. También puedo descargar música de la red y esto me sale más económico que comprar discos compactos. El correo electrónico y el mensajero instantáneo los encuentro muy útiles porque puedo chatear y estar en contacto con mis amigos. Además, los deberes se hacen mejor en el ordenador. ¿Y las desventajas? El correo basura que recibes automáticamente con el email. Esto es muy desagradable.

Isabel, 17 años

1a 📖 🎧 Read the article and find the Spanish equivalents of these words and phrases. Then separate them into two lists: words useful for **this topic**, and words useful for **all topics**.

1b 📖 🎧 Read the article again and find who (Sara, Jorge or Isabel) says that:

1 they didn't get their favourite device from their family.
2 they are hoping for a present.
3 the main advantages and disadvantages are to do with security.
4 their parents are happy with them using it.
5 it is educational as well as fun.

2 🅖 Identify any direct and indirect object pronouns in these sentences. Then translate the sentences into English.

1 Mi nueva cámara digital es genial. Me la regalaron mis padres en Navidad.
2 ¿Me mandaste un mensaje? Sí, te lo mandé anoche.
3 Mis abuelos no tienen Internet. Les voy a escribir una carta.

3 🎧 Listen to the report then read the following sentences. Find the three that are true.

1 Reading on a screen hurts your eyes.
2 Older people have seen computers evolve.
3 It's better to read on a screen.
4 Young people are better at computers.
5 Old people find it hard to adapt.
6 Technology can help you keep in touch with family members.
7 New technology makes older people anxious.

4 ✏ Read the survey questions about technology on page 66. Write your own response, similar to those written by Sara, Jorge and Isabel.

they gave it to me	they improve
more than anything	indispensable
messages	advantages
calls	broadband
they feel	even
yet	download
probably	email
they complain	spam
entertaining	

Gramática · página 178

Direct and indirect object pronouns

Direct object pronouns

me – me	*nos* – us
te – you	*os* – you
lo / la – he / she / it	*los / las* – them

Indirect object pronouns (to me, to you, to him …) are the same except for:

le – to him / to her / to it   *les* – to them

*Adoro mi móvil. Mis padres **me lo** regalaron.* – I love my phone. My parents gave it to me.

Both pronouns go in front of a conjugated verb. In the example above, *me* (to me) is the indirect object and comes first; *lo* (it) is the direct object.

For more on handling pronouns, see page 69.

Estrategia 3

Avoiding traps when listening

Predicting answers is good, but do not automatically put what you assume should be the answer.

Listening for key words from the question is good, but not if they are being used as a distractor.

Answers that don't appear to have any of the words from the listening passage may turn out to be a correct summary of what was said.

Estrategia 4

Justifying opinions and adding extra information

In Activity 1a, you identified expressions that would be useful for any topic, e.g. *más que nada* or *incluso*.

Keep a list of these words and use them in your own writing.

Free time and the media

1 Copy and complete the sentences using the correct Spanish verb.

1 <u>I went</u> a la playa el fin de semana.
2 El sábado Guillermo <u>watched</u> un partido de fútbol.
3 <u>¿You did</u> los deberes por la mañana?
4 <u>I watched</u> un programa en la televisión.
5 Montse <u>went</u> a una fiesta.

> ### Irregular verbs in the preterite
>
> On pages 56–57 you will have noticed some irregular preterite verb forms:
>
> *fui* – I went
> *hice* – I did or made
> *vi* – I saw or watched
> *fuiste* – you went
> *hiciste* – you did or made
> *viste* – you saw or watched
> *fue* – he / she / it went
> *hizo* – he / she / it did or made
> *vio* – he / she / it saw or watched
>
> **Gramática** *página 182*

2 Read this dialogue and explain to a partner (or make notes on) exactly what the underlined words mean.

– ¿Dónde está la sección de vestidos?
– <u>Allí</u>, a la izquierda.
– ¿Por <u>aquí</u>?
– Sí, <u>allí</u>.
– ¿Y los probadores?
– Están <u>aquí</u>.
– También necesito unos zapatos.
– Los zapatos están <u>allá</u>, al fondo.

> ### Expressions of place
>
> On page 61 you saw how Spanish has three different ways of saying 'this / that'.
>
> There are three words for **here / there**, following the same pattern.
>
> | Near me | Near you | Not near either of us |
> |---------|----------|-----------------------|
> | *éste* | *ése* | *aquél* |
> | this one | that one | that one (over there) |
> | *aquí* | *allí* | *allá* |
> | here | there | (over) there |
>
> **Gramática** *página 177*

3 Decide which word **you** would choose to complete these sentences. Copy and complete the sentences.

1 Nos comunicamos _____ por teléfono que por Internet. (mejor / peor)
2 Es _____ ver una película en DVD que en el cine. (mejor / peor)
3 Hay muchos videojuegos y los juegos violentos son _____. (los mejores / los peores)
4 La música se escucha _____ en CD que en MP3. (mejor / peor)

> ### *Mejor* and *peor* – comparative / superlative adjectives and adverbs
>
> *Mejor* means 'better' or 'best'.
>
> *es muy bueno – es mejor – es el mejor*
> it is very good – it is better – it is the best
> *juega bien – juega mejor*
> he plays well – he plays better
>
> Remember to make *el mejor* agree in gender and number: *el / la mejor, los / las mejores*
>
> *Peor* means 'worse' and *el peor* means 'the worst'.
>
> **Gramática** *página 175*

4 Copy the sentences and fill in the gaps with the correct preterite form of the verb *jugar*, *tocar* or *sacar*.

1 En el concierto, _____ la batería y mi amiga Ángela tocó la guitarra.
2 _____ fotos de mi perro para un concurso.
3 El sábado _____ en un torneo de tenis, pero no llegué a la final.
4 Mis hermanos _____ un partido de fútbol.

página 182

Gramática

Regular verbs with spelling changes in the preterite

Some regular verbs have spelling changes in the first person form of the preterite. The changes are needed to maintain the sound pattern for the verb when it is pronounced. For example, *jugar* is a regular -*ar* verb so the first person singular ending in the preterite is -*é*. If just -*é* were added to *jug*-, the sound of the *g* would change. So the *u* must be added to keep the hard *g* sound: *jugué*.

jugar – to play (a sport or game) *jugué* – I played
sacar – to take (out) *saqué* – I took out
tocar – to play (an instrument) *toqué* – I played
empezar – to start *empecé* – I started

5 Translate these sentences into English and identify the comparative adjectives.

1 Los jóvenes que trabajan gastan el dinero más responsablemente.
2 Hoy todo tiene que hacerse más rápidamente.
3 Los jóvenes entienden mejor Internet que sus padres.

página 177

Gramática

Comparative and superlative adverbs

Adverbs are formed by adding -*mente* to the feminine singular form of an adjective.

– *rápido* – *rápidamente*

Use *más* or *menos* to make comparatives:

*Gracias a Internet, se puede comprar **más fácilmente**.*

Some irregular adverbs have irregular comparative and superlative forms:

bien – *mejor* *mal* – *peor*

6 Shorten these sentences by replacing the names of things and people with pronouns.

1 Voy a comprar el videojuego para mi hermano.
2 Regalé mi antiguo móvil a Miguel.
3 Leí las instrucciones a mi abuelo.
4 Me robaron la videoconsola.

página 178

Gramática

Using direct and indirect object pronouns together

The direct object pronoun for 'it' is *lo* or *la*. Normally the indirect object pronoun for 'to him' or 'to her' is *le*. But if you want to say 'He gave it to her', then you would get '*le lo*'. This sounds odd, and so does *le los*, *les lo*, etc. So the rule is that the *le / les* will change to *se*: *Se lo regaló*.

With a non-conjugated verb (an infinitive, imperative or present participle), the pronouns will attach to the end of the verb.

Voy a comprártelo. – I am going to buy it for you.
¡Cómpraselo! – Buy it for him!
Estoy comprándoselo. – I am buying it for him.

The accent makes sure the stress falls on the same part of the verb as it did before the pronouns were added.

Free time and the media

Topic 3.1 Free time activities

3.1 F ¿Qué tal el fin de semana? ➡ *pages 56–57*

	anoche	last night
	ayer	yesterday
la	batería	drums
el / la	cantante	singer
	cenar	to have dinner
	después de	after
el	equipo	team
el	fin de semana	weekend
	fui	I went
	ganar	to win
	hice	I did / I made
el	jugador	player
	libre	free
	luego	then
el	partido	match
la	película	film
la	semana pasada	last week
	por la tarde	in the afternoon
	a veces	sometimes
	vi	I saw / I watched

3.1 H ¿Qué hicisteis? ➡ *pages 58–59*

	acostarse	to go to bed
	apagar	to turn off
	caer(se)	to fall
	cerrar	to close
el	cumpleaños	birthday
	despertarse	to wake up
los	dibujos animados	cartoons
en	directo	live
el	documental	documentary
	empezar	to start
el	espectáculo	show
	llegar	to arrive

	llorar	to cry
las	noticias	news
las	palomitas	popcorn
	pasar la aspiradora	to vacuum
la	película de acción	action movie
la	película romántica	romantic film
el	ruido	noise
la	telenovela	TV soap
	trabajar	to work

Topic 3.2 Shopping, money, fashion and trends

3.2 F ¿Te gusta estar de moda? ➡ *pages 60–61*

los	calcetines	socks
el	efectivo	cash
el	escaparate	shop window
el	estilo	style
al	fondo	at the back
	gastar dinero	to spend money
los	grandes almacenes	department stores
el	maquillaje	make-up
de	marca	branded
	mismo/a	same
de	moda	fashionable
	nunca	never
	pagar	to pay
el	peinado	hairstyle
el	precio	price
	probarse	to try on
la	revista	magazine
la	ropa	clothes
de	segunda mano	second hand
	tampoco	neither
las	tendencias	trends
	vale la pena	it's worth it

3.2 H ¿En qué gastas tu dinero? ➡ *pages 62–63*

	ahorrar	to save
	alrededor de	around
	cambiar	to change
	dar	to give
la	encuesta	survey
	ganar	to earn
	igual	equal
	más	more
los	mayores	older people
	medio/a	average
	menos	less
el	mes	month
la	mitad	half
el	ocio	leisure
la	paga	pocket money
la	'pasta'	'dosh' / money
	pedir	to ask for
un	poco	a little
la	publicidad	advertising
	seguir + -ando /+ -iendo	to carry on

Topic 3.3 Media and new technology

3.3 F Los medios y la comunicación
➡ *pages 64–65*

el	aparato	device
la	cámara	camera
el	correo electrónico	email
el	disco compacto	CD
	enviar	to send
	imprescindible	indispensable
la	llamada	call
	mejor	better
el	mensaje	message
	nada	nothing
	peor	worse
el	periódico	newspaper
el	programa	programme
la	red	network

el	sitio web	website
el	tebeo	comic
	usar	to use
	utilizar	to use
la	videoconsola	games console

3.3 H La tecnología y las diferentes generaciones ➡ *pages 66–67*

	aislado/a	isolated
la	banda ancha	broadband
el	correo basura	spam
la	destreza	skill
la	gente	people
	incluso	even
la	informática	IT
los	jóvenes	young people
la	luz	light
	más que nada	more than anything
	a lo mejor	probably
	a menudo	often
el	ordenador	computer
los	nietos	grandchildren
la	pantalla	screen
	quejarse	to complain
	regalar	to give a gift
	sentirse	to feel
el	tamaño de la letra	font size
	todavía	still
la	ventaja	advantage

4.1 F ¡Estamos de vacaciones!

1 🅥 Categorise the following activities according to the type of holiday you would do them on. Some could go in more than one column.

tomar el sol	visitar monumentos	sacar fotos	nadar en el mar
comprar recuerdos	ir a la playa	comer en restaurantes típicos
esquiar	caminar por el bosque	visitar a la familia	comer helados
ir al mercado	bailar en discotecas	leer libros

en la costa	en la montaña	en la ciudad
tomar el sol	esquiar	

2a 📖 🎧 Read the responses to the forum post. Then look carefully at the pictures and note in which order they are mentioned.

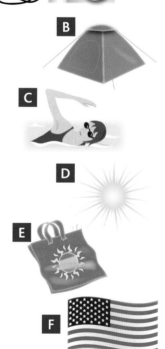

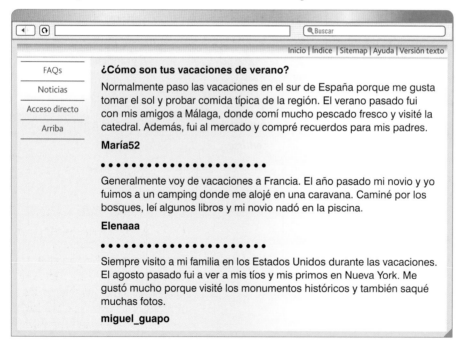

Inicio | Índice | Sitemap | Ayuda | Versión texto

FAQs
Noticias
Acceso directo
Arriba

¿Cómo son tus vacaciones de verano?

Normalmente paso las vacaciones en el sur de España porque me gusta tomar el sol y probar comida típica de la región. El verano pasado fui con mis amigos a Málaga, donde comí mucho pescado fresco y visité la catedral. Además, fui al mercado y compré recuerdos para mis padres.

María52

• •

Generalmente voy de vacaciones a Francia. El año pasado mi novio y yo fuimos a un camping donde me alojé en una caravana. Caminé por los bosques, leí algunos libros y mi novio nadó en la piscina.

Elenaaa

• •

Siempre visito a mi familia en los Estados Unidos durante las vacaciones. El agosto pasado fui a ver a mis tíos y mis primos en Nueva York. Me gustó mucho porque visité los monumentos históricos y también saqué muchas fotos.

miguel_guapo

2b 📖 🎧 Read the responses to the forum post again, then read the following sentences. Decide if each sentence is true (**T**), false (**F**) or not mentioned (**?**).

1 María likes to sunbathe and drink wine.
2 María prefers going on holiday with her friends.
3 Elena stayed in a caravan last year.
4 Elena swam in the pool.
5 Miguel travelled by plane to America.
6 Miguel did lots of sightseeing.

3a **G** Can you find all the preterite tense verbs in the forum posts in Activity 2? Hint: There are 14!

3b **G** Choose the correct verb in the preterite tense to complete these sentences. Then translate the sentences into English.

1   El año pasado yo visité / visito / vistamos Grecia con mis padres.
2   Paso / Pasé / Pasas dos semanas de vacaciones en el sur de Italia.
3   Normalmente voy a Escocia con mi madre pero el verano pasado viajo / viajé / viajaste con mi padre a Gales.
4   El mes pasado en Roma mi hermano compro / compró / compré muchos recuerdos cuando fuimos al mercado.
5   Durante las vacaciones fui a restaurantes típicos y comiste / comí / comisteis paella por primera vez.

4a Listen to Ana and Juan talking about their holidays and note down which three things are mentioned from the list below.

1   languages   4   skiing
2   travel arrangements   5   plans for next holiday
3   going to the beach   6   visiting grandparents

4b Listen again and answer the following questions in English.

1   Where did Juan go last year and why?
2   Where did he stay?
3   What did he do there?
4   Why was Ana's holiday different last year?
5   Who did she go with?
6   What will she do after her exams?

5 Write a reply to the forum post in Activity 2a.

■   Describe what you normally do on holiday.
■   Say what you did last time you went on holiday.
■   Say if you liked it or not and why.

Normalmente En general Generalmente	voy de vacaciones a … visito monumentos / museos / a mi familia. me gusta (+ infinitive).	
El año / mes pasado El verano / invierno pasado	fui de vacaciones a … pasé una semana / dos semanas en … me alojé en … nadé en el mar. comí pescado fresco / en restaurantes típicos.	
Me gustó (mucho) No me gustó (nada)	porque ya que	fue una experiencia inolvidable / horrible. lo pasé muy bien / fatal.

Revision of the preterite tense

This tense is key to describing what you did on holiday. Remember, to form the regular preterite tense, remove the infinitive endings -ar, -er or -ir, to leave the stem and add the following endings:

-ar verbs	-er / -ir verbs
-é	-í
-aste	-iste
-ó	-ió
-amos	-imos
-asteis	-isteis
-aron	-ieron

For more on the preterite tense, see page 84.

Gramática página 181

Showing off the language you know

If you can't remember exactly what you originally planned to say, or you don't have an opinion on something you are asked about, don't panic. The key thing to remember is to produce information in accurate Spanish – you don't have to tell the truth! It is perfectly possible to do well at this writing activity even if you have never been on holiday in your life!

Estrategia 5

Enlace

4.1 Groundwork is available in the Foundation book.

4.1 H ¿Qué tipo de vacaciones prefieres?

Para mí, lo ideal son las vacaciones de sol y playa. Y mi lugar de veraneo preferido es Nerja, que está cerca de Málaga en el sur de España. Estuve en Nerja el mes pasado. Fui sola y además de tomar el sol, bañarme y practicar la vela, visité la famosa Cueva prehistórica. La Cueva de Nerja fue descubierta en 1959. También hay muchos parques temáticos como 'Tivoli World' que tiene más de cuarenta atracciones. Cuando estuve allí monté en la Torre de Caída y la Noria. ¡Qué miedo! Me gusta veranear en Nerja porque me olvido del estrés de los estudios.

Lucía

A mí me encanta la naturaleza y siempre hago eco turismo. Durante las vacaciones de Semana Santa estuve de vacaciones en los Picos de Europa, las montañas en el norte de España. Fui con mis amigos. Sólo llevamos mochilas, sacos de dormir y un libro de guía. Nos alojamos en albergues juveniles. Conocimos a gente nueva y lo pasamos estupendamente. Practicamos senderismo, alquilamos bicicletas de montaña, montamos a caballo e hicimos piragüismo. Un día fuimos de excursión a un pueblo antiguo con un castillo que fue construido en el siglo X.

Cristóbal

Prefiero ir de camping cuando estoy de vacaciones porque estás al aire libre. Este verano fui de camping a Los Pirineos con mi novia. Quisimos unas vacaciones baratas. Fuimos en moto. En el camping hay de todo: desde canchas de baloncesto y mini golf hasta peluquería y tienda de regalos. Alquilé una tienda muy cómoda. Durante el día nadamos en el lago cercano, fuimos de paseo, practicamos la pesca y sacamos fotos. Compramos comida en el supermercado del camping e hicimos barbacoas para cenar. Una noche tuvimos mala suerte porque hubo tormenta.

Eduardo

1a 📖 🎧 Read the speech bubbles. Find the Spanish equivalents of the following phrases.

1 my favourite summer place
2 was discovered
3 more than forty
4 how scary!
5 we only took

6 we met new people
7 we had a great time
8 was built in the tenth century
9 we wanted a cheap holiday
10 bad luck

1b 📖 🎧 Match up each speech bubble with the correct photo (A–D). (There is one extra photo.)

1c 📖 🎧 Write the name of the person who …

1 went on a walking holiday.   4 stayed in youth hostels.
2 went sailing.   5 visited a cave.
3 met new people.   6 fished.

2 🇬 Identify which of the following sentences are in the passive voice, then translate them into English.

1 La catedral es admirada por todo el mundo.
2 Los cheques de viajero fueron cambiados en el banco.
3 Los jóvenes fueron a la oficina de turismo para informarse.
4 El museo fue cerrado durante dos meses.
5 A mi amiga le regalé un abanico.
6 El portero trae las maletas a la habitación.

3a 🎧 Listen to Gema, Antonio, Paloma and Joaquín talking about their holiday experiences. Are their comments positive (**P**), negative (**N**) or both (**P + N**)?

3b 🎧 Listen again and write the name of the person who …

1 got sunstroke.
2 lost luggage.
3 had their flight cancelled.
4 had their passport stolen.

4 🗨 Work with a partner. Ask questions to find out about their last holiday and what they did, then swap partners and tell your new partner what the first person did on holiday.

¿Adónde fuiste de vacaciones el año pasado?

El año pasado fui de vacaciones a …

¿Qué hacías durante el día?

Durante el día … y … pero … sin embargo … Me gustó (mucho) porque …

¿Y por la noche?

Por la noche … y… pero … sin embargo … Me gustó (mucho) porque …

Gramática   *página 186*

Recognising the passive voice

In a passive sentence the subject has something done to it, him or her:

El castillo fue construido por los romanos. – The castle was built by the Romans.

Remember that the passive is formed with *ser* and a past participle.

Also learn about interrogative pronouns.   *See page 85*

Estrategia 4

Using questions to help you to answer

Use the questions to help you to formulate your answers. Listen to a question very carefully in the Speaking assessment as they often contain clues about what you can include in your answer. If you get stuck on where to start when you are trying to answer your Controlled assessment questions, listen carefully to the question you have been asked as you can use the structure in your answer. This is also a useful tip for the unpredictable question. Look at the questions below. Can you see how the beginning of the answer is similar to the question?

¿Qué te gusta hacer durante el día? Durante el día me gusta …

¿Qué tiempo hizo? Hizo buen tiempo todo el día pero un día llovió.

How would you answer the following questions:

¿Adónde fuiste de vacaciones el año pasado?

¿Adónde vas a ir de vacaciones el año que viene?

4.2 F   Vamos de visita

1 **V** Categorise the following vocabulary into two separate lists: transport or places in town.

el ayuntamiento	en barco	el hotel	el castillo
	en avión	en coche	la plaza mayor
la estación de trenes	el zoológico	la galería de arte	
en ferrocarril	en tren	a pie	el teatro
la plaza de toros	el puerto	el estadio	
el centro comercial	en bicicleta	en autocar	
en autobús	en tranvía	la oficina	de Correos
los grandes almacenes	el restaurante		

2a 📖 🎧 Read the conversation, then look at pictures A–D below and choose which speech bubble each picture refers to.

1 Mira, Anita. Este plano es de mi pueblo. Esta plaza es la Plaza Mayor. Aquí está el ayuntamiento.

¿Qué es ese edificio, Paco?

2 Es la biblioteca y al lado están Correos y la comisaría.

¿Hay un centro comercial?

3 No, pero esta calle es la calle principal con bancos y unos grandes almacenes.

¿Hay metro?

4 Todavía no hay. Esa estación es de autobuses. Aquella estación, en las afueras, es la del tren.

¿Qué es aquéllo?

5 Era una fábrica pero ahora es un hotel. Y aquel hospital es nuevo.

¿Y para diversión?

6 Hay cines, restaurantes, discotecas … de todo.

A

B

C

D

2b 📖 🎧 Read the conversation again. There is one error in each of the following sentences. Rewrite each sentence correctly.

1 The town hall is on the High Street.
2 The police station, post office and bookshop are close to each other.
3 There is no department store.
4 The town has an underground train system.

3 **G** Copy the sentences and fill in the gaps with the correct demonstrative adjective.

1 _____ (*this*) restaurante se llama Las Fuentes.
2 _____ (*this*) calle, con bares y cafeterías, es la calle principal.
3 _____ (*that*) hotel allí es nuevo.
4 _____ (*those*) tiendas son bastante grandes.
5 _____ (*these*) películas se ponen hoy en el cine.

4 🎧 Listen to the conversations and answer the following questions in English.

1 What platform does the Malaga train leave from?
2 What do you have to do at the crossroads?
3 What is cheaper than driving?
4 What is after the traffic lights?
5 What is the person looking for?
6 How does the person suggest travelling?

5 💬 Work with a partner. Discuss what there is to visit in your town. Mention where it is located and how you can get there. Use the vocabulary in Activity 1 to help you. Try to use as many linking words from the language structure box to help you extend your sentences.

En mi pueblo / ciudad hay	un centro comercial un castillo una plaza, etc.	sin embargo hay … aunque también hay … además hay …	
Se puede ir a …	a pie en bicicleta en tren en autobús, etc.	luego entonces	se puede ir en … a …

Demonstrative adjectives

Gramática *página 176*

Demonstrative adjectives ('this, that'; 'these, those') are used with a noun and must agree with it.

este	esta	estos	estas	this / these
ese	esa	esos	esas	that / those
aquel	aquella	aquellos	aquellas	that / those

Aquel refers to something further away:

Ese polideportivo es viejo pero aquél es nuevo.

The same words are also used as demonstrative pronouns, appearing in place of a noun ('this one' and 'that one', 'these ones' and 'those ones').

Remember that these words have an accent when they are used as pronouns.

Also learn how to use *vamos* to mean 'let's'.

See page 84

Using linking words

Estrategia 5

Make your work more advanced by including a wider range of vocabulary that will help your language to flow better, for example: *sin embargo, aunque, además, luego, entonces, después de* + infinitive, *antes de* + infinitive.

 **Enlace**

4.2 Groundwork is available in the Foundation book.

Objetivos
Sightseeing and activities
Using the perfect tense
Giving opinions

4.2 H ¡Vamos de excursión!

1a 📖 🎧 Read the dialogues and find the correct word for each gap from the lists at the bottom of the page. Then listen and check.

En la oficina de alquiler de coches

Cliente: Quisiera alquilar un coche. ¿Me puede decir cuánto cuesta?

Empleado: ¿Qué modelo de coche quiere alquilar?

Cliente: Un SEAT Ibiza.

Empleado: ¿Por cuántos días quiere alquilarlo?

Cliente: Por cuatro días.

Empleado: La tarifa por un SEAT Ibiza es 73.25 euros por día pero por cuatro días son 219.76. Incluye seguros de robo y colisión y el IVA.

Cliente: ¿Tiene aire (1) …?

Empleado: Sí, y equipo de música.

Cliente: Está bien.

Empleado: Rellene esta (2) …, por favor. Y déme su carnet de (3) …

Cliente: Tome usted.

Empleado: Enséñeme su (4) … de identidad o su pasaporte.

Cliente: Tenga.

Empleado: ¿Va a pagar con tarjeta de crédito o en efectivo?

Cliente: Con tarjeta de crédito.

Empleado: Perfecto. Firme aquí.

Cliente: Queremos ir a Ávila.

Empleado: Mire el mapa de la región. Tome la (5) … con dirección a Burgos.

| documento | ficha | acondicionado |

| autopista | conducir |

En la taquilla de RENFE

Viajero: Quiero ir a Barcelona pasado mañana.

Taquillero: Hay varias opciones. El tren más rápido es el AVE.

Viajero: ¿A qué hora sale el primer tren?

Taquillero: A las 6h. Hay trenes cada media hora hasta las 22h.

Viajero: ¿Cuánto tarda el (6) … ?

Taquillero: Dos horas 43 minutos. La llegada a Barcelona es a las 8h43.

Viajero: ¿Hay que cambiar?

Taquillero: No, es (7) …

Viajero: ¿Hay (8) … para jóvenes?

Taquillero: Sí, un 20%. ¿Tiene carné joven?

Viajero: Sí, tome. Déme un (9) … de ida y vuelta en el AVE para el jueves a las 13h30.

Taquillero: ¿Cuándo va a regresar?

Viajero: El domingo.

Taquillero: Son 125 euros.

Viajero: Tome usted.

Taquillero: Hay máquinas de auto check-in en la estación. Puede utilizar su billete también en los trenes de cercanías.

Viajero: Hay servicio de cafetería en el (10) …, ¿no?

Taquillero: Sí, y hay música y vídeo por canal individual.

Viajero: ¡Qué bien!

| tren | billete | viaje | descuento | directo |

1b 📖 🎧 Read the dialogues again then read the following sentences. Decide if they are true (**T**), false (**F**) or not mentioned (**?**).

1 The car is hired for 5 days.
2 The car hire includes insurance.
3 The car hire is paid for in cash.
4 The car has to be returned on Wednesday.
5 The train is a direct train to Barcelona.
6 The train leaves from platform 7.
7 There is no discount for young people.
8 The return train journey is on Saturday.

2 🄖 Copy the sentences and fill in the gaps with the correct form of the verb *haber* and the correct past participle.

1 Javier y Pili _____ _____ un plato de paella valenciana.
2 ¿Vosotros _____ _____ el espectáculo de flamenco?
3 Yo _____ _____ el museo de la ciencia.
4 ¿Tú _____ _____ en Valencia?
5 A Marcos le _____ _____ mucho el acuario.
6 Nosotros _____ _____ a las corridas de toros.

3 🎧 Listen to the conversation and answer the following questions in English.

1 Why hasn't Sara seen Marcos?
2 How many days running has he visited the City of Arts and Sciences?
3 Which museum is in the shape of a dinosaur?
4 What has impressed him about the aquarium?
5 What two things impressed him about the flamenco show?
6 Why did he like the planetarium best?

4 ✏️ Write an article for a tourist magazine to advertise a holiday resort that you have visited. Include where you went, what you did there and your opinions on it. Read the example below for ideas.

> El año pasado fui a Palma de Mallorca con mis amigos. Nos alojamos en un hotel de tres estrellas que era muy cómodo y tenía una piscina enorme y un buen restaurante. En mi opinión, el hotel era fantástico porque cada día organizaba excursiones al centro donde se podía visitar los museos. Me gustó mucho porque fue muy interesante. Además, fui a la playa casi cada día ya que me encanta tomar el sol y relajarme con un buen libro.

Gramática — *página 182*

Using the perfect tense

To form the perfect tense, use the appropriate form of *haber* and the past participle.

To form the past participle add -*ado* to the stem of -*ar* verbs and -*ido* to the stem of -*er* and -*ir* verbs:

He estado de vacaciones. – I've been on holiday.

Also learn about using the imperative.

See page 85

Estrategia 4

Giving opinions

In order to gain a C grade or higher, you should include at least two opinions in your assignments. Aim to include more if you want more than a C. In order to develop your response further and show complexity of language, say why you have that opinion. Don't forget, you can change the tense of your opinion as well! For example:

Me gusta viajar en avión porque, en mi opinión, es más rápido que viajar en coche.

No me gustó visitar los monumentos porque pensé que era aburrido.

4.3 F ¿Qué vas a hacer de vacaciones?

1 **V** Look at the phrases below and categorise them according to whether they are an activity or a type of accommodation.

un hotel de cinco estrellas	broncearme en la playa
un apartamento en la playa	nadar en el mar un albergue juvenil
salir de marcha hacer snowboard	un chalet
pasear por las calles estrechas una pensión	asistir a una escuela de salsa
aprender a bailar salsa hacer un curso de buceo	

Este invierno voy a pasar una semana en la nieve. Voy a una estación de esquí en Sierra Nevada que para mí es el lugar número uno para deportes de invierno. Aunque está tan sólo a dos horas de la Costa del Sol, Sierra Nevada es una de las mejores estaciones de esquí en España. Voy a ir con un grupo de amigos y nos vamos a alojar en un chalet con vistas a las pistas. Vamos a poder esquiar y hacer snowboard no sólo por el día sino también por la noche. Para nosotros es importante la vida nocturna y es muy animada en Sierra Nevada. Después de un duro día en la pista vamos a salir de marcha a los bares, pubs y clubes. Vamos a pasarlo estupendamente.

Sergio

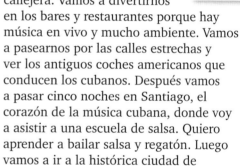

Voy a ir a la isla de Cuba a pasar mis vacaciones este año. Mi hermano viene conmigo. Vamos a pasar unos días en La Habana en un hotel de cinco estrellas en el Malecón, el paseo que bordea el mar. La Habana es una ciudad con mucha vida callejera. Vamos a divertirnos en los bares y restaurantes porque hay música en vivo y mucho ambiente. Vamos a pasearnos por las calles estrechas y ver los antiguos coches americanos que conducen los cubanos. Después vamos a pasar cinco noches en Santiago, el corazón de la música cubana, donde voy a asistir a una escuela de salsa. Quiero aprender a bailar salsa y regatón. Luego vamos a ir a la histórica ciudad de Trinidad donde mi hermano va a hacer un curso de buceo. Yo voy a descansar y broncearme en la playa.

Marisa

2a Who is going to do what on holiday this year? Write **S** (Sergio) or **M** (Marisa).

Who is going to …

1 sunbathe?
2 do sports?
3 go to dance classes?
4 take a walk around the city?
5 enjoy themselves in the night clubs?
6 stay in a house?

2b 🖊 🎧 Using the immediate future, write two more things that Sergio and Marisa are each going to do. Look at the grammar box for further help.

Ejemplo: Sergio va a ir con un grupo de amigos.

3a **G** Copy the sentences and fill in the gaps with the correct form of the verb *ir* and the correct infinitive.

Ejemplo: 1 Consuelo <u>va</u> a <u>jugar</u> al tenis.

1 Consuelo _____ a _____ al tenis.
2 Esta Semana Santa Emilio y yo _____ a _____ a Sevilla.
3 ¿Dónde _____ vosotros a _____ las vacaciones?
4 Lorenzo y Luisa _____ a _____ el tren de las 6.00.
5 ¿Y tú? ¿Qué _____ a _____ por las tardes?
6 Yo _____ a _____ en una pensión de dos estrellas.

va	van	vas	vais	voy
vamos	jugar	alojarme	ir
hacer	coger	pasar

3b **G** Translate the sentences in Activity 3a into English.

Ejemplo: 1 Consuelo is going to play tennis.

4 🎧 Listen to Benjamín talking about his holiday plans. Decide whether the following statements are true (**T**) or false (**F**). Correct the false statements.

1 Benjamín is going to go to the coast for his holiday.
2 He is going to find it difficult to understand what people are saying.
3 Benjamín is going to be travelling by ferry.
4 Patrick is going to stay for a fortnight with Benjamín.
5 Going to the countryside will be the highlight of Benjamín's stay.
6 Benjamín expects the weather will be good during his visit.

5 🗣 Describe your plans for your next holiday to your partner. You could include the following:

- where you are going to go
- what you plan to do
- who you plan to go with
- where you are going to stay
- how you are going to travel.

🔗 *Enlace*

4.3 Groundwork is available in the Foundation book.

Gramática · *página 183*

Revision of the immediate future

To talk about the immediate future use *ir a* + infinitive:

voy a aprender – I'm going to learn

vas a bailar – you are going to dance

va a divertirse – he / she is / you (formal) are going to have a good time

vamos a ir – we are going to go

vais a pasar – you are going to spend

van a salir – they / you (formal, plural) are going to go out

Este invierno voy a pasar una semana en la nieve. – This winter I'm going to spend a week in the snow.

Also learn about disjunctive pronouns.
See page 84

Estrategia 4

Prefixes

To work out the meaning of an unfamiliar word, note prefixes that are the same or similar in Spanish (*re-*, *pre-*, *des-*). Recognising the root verb will also help you to conjugate the verb. To work out the meaning of *rellenar* in the sentence *¿Puedes rellenar la ficha?*, remove *re-* from *rellenar*. *Llenar* means 'to fill' so *rellenar* must mean 'to fill in'.

Make a note of any other verbs that you have found that have a prefix.

Listening for negatives

Whenever you are listening to Spanish, listen out for the speaker using any negative words or linking words that could indicate a different view, as this will change the meaning of what they are saying.

no – no

nada – nothing, at all

sin – without

pero – but

sin embargo – however

4.3 H Mis vacaciones ideales

1a 📖 🎧 Read Isabel's email. Find the Spanish equivalents of the following words and phrases.

1 I wanted to travel
2 the flights cost too much
3 I queued to buy them
4 on arriving in London
5 the taxi driver charged us
6 very tired
7 the nightmare continued
8 ask for a different room for us
9 it was very difficult
10 I lost my purse

◀ ⟳ [   ] 🔍 Buscar

Inicio | Índice | Sitemap | Ayuda | Versión texto

Querido Pablo,

¡No te vas a creer lo que me ha pasado recientemente! Pues, el mes pasado pasé una semana en Londres, la famosa capital de Inglaterra. Quería viajar en avión desde el aeropuerto de Edimburgo porque está cerca de mi casa, pero los vuelos costaban demasiado y mi madre nos dijo que teníamos que ir en tren.

Cuando llegamos a la estación tuvimos que comprar los billetes, así que me puse en la cola para comprarlos, pero había tantas personas esperando que perdimos el tren y tuvimos que esperar una hora para el siguiente. Al llegar a Londres teníamos mucha hambre, pero era muy tarde y las tiendas y las cafeterías ya estaban cerradas, así que cogimos un taxi para ir al hotel. Todo es muy caro en Londres ¿no? ¡El taxista nos cobró diez libras por un viaje de sólo cinco minutos!

Finalmente llegamos al hotel con mucho sueño, pero la pesadilla continuó. Primero, las llaves no funcionaban y luego cuando entramos en la habitación las camas no estaban hechas y el cuarto de baño estaba sucio y no había toallas ni papel higiénico tampoco. Tuve que hablar con la recepcionista y pedir que nos cambiara de habitación.

Mientras estábamos en Londres el tiempo fue horrible. Todos los días hacía mucho frío y nevaba también, así que había problemas con el transporte público y resultaba muy difícil llegar a los museos y a los otros lugares de interés. Un día fui de compras a la gran y famosa calle que se llama Oxford Street y fui a varias tiendas, pero en una perdí el monedero con todo mi dinero. ¡Vaya vacaciones! La verdad es que me gustaría volver a Londres, pero quizás durante el verano cuando haga sol. Si pudiera, iría sin mi familia porque sería menos complicado.

¡Espero que tú hayas tenido unas vacaciones mejores que las mías!

Un beso,

Isabel

1b 📖🎧 Read the email again and answer the following questions in English.

1 Where was Isabel spending a week?
2 How did she travel there and why?
3 Why did they miss the train?
4 What was the issue with the taxi driver?
5 What problems were there at the hotel? (Give details of three.)
6 What was the weather like during her stay?
7 What happened when she went shopping?
8 Does she want to go back? Give one detail explaining your answer.

2 🅖 Copy the sentences and fill in the gaps with the correct form of the conditional from the boxes below.

1 Yo _____ en avión y luego en tren.
2 Nosotros nos _____ en un hotel de cinco estrellas.
3 Mis vacaciones ideales _____ en una isla privada.
4 La isla _____ playas blancas y mares azules.
5 _____ mucho sol y calor.
6 _____ cócteles mientras _____ un libro.
7 Yo _____ de excursión a lugares interesantes.
8 Yo _____ de las diferentes culturas.

viajaría	bebería	serían	leería	iría
quedaríamos	aprendería	tendría	haría	

3 🎧 Listen to Alicia (**A**), Juan (**J**) and María (**M**) talking about their ideal holiday plans. Make a note of the person who …

1 would like to stay in a hotel.
2 would go shopping.
3 wants to visit New York.
4 would like to cook.
5 would like to stay in an apartment.
6 goes on holiday with their family.
7 would like to do winter sports on holiday.
8 would spend the day relaxing.

4 🖊 Describe your own disastrous holiday and explain what you would like to do next time you go on holiday. Use the email in Activity 1 to help you.

Using the conditional tense

The conditional translates as 'would' in English:

Me gustaría volver el año que viene. – I would like to return next year.

Regular verbs are very easy to form as you just put the endings onto the infinitive, and the endings are the same for *-ar*, *-er* and *-ir* verbs.

yo	-ía
tú	-ías
él / ella	-ía
nosotros	-íamos
vosotros	-íais
ellos/as	-ían

e.g. *hablaría, comería, viviría*

You will need to know some of the irregulars as well. Just add the endings on to their stems.

Hacer > har > haría
Tener > tendr > tendría

Also learn about using a variety of tenses. *See page 85*

Gramática *página 184*

Using a variety of tenses

In your Controlled assessments you will achieve a higher grade if you can show that you can use a variety of tenses accurately. Try to use three tenses at least four times each throughout your work to show that you can use them correctly.

Si clauses

Si means 'if' in Spanish (not to be confused with *sí*, which means 'yes') and can be used with the conditional tense to make Higher sentences, like the examples below.

Si pudiera, iría al estadio de fútbol durante la visita.

Si me tocara la lotería, compraría un coche nuevo y una casa enorme.

Si tuviera mucho dinero, me compraría un yate y viajaría por todo el mundo.

Estrategia 4

ⓖ Holidays

1 Copy the sentences and fill in the gaps with the correct form of the verb in the preterite tense, using the words below.

1 (*I was*) _____ de vacaciones en el extranjero, en Alemania.
2 El policía me (*he gave*) _____ un documento.
3 No (*it was*) _____ buen tiempo.
4 Juan (*he had*) _____ mala suerte.
5 Ana dijo que (*it was*) _____ una experiencia inolvidable.
6 Durante mi estancia (*I played*) _____ el tenis e (*I did*) _____ buceo también.

| tuvo | hizo | fue | practiqué |
| estuve | dio | hice | |

2 Look at the pictures and write a caption for each one using *vamos a ...* . Then write five more sentences using *vamos (a) ...* .

3 Copy the sentences and fill in the gaps with the correct disjunctive pronoun.

1 La paella es _____ (*for us*).
2 Esta postal es _____ (*for you, singular informal*).
3 ¿Las limonadas son _____ (*for you, plural informal*)?
4 Va a ir a la montaña _____ (*with them*).
5 ¿Quieres venir _____ (*with me*)?
6 Yo hablé _____ (*with him*).

4 Choose the correct interrogative pronoun to complete these questions. Then work with a partner and make up more questions.

1 ¿_____ te gusta más? (*which*)

2 ¿_____ te dio el regalo? (*who*)

3 ¿_____ quieres ir a los Estados Unidos? (*why*)

4 ¿_____ vamos a ir al aeropuerto? (*how*)

5 ¿_____ es la fiesta de San Fermín? (*when*)

6 ¿_____ quieres hacer hoy? (*what*)

Gramática *página 180*

Interrogative pronouns

To ask a question, use an interrogative pronoun at the beginning of the sentence. Remember that these words have accents when they are used as interrogatives.

¿Cómo? – How?

¿Cuál? ¿Cuáles? – Which?

¿Cuándo? – When?

¿Cuánto/a/os/as? – How many / much?

¿Dónde? – Where?

¿Adónde? – To where?

¿Qué? – What?

¿Por qué? – Why?

¿Quién(es)? – Who?

¿De quién? – Who from?

5 Choose the appropriate form of the imperative by deciding whether the requests are formal or familiar.

1 No beba / bebas tanta cerveza, Manolo.

2 ¡Ve / Vaya al hospital enseguida, señora!

3 Cruce / Cruza la plaza, Mónica.

4 Rellena / Rellene el formulario, señor.

5 Señores, visitad / visiten nuestro pueblo.

6 Patricio, pon / ponga los platos en el lavaplatos.

Gramática *página 184*

Imperatives

Imperatives give commands and instructions.

To form *vosotros* imperatives, remove the *-r* from the infinitive and replace it with *-d*.

To form *tú* imperatives just remove the *-s* from the present tense *tú* form.

Usted(es) imperatives work differently: they use the subjunctive form.

	Familiar	Formal			
	tú	*vosotros*	*usted*	*ustedes*	
-ar	cierra	cerrad	cierre	cierren	close
-er	come	comed	coma	coman	eat
-ir	abre	abrid	abra	abran	open

Compra este recuerdo. – Buy this souvenir.

6 Copy the paragraph and fill in the gaps with the correct verb from the selection given below.

Normalmente (**1**) _____ en España para las vacaciones de verano pero el agosto pasado (**2**) _____ de vacaciones a Italia con mi hermana Luisa. (**3**) _____ en avión porque (**4**) _____ más rápido que viajar en tren. Durante las vacaciones (**5**) _____ en la casa de nuestra tía que (**6**) _____ en Sorrento y (**7**) _____ mucho con los primos. En diciembre mis primos (**8**) _____ en España y (**9**) _____ aquí para dos semanas. (**10**) _____ muy divertido estar con toda la familia durante las navidades.

nos divertimos	vive	viajamos	estarán
nos quedamos	será	fui	van a visitarnos
me quedo	era		

Gramática *páginas 180–185*

Using a variety of tenses

Being able to recognise and use a variety of tenses is an important skill to develop. You will be able to use the present tense, the preterite tense and the immediate future tense to describe your holidays, but consider using time markers to help focus the examiner's attention on which tense you have used.

e.g. *el año que viene* – next year
el mes pasado – last month

Holidays

Topic 4.1 Holiday experiences

4.1 F ¡Estamos de vacaciones! ➡ *pages 72–73*

el	albergue juvenil	youth hostel
	alojarse	to stay
	bailar en discotecas	to dance in night clubs
	caminar por el bosque	to walk in the woods
el	camping	campsite
la	caravana	caravan
	comer en restaurantes típicos	to eat in traditional restaurants
	comer helados	to eat ice cream
	comprar recuerdos	to buy souvenirs
el	idioma	language
	ir a la playa	to go to the beach
	ir al mercado	to go to the market
	leer libros	to read books
el	museo	museum
	nadar en el mar	to swim in the sea
	pasar	to spend (time)
	quedarse	to stay
	sacar fotos	to take pictures
	tomar el sol	to sunbathe
	visitar a la familia	to visit family
	visitar monumentos	to visit monuments

4.1 H ¿Qué tipo de vacaciones prefieres?
➡ *pages 74–75*

el	aire libre	open air
	alojarse	to stay
	alquilar	to rent
	averiado	broken down
	bañarse	to swim
la	cancha (de baloncesto)	(basketball) court
la	ficha	form
la	guía	guidebook
	hacer piragüismo	to go canoeing

la	insolación	sunstroke
	ir de excursión	to go on a trip
	montar una atracción	to go on a ride
el	parque temático	theme park
	practicar la vela	to go sailing
el	retraso	delay
el	saco de dormir	sleeping bag
la	Semana Santa	Easter
el	senderismo	hiking
	solo / solamente	only
	veranear	to spend the summer holidays

Topic 4.2 What to see and getting around

4.2 F Vamos de visita ➡ *pages 76–77*

el	andén	platform
el	autobús	bus
el	autocar	coach
el	AVE	high-speed train
el	ayuntamiento	town hall
el	barco	boat
el	centro comercial	shopping centre
	coger	to take / catch
el	cruce	crossroads
la	estación de trenes	train station
el	estadio	stadium
la	fábrica	factory
el	ferrocarril	railway / train
los	grandes almacenes	department stores
la	oficina de correos	post office
	a pie	on foot
la	plaza de toros	bullring
el	puerto	port
la	sala de espera	waiting room
el	tranvía	tram

4.2 H ¡Vamos de excursión! ➡ *pages 78–79*

el	*acuario*	aquarium
el	*aire acondicionado*	air conditioning
	alquilar	to hire
el	*billete*	ticket
el	*carnet de identidad*	ID card
el	*carné joven*	young person's card
el	*concierto*	concert
en	*efectivo*	in cash
el	*espectáculo*	show / performance
	firmar	to sign
	de ida	single (ticket)
	de ida y vuelta	return (ticket)
la	*llegada*	arrival
	pagar	to pay
	regresar	to return
	rellenar	to fill in
la	*salida*	departure
el	*seguro*	insurance
	tardar	to take (time)
la	*tarjeta de crédito*	credit card

Topic 4.3 Planning holidays

4.3 F ¿Qué vas a hacer de vacaciones?
➡ *pages 80–81*

el	*ambiente*	atmosphere
	aprender	to learn
	asistir	to attend / go to
	broncearse	to sunbathe
el	*buceo*	diving
un	*chalet*	villa, chalet
	descansar	to rest
el	*equipaje*	luggage
	estrecho/a	narrow
el	*intercambio*	exchange
la	*isla*	island
el	*lugar*	place

la	*nieve*	snow
el	*paraguas*	umbrella
	pasear	to go for a walk
la	*pista*	ski slope
la	*vida nocturna*	nightlife
la	*vista*	view
	en vivo	live (music)
	volar	to fly

4.3 H Mis vacaciones ideales ➡ *pages 82–83*

la	*cama*	bed
la	*capital*	capital
	cobrar	to charge
la	*cola*	queue
la	*Estatua de la libertad*	Statue of Liberty
la	*excursión*	trip
	tener ganas de	to want to
la	*habitación*	room
	tener hambre	to be hungry
la	*llave*	key
	lujoso/a	luxurious
el	*monedero*	purse
el	*papel higiénico*	toilet paper
	perder	to lose / miss
la	*pesadilla*	nightmare
	probar	to try
el	*tiempo*	weather
el	*transporte público*	public transport
la	*toalla*	towel
el	*vuelo*	flight

Higher – Exam practice

Queridos primos:

Estoy de vacaciones en Cancún en Méjico con mis padres. Es la primera vez que visito el extranjero, y para mí es una aventura porque siempre he querido visitar un país latinoamericano. Nuestro hotel es de cinco estrellas. Además, tiene dos piscinas, tres restaurantes, y varias tiendas de recuerdos.

Las playas son de arena blanca y el azul del mar Caribe. ¡Es fantástico! Ha hecho sol y calor todo el tiempo, así que pasamos los días tomando el sol o haciendo deportes acuáticos.

No tenemos pensión completa sino media pensión. Hemos cenado en diferentes restaurantes y hemos probado platos típicos como el guacamole o los tacos. Aunque tengo que admitir que para mí la comida de aquí no es muy buena ni tampoco barata.

En Noviembre se celebra el Día de los Muertos. Es una fiesta muy alegre donde la gente visita los cementerios con comida y flores para los muertos. La gente se viste de esqueletos y hay muchos bailes divertidos. Por lo general la vida nocturna es muy animada ya que hay muchas discotecas y clubes que abren toda la noche.

Hay un mercado con mucho ambiente donde venden artículos de artesanía, pero todo es caro. Sin embargo, hemos comprado algunas joyas de plata. Hoy hemos ido en ferry a la Isla de Mujeres donde hemos practicado el buceo. Me ha divertido mucho aprender un deporte nuevo pero lo mejor ha sido ver los peces tropicales. Mañana vamos de excursión con guía en autocar a ver las ruinas mayas. Quiero conocer más sobre la cultura y las costumbres de los mayas. Va a ser impresionante. Voy a sacar muchas fotos.

Un beso,

Guadalupe

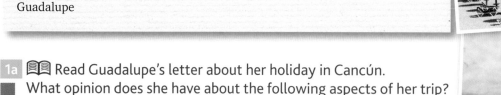

1a  Read Guadalupe's letter about her holiday in Cancún.
What opinion does she have about the following aspects of her trip?
Write **P** (positive), **N** (negative) or **P + N** (positive and negative).

1 her first trip abroad

2 the food

3 the market

4 tomorrow's excursion

Total = 4 marks

1b 📖 Answer the following questions in English.

1   Why is Guadalupe excited to be in Mexico? (2)
2   What have Guadalupe's family booked at the hotel?
    a B&B   b half board   c full board
3   What does Guadalupe think of the Day of the Dead celebrations? They are …
    a fun.   b sad.   c boring.
4   Why exactly is the nightlife so lively in Cancún?
5   What did Guadalupe like the most about today's trip?
    a learning a new sport   b seeing the fish   c seeing the ancient ruins
6   What does Guadalupe hope to gain from her visit to see the ancient ruins?

(**Total** = 7 marks)

2   🎧 Listen to five people talking about communication technology. What is the attitude of each person 1–5? Choose the correct letter.

a   It's essential to my life.
b   It's useful.
c   There are disadvantages.

(**Total** = 5 marks)

3a   🎧 Listen to five teenagers talking about different aspects of technology. Match up each speaker 1–5 with the correct aspect a–e below.

a   Technology can improve your skills
b   Technology can help people
c   Technology can help you save money
d   Addiction to technology
e   Making friends thanks to technology

(**Total** = 5 marks)

3b   🎧 Listen again and answer the following questions in English.

1   Does the first speaker's mum like technology? How do you know? (2)
2   Does the second speaker live far away? How do we know? (2)
3   How does the third speaker describe herself? (2)
4   Was the fourth speaker young when he started playing video games? How do we know? (2)
5   Why does the fifth speaker hardly ever call her friends? (2)

(**Total** = 10 marks)

(**Total for Reading and Listening** = 31 marks)

Estrategia 1a–1b

Use cognates to help you

You might find words that are not exactly the same in English but can give you a clue: these are called cognates.

For example, the word *muertos* (the dead) might make you think of 'mortuary' or 'mortality', so it is likely it has something to do with the dead. Also the word *costumbres* might look like 'costumes' in the first instance, but that obviously doesn't make sense. Keep thinking of words like it that will make sense in context, and you are likely to find 'customs'.

Estrategia 3a–3b

Infer meaning when listening

In the Higher Listening exam you are sometimes expected to infer meaning (work something out) rather than just find the right piece of information and translate it into English. Here is an example from question 3b:

4 Was the fourth speaker young when he started playing video games? How do we know?

The fourth speaker says he already played video games before going to school, which implies he was very young indeed.

You will find two more examples of this type of question in question 3b.

Higher – Speaking

Las vacaciones

You are talking to a Spanish friend about holidays. He / She wants to know:

1. what type of holiday you prefer
2. what you did last summer
3. what destination you would recommend and why
4. how to get to your suggested destination
5. where you will be going on your next holiday
6. what is important for you when choosing a type of holiday.
7. !

! Remember you will have to respond to something that you have not yet prepared.

> **ⓘnfo**
>
> **Important information:**
> This sample task is for practice purposes only and should not be used as an actual assessment task. Study it to find out how to plan your Controlled Assessment efficiently to gain maximum marks and / or work through it as a mock exam task before the actual Controlled Assessment.

1. **What type of holiday you prefer.**
   - mention the type of holiday you like and why
   - say where you have been recently and what it was like
   - mention the type of accommodation you usually stay in
   - say how long you normally go for and who with, and whom you would like to go with when you are 18

> **Estrategia**
>
> Start your plan. Remember that the maximum number of words allowed in your plan is 40. Write a maximum of six words for each bullet point. Here are some suggested words for bullet point 1: *esquí, encantar, relajante, chalet, semanas, padres.*
> Remember to include one verb in each list of words. The verbs must be either infinitives or past participles.
> Use the perfect tense to describe what you have done recently, e.g. *He ido a Grecia, he visitado las Islas Canarias.* See page 182.
> Use *para* to say how long you go on holiday for. See page 187.
> See also Exam technique S5.

2. **What you did last summer.**
   - describe where you went for your last summer or winter holiday
   - describe what you did there and whether you would like to do these activities again
   - say whether you had a good time or not and why
   - describe any good or bad experiences you had

> **Estrategia**
>
> Suggested words for this bullet point: *pasarlo bien, divertirse, disfrutar, excursión, broncearse, descansar.*
> Remember to use the preterite tense of the verb *ir* to say where you went. You could use alternative verbs in your list to help you remember to give details of what you did such as: *ir, comer, jugar, practicar, visitar, comprar.*

3. **What destination you would recommend and why.**
   - suggest a holiday destination and say where it is
   - describe what the weather is like there normally, and say if it changes
   - say what there is to do and see and what it is like
   - describe the type of food you can eat there

> **Estrategia**
>
> Suggested words for this bullet point: *recomendar, tormenta, impresionante, espectáculo*; add two more of your own.
> Mention any local dishes and specialities and say if the food is good (*bueno*), spicy (*picante*), tasty (*rico*), fresh (*fresco*).

4 How to get to your suggested destination.
- describe the best way to get to the location
- compare other types of transport, and say what you think of them
- mention ticket prices
- say how to get from the airport / port / station to the hotel or other accommodation

Estrategia

Suggested words for this bullet point: *aeropuerto, carretera, alquilar*; add three more of your own.

Make sure you know your high numbers and how to say 24-hour times so that you can give prices and departure and arrival information.

Use *hay que* and *debes* to give instructions, e.g. *Debes alquilar un coche. Hay que tomar la autopista hasta Gerona.*

5 Where you will be going on your next holiday.
- describe where you will be going
- say why you will be going there, and if you have ever been before
- mention when you will be going and with whom
- describe several things you plan to do there

Estrategia

Suggested words for this bullet point: *verano, tomar el sol*; add four more words of your own.

Use the immediate future tense to talk about future plans: *Voy a ir a (Italia)*. See page 183.

Don't repeat words in your plan. Repeating information more than once won't get you extra marks. You don't have to tell the truth, so give alternative activities to those already mentioned.

6 What is important for you when choosing a type of holiday.
- describe any local festivals and attractions
- mention learning new things
- talk about ways to relax and be active
- describe your preferred weather and company

Estrategia

Write down five or six words for this bullet point.

To say what is important / good / fun / interesting, use: *Para mí, lo importante / bueno / divertido / interesante es …*

When talking about festivals mention dates and special attractions such as fireworks or parades.

Don't just copy the models in textbooks or online. You will find it easier to remember information that is personal and that you have prepared yourself.

7 ! At this point, you may be asked to …
- describe your friend's last holiday
- describe what your ideal holiday would be
- talk about the benefits of taking holidays
- talk about your local area as a holiday destination.

Estrategia

Listen carefully to what the examiner is asking you. Make sure you know a variety of interrogative pronouns such as *¿Cómo?, Cuándo?, ¿Cuánto?, ¿Dónde?*, and shape your answer to the question.

Make sure you prepare answers for all the above possibilities by making three different points for each possibility, e.g. for the third sub-division: meeting new people, enjoying the nightlife, resting. Write three or four words for each of the two most likely options. Check the total number of words. It should not be more than 40.

See also Exam technique S6

Enlace

Foundation sample assessment tasks for this Context can be found in the Foundation book.

Higher – Writing

El tiempo libre

You are writing a section of an article for a Spanish online magazine on teenagers in the EU. The title of the article is '*Los jóvenes y el tiempo libre*'. In your section you could include:

1. what you do at home on a typical weekend
2. what you do outside the home in your free time
3. money, how you get it and what you spend it on
4. your views on fashion
5. your own tastes and style
6. how you use communication technology
7. an overview of how young people spend their leisure time.

---

1. **What you do at home on a typical weekend.**
   - say what time you usually get up, and if it was different last weekend
   - describe your usual free-time activities
   - say what you and your family did last weekend
   - say what your plans are for next weekend

Estrategia

Start your plan. Remember that the maximum number of words allowed in your plan is 40. Write a maximum of six words for each bullet point. Here are some suggested words for bullet point 1: *a veces, dibujos animados, normalmente, videoconsola, levantarse.*

Use the preterite tense to describe what you or your family did: *toqué el piano, arreglé mi dormitorio, mi padre lavó el coche …*

See also Exam technique W4.

---

2. **What you do outside the home in your free time.**
   - describe the sports you do and when you do them
   - describe a weekend when you did something special
   - say whether you enjoyed the weekend or not
   - say if there are any things you would like to learn to do in the future

Estrategia

Suggested words for this bullet point: *el sábado, el fin de semana, genial, natación, bailar.*

You can use *el sábado* or *los sábados*, *el fin de semana* or *los fines de semana* to say 'on Saturday' or 'on Saturdays', 'at the weekend' or 'at the weekends'. Remember to use the preterite tense to say what you did and where you went.

See also Exam technique W5.

---

3. **Money, how you get it and what you spend it on.**
   - say if you work to earn money or if your parents give you money
   - say how much money you have each week or each month
   - say what you spend your money on
   - say if you save money regularly, how much and what for, and what you want to buy with it

Estrategia

Suggested words for this bullet point: *ganar, gastar, ahorrar, la paga*; add two more of your own.

Use *a la semana* or *al mes* to say how much money you earn, receive or spend 'a week' or 'a month': *Trabajo en una cafetería y gano 50 libras a la semana.* Use future or conditional to say what you want to buy, e.g. *voy a comprarme … / me gustaría comprar...*

4 Your views on fashion.

- say whether you are interested in fashion or not and why
- describe what kind of clothes, colours and accessories are fashionable at the moment, and speculate on what will be fashionable next year
- explain your views on designer labels
- say whether you think males and females are equally interested in fashion, and explain why

Suggested words for this bullet point: *calidad, precio, estar de moda*; add three more of your own.

Discuss quality and cost when weighing up the pros and cons of designer labels.

---

5 Your own tastes and style.

- describe your own fashion style
- describe your shopping habits: how often you go shopping, where you usually buy your clothes, whether you like shopping for clothes, etc.
- describe the kind of clothes and accessories you like to buy and wear
- say what else you spend money on and what you plan on buying next

Suggested words for this bullet point: *maquillaje, grandes almacenes, segunda mano*; add three more of your own.

Look back at the pages which give opinions on fashion and personal style. Notice the expressions they use and adapt them to give your own views. Use a variety of verbs and phrases to describe your likes and dislikes.

---

6 How you use communication technology.

- say which items you use most: mobile, laptop, MP3, etc.
- explain why they are useful to you
- describe the advantages and disadvantages of communication technology
- explain why you think communication technology is important for young people

Suggested words for this bullet point: *comunicarse, navegar*; add four more of your own.

Find the expressions in the book that match your own views on communication technology. For example: *Para mí es imprescindible (el portátil). Adoro (mi móvil). Lo uso para …*

---

7 An overview of how young people spend their leisure time.

- describe how other people you know spend their free time and give examples
- say which leisure facilities in your local area are good and explain why
- say what you would like to be improved to offer young people facilities in your area
- say why you think having free time is important

Write down six words on bullet point 7 for your notes. Being able to express opinions raises the level of your writing. For example: *Creo que el tiempo libre es importante porque …*

para evitar el estrés es necesario descansar / de lunes a viernes trabajamos mucho y tenemos muchos deberes / es importante estar con la familia y con los amigos.

Use *se necesita* or *hace falta* to explain what your area needs, e.g. *hace falta una bolera* and the conditional to say what you would like, e.g. *sería bueno tener un / una …*

See also Exam technique W6.

Enlace

Foundation sample assessment tasks for this Context can be found in the Foundation book.

Exam technique – Speaking

S4 Help available

Your teacher is allowed to discuss each task with you in English, including the kind of language you may need and how to use your preparatory work. You can have access to a dictionary, your Spanish books, Kerboodle and internet resources. This is the stage when you will prepare your plan using the Task Planning Form.

When you actually perform the task, you will only have access to your plan and your teacher's comments (i.e. the Task Planning Form).

S5 AQA administration

For the Speaking part of your exam, you have to do two different tasks (at two different times). One of the tasks will be recorded and sent to a moderator. Each task will last between four and six minutes. When your teacher thinks that you have been taught the language you need and feels that you are ready, you will be given the task to prepare. It could be a task designed by the AQA Examination Board or a task designed by Spanish teachers in your school.

S6 Marking of the tasks

Your teacher will mark your work. A moderator (i.e. an examiner) will sample the work of your school and check that it has been marked correctly. A senior examiner will check the work of the moderator. This complicated but secure system ensures that candidates are given the correct mark.

The Speaking part of your exam counts for 30% of the Spanish GCSE. Each task is marked out of 30 marks. As there are two Speaking tasks, the total number of marks available for Speaking is 60.

For each task, the marks are divided in the following way, with the maximum number of marks available shown in each case: 10 marks for Communication, 10 marks for Range of language and Accuracy, 5 marks for Pronunciation and Intonation, 5 marks for Interaction and Fluency.

Grade booster

To reach grade B, you need to …

■ Develop most of your answers well, using some complex sentences, e.g. for bullet point 3 of the sample Controlled Assessment on page 90. Link up opinions and reasons.

■ Answer without hesitation, using a good range of vocabulary, e.g. bullet point 2. Describe all the different activities different family members did. Use different verbs each time, e.g. *ir, hacer, jugar, visitar,* …

To reach grade A, you need to …

■ Attempt a variety of verb tenses, e.g. bullet point 6: present, past, future, conditional.

■ Express ideas and points of view using complex sentences and a very good range of vocabulary, e.g. bullet point 4. Opinions combined with comparisons.

To reach grade A*, you need to …

■ Have a wide range of vocabulary and use a number of more complex structures, e.g. bullet point 5. Show off your vocabulary by using a variety of different activities you and different people plan to do.

■ Respond readily and show initiative on several occasions, e.g. bullet point 1. Initiative can be shown in different ways, e.g. by asking a question.

Exam technique – Writing

W4 Responding to the bullet points

In a Writing task, there are typically between six and eight bullet points. All bullet points are written in English. Although you have to write a response to the title of the task, it is recommended that you deal with every bullet point that is given below it so that you don't miss out any important information.

W5 Using different tenses

If you are aiming at grade A, as well as a knowledge of the present, you should also show that you know the future tense, the perfect, the preterite and imperfect, and the conditional.

W6 How much to write

For grades C–A*, you should produce 400–600 words across the two tasks (i.e. 200–300 words per task). Although there is flexibility, aim to write approximately 40 words per bullet point.

You may produce a draft, but this is for your use only. Your teacher cannot comment on it and you cannot have access to any draft when you write the final version.

To reach grade B, you need to ...

- Be able to explain ideas, using appropriate vocabulary and complex sentences, e.g. for bullet point 6 of the sample Controlled Assessment on page 93. How young people use communication technology, any issues with it, what the advantages and disadvantages are.
- Write with some accuracy. There may be errors in your attempt at more complex sentences but verb and tense formations are usually correct, e.g. bullet point 2. You can potentially use the present, past and conditional tenses here. Take care with the accuracy of verb endings.

To reach grade A, you need to ...

- Write 40 to 50 words per bullet point, conveying a lot of relevant information clearly, e.g. bullet point 1. You could give a lot of details here. Limit yourself to 40–50 words and focus on quality of communication.
- Be generally accurate in your attempts at complex sentences and verb tenses.

To reach grade A*, you need to ...

- Use a wide variety of vocabulary and structures with accuracy, e.g. bullet point 6. Use vocabulary that describes the various functions of your mobile: taking photos, internet access, downloading music, etc. Use complex structures that you know are correct, e.g. *Como tenemos banda ancha puedo conectarme fácilmente a Internet.*
- Use more complex sentences and verb tenses successfully, e.g. bullet point 4. Combine complex structures and verb tenses, e.g. *La falda que compré recientemente no era muy cara, y además era de muy buena calidad.*

5.1 F   Mi casa y mi barrio

Objetivos

Describing where you live

Ser and *estar*

Using logic when reading

1 **V** Look at the word snake below. Can you find the seven different types of home in it?

casabloquecasaadosadachaletpisotorrepisodúplex

2a 📖📖 🎧 Read the descriptions and name the person who says each of the sentences below.

1   I live in a street of two-storey houses.
2   We are moving to a three-storey house next year.
3   I live in a village not far from the city.
4   I used to live in a terraced house but now I live in a flat.
5   I live on the outskirts of the city.
6   I'd like to live somewhere with more space.
7   Our flat is on two floors.
8   I live on the third floor.

Matilde
Mi dirección es Calle Francisco de Goya, número 10, 3°. Vivo en un piso moderno. Mi bloque es de cinco plantas y vivimos en la tercera planta. Es parte de una construcción nueva. Antes vivía en una casa adosada en otro barrio. Me gusta vivir aquí más que en la otra casa porque el piso es más grande.

Ignacio
¿Cómo es mi casa? Pues, es una casa adosada antigua de dos plantas en un pueblo cerca de Cáceres. Todas las casas en la calle son iguales. Preferiría vivir en una casa más grande. Necesitamos más espacio. Esta casa es muy pequeña.

Elvira
El año que viene mi familia y yo vamos a mudarnos a una casa nueva en las afueras de Segovia. Ahora vivimos en un piso dúplex con dormitorios arriba y los demás cuartos abajo. Vamos a comprar un chalet de tres plantas, con sótano y desván.

2b 📖📖 🎧 Read the descriptions again. Decide who likes their house, who dislikes it, or whether you can't tell. Write **P** (positive), **N** (negative) or **?** (can't tell).

3 **G** Choose the correct verb to complete these sentences correctly.

1   Mi casa es / está grande.
2   Mi casa es / está en Madrid.
3   Mis hermanos son / están enfermos.
4   Soy / Estoy pequeño.
5   Soy / Estoy contento.
6   Somos / Estamos tristes.

Estrategia 2a–2b

Using logic when reading

Think about these points before you look at the answers, and discuss them with your partner.

a If someone says *'Esta casa es demasiada pequeña'*, is it likely that they like it or not?

b If someone says *'Necesitamos más espacio'*, what type of house do they probably want to move to?

c If someone says *'Vivo en un piso en la tercera planta de un bloque'*, what is it fairly likely that they don't have?

(a not – they say it is too small)

(b a big one – they say they need more space)

(c a garden – not many third floor flats have one)

Gramática   página 187

Ser and estar

Ser and *estar* both mean 'to be'.

Ser is used to describe what things and people are and what is unlikely to change:

Mi bloque es de cinco plantas.
Mi casa es grande.

Estar is used to to talk about location, or something which is likely to change:

Estoy muy mal. Mi casa está en el centro de la ciudad.

For more on *ser* and *estar*, see page 108.

4a 🎧 Listen to the four speakers and match up each one with the correct picture A–D showing where they live.

Antonio

Javi

María

Mercedes

4b 🎧 Listen again. Where would each person prefer to live? Answer in English.

5 🗣 Prepare an interview with your partner about the house they live in. One of you plays the interviewer. Ask and answer questions on the points below. Add one extra question that your partner has not been able to prepare for, but which is related to the subject. Then swap roles.

- the type of house you live in
- how long you have lived there
- how big or small it is
- what type of area it is in
- what you think of it
- where (if anywhere) you would prefer to live

¿Cómo es tu casa?

¿Qué opinas de tu casa?

Vivo en una casa adosada.

Me gusta mi casa porque es más grande que mi piso antiguo.

Estrategia 5

Extending your sentences when speaking

When you are asked a question, don't just give a short answer. Extra information will gain you a higher grade. You could give a reason for your answer, using *porque* (because), or you could include extra detail by adding adjectives or further information using *y* (and) or *también* (also). Similarly you could qualify your answer, using *pero* (but), e.g. *Mi casa me gusta mucho, pero es bastante pequeña.* (I like my house very much, but it is rather small.)

¿Dónde vives?	Vivo en un piso.
¿Cuánto tiempo hace que vives allí?	Vivo aquí desde hace dos años.
¿Cómo es tu casa / piso?	Es muy pequeña / pequeño y antiguo.
¿Dónde está?	Está en el centro del pueblo, cerca del parque.
¿Te gusta?	Sí, me gusta porque es confortable. Sí, me gusta pero es muy pequeño. No, no me gusta porque no hay jardín.
¿Dónde preferirías vivir?	Me gustaría vivir en un chalet / cerca de la playa / en la capital.

🔗 **Enlace**

5.1 Groundwork is available in the Foundation book.

5.1 H ¿Cómo es tu casa?

Objetivos

Describing what your home is like

Possessive pronouns – singular forms

Remembering to listen out for quantifiers and intensifiers

1a Read Trini's blog and find the Spanish equivalents (one in each paragraph) of the sentences below. Work with a partner: test each other on these words and phrases from the text.

1 It's like a palace.
2 There are lots of stairs to climb.
3 Ours is rented.
4 There is only a shower.
5 It's very cosy.

■ La casa de Julia Pérez

Inicio | Índice | Sitemap | Ayuda | Versión texto

FAQs
Noticias
Acceso directo
Arriba

El blog de Trini

A

Julia Pérez es mi cantante preferida y ésta es su casa. Es igual que un palacio, ¿verdad? ¿Cuántas habitaciones y cuartos de baño tiene? Demasiados. ¿Tendrá gimnasio, cine o biblioteca? No tengo idea, es enorme. Sin embargo mi piso aquí en Madrid es muy pequeño con dos dormitorios, el de mis padres y el mío que comparto con mi hermana mayor. Hay un cuarto de baño y tiene un salón comedor.

B

Mira la piscina y las fuentes en el césped de la casa de Julia. Mi casa no tiene patio, sólo tiene una terraza. Su casa es de dos plantas con ático. Nuestra casa está en el séptimo piso y da a la calle mientras que la mansión de Julia tiene jardines con árboles y flores. El ascensor en mi bloque está roto y hay muchas escaleras que subir. No tenemos aparcamiento mientras que su casa tiene garajes para todos sus coches.

C

Su casa vale millones de dólares, la nuestra es alquilada. La suya está lejos de sus vecinos. Tiene paredes altas y cámaras de seguridad. Nuestro bloque tiene la mínima seguridad y puede entrar cualquiera.

D

¿Cómo está decorada la casa de Julia? Sin duda tiene alfombras caras, muebles de lujo, lámparas de cristal, cortinas de seda y espejos gigantescos por toda la casa … Mi piso está pintado todo de blanco con una moqueta azul y persianas en las ventanas. Nuestra cocina es tan pequeña que no cabe la nevera, la tenemos en el pasillo. No tenemos ni lavaplatos ni tampoco microondas. Y no hay bañera en el cuarto de baño, sólo hay una ducha.

E

¿Me gusta más la casa de Julia que la mía? Es claramente más grande, más lujosa y cómoda que la mía. Aunque mi casa es pobre y pequeña es muy acogedora. No me gusta tanto la mansión de Julia como mi hogar querido.

1b Read the sentences and identify which home, if any, is being referred to in each case. Write **J** for Julia's house, **T** for Trini's flat or **N** for neither of them.

1 It's like a palace.
2 It's semi-detached.
3 The lift doesn't work.
4 It's less isolated.
5 The building is old.
6 There is better furniture.
7 There aren't many household appliances.
8 It's the biggest.

2 **G** Choose the correct possessive pronoun to complete these sentences.

1   No me gusta su casa pero me gusta mucho la tuya / el tuyo.
2   Nuestro piso es pequeño, pero la suya / el suyo es también.
3   Mi cocina es grande. ¿Y la tuya / el tuyo?
4   ¿Es éste tu dormitorio? Sí, es el mío / la mía.
5   El chalet es muy moderno. No es como el mío / la mía.

3a 🎧 Listen to the interview with María Ángeles about her house. Answer the questions in English.

1   What type of village is it?
2   How many people live there?
3   How old is her house?
4   What can she see from her bedroom?
5   What was it before they lived there?
6   What do they have now that they didn't have before?
7   What household appliances does she mention?
8   Apart from five bedrooms, what other rooms are there?

3b 🎧 Listen again. In which section of the interview (a–e) are the following mentioned?

1   The house is warm in winter and cool in summer.
2   The house didn't have lighting and heating before.
3   María Ángeles lives in a village.
4   Her home is modernised.
5   Her room is on the top floor.

4 ✏️ Compare the differences between your house and where you live with one of the houses shown in the pictures. Imagine what type of person lives there. Include:

■ who they are
■ where they / you live
■ what type of houses they are
■ a description of the rooms in the different houses
■ some furniture
■ which you prefer and why.

Gramática *página 179*

Possessive pronouns – singular forms

You use these to replace a possessive adjective and its noun.

mío – mine, *tuyo* – yours, *suyo* – his / hers. Use these with *el / la / los / las* and remember to make them agree with the nouns they replace.

La casa de Julia es más grande que **la mía**.

Mi jardín es más pequeño que **el tuyo**.

Mi piso es más bonito que **el suyo**.

NB: The possessive pronoun agrees with the **noun** it replaces, not the person it refers to. Thus *el mío* means 'mine' for both males and females, and *el suyo* and *la suya* can both mean 'his' and 'hers'.

Mi casa es más antigua que la casa de Roberto.

Mi casa es más antigua que la suya. – My house is older than his.

For more on possessive pronouns, see page 109.

Estrategia 3a–3b

Remembering to listen out for quantifiers and intensifiers

Sometimes you need to listen for clues to the speaker's emotional attitude to her house. Words like *muy, bastante, demasiado, poco* and *mucho* can help you understand the speaker's opinions.

María Ángeles refers to her house as *bastante grande*, then says it has three floors and five bedrooms. Would you describe that as *bastante grande* or *muy grande*?

She describes her bedroom as *muy cómodo*. How do you think she feels about her room? Would you think she felt differently about it if she described it as *bastante cómodo*?

5.2 F   Mi región

1 🅥 Match up the Spanish words with their English equivalents. Then categorise them in three lists: landscape, buildings and weather.

| bosque | cielos despejados | grados | granja | llana | mezquita | nieve | palacio | tormentas | valle |

| *valley* | *degrees* | *farm* | *palace* | *forest* | *mosque* | *flat* | *snow* | *storms* | *clear skies* |

En el norte

Vivo en una zona rural a 120 kilómetros al norte de Barcelona. Es un lugar tranquilo pero hay una ciudad a poca distancia, con todos los servicios, y es fácil llegar a las playas de la Costa Brava. Además hay buen acceso a la autopista.

El pueblo está situado en un valle muy bonito con muchas granjas y casas de piedra. Alrededor hay bosques, ríos y montañas. A lo lejos se ven los picos de los Pirineos. Normalmente, desde diciembre a abril, están cubiertos de nieve y se puede ir a esquiar. Pero este año no hacía mucho frío en invierno y casi no nevaba.

El valle está a 500 metros sobre el nivel del mar y tiene un clima bastante variable. Este verano hacía mucho calor, con temperaturas de más de 30 grados. Pero en invierno la temperatura baja mucho por la noche, hasta quince grados bajo cero.

Lo mejor de mi zona son las noches de luna llena, con cielos despejados y miles de estrellas.

En el sur

Vivo en las afueras de Sevilla, en el sur de España. La zona alrededor de la ciudad es muy llana pero a unos kilómetros hacia el oeste se encuentra la Sierra de Aracena y al este están las montañas de Sierra Nevada.

Al sur de Sevilla hay pueblos pequeños, con casas antiguas, todas pintadas de blanco y muy típicas de la región. Además hay ciudades antiguas con monumentos históricos, como La Mezquita de Córdoba y la Alhambra de Granada, un impresionante palacio árabe.

Lo bueno de mi región es que tiene un clima estupendo con más de un noventa por ciento de días de sol al año. En verano a veces hace más de 40 grados. Los inviernos son suaves – no hace frío y raras veces se baja de los 0° Celsius. Pero hay excepciones, por ejemplo, fuimos de excursión a la sierra en septiembre y hacía mal tiempo casi toda la semana: había tormentas y hasta inundaciones.

2a 📖 🎧 Match up each caption 1–6 with one of the two parts of the article.

1 La autopista está cerca y es fácil llegar a Barcelona o a Francia.
2 En mi región hay ciudades interesantes con monumentos históricos.
3 La región tiene un clima muy agradable: hace buen tiempo todo el año.
4 La zona alrededor de la ciudad es muy llana.
5 Mi pueblo está en el campo, en medio de granjas, bosques, ríos y montañas.
6 Hace mucho frío en invierno.

2b 📖 🎧 Answer the following questions in English.

En el norte
1 How high is the valley?
2 How hot is it in summer?
3 How cold is it in winter?

En el sur
1 Is it sunny most of the year in Seville? How do you know?
2 How hot is it in summer?
3 What is the weather like in winter?

3 **G** Copy and complete the sentences using the appropriate verbs in the past: *hacía* (use three times), *estaba* (use once), *nevaba* (use once).

Este año no (**1**) <u>hacía</u> mucho frío en invierno y no

(**2**) _____  en las montañas hasta finales de marzo.

Sin embargo, durante el verano (**3**) _____ 38° mucho calor.

Pero según Sandra, (**4**) _____ -20° frío por la noche en los

Pirineos y durante el día (**5**) _____ ☀ sol y el cielo

(**6**) _____ ☁ despejado.

4a 🎧 Listen to Carlos, Sandra, José María and Noemí talking to their friends about their recent holidays. Note down which of the following things each person mentions. (There are more than you need.)

1   camping   4   pony-trekking
2   culture   5   skiing
3   a famous waterfall   6   sunbathing

4b 🎧 Listen again. Match up each person with the picture A–D which best depicts the weather they experienced on their holidays.

A   B   C   D

5 ✏ Write a factual description of your region for a Spanish information booklet. Then adapt your piece for a tourist brochure aiming to attract visitors to the region. What changes do you need to make? Include:

■ where exactly you live
■ what the region is like
■ what you can do there
■ what the weather is like in summer and winter.
■ what the weather was like last summer / winter / year
■ what the best bits of your region are.

Gramática   *página 183*

Describing past weather conditions

To talk about weather in the past, with *buen / mal tiempo, calor, frio, sol, viento,* use *hacía*:

Hacía mal tiempo casi toda la semana.

With *despejado, nublado (nuboso),* use *estaba*:

Estaba casi siempre nublado.

Here are two more verbs for describing weather:

llover – to rain
llueve – it rains
llovía – it rained
nevar – to snow
nieva – it snows
nevaba – it snowed

Also learn how to use numbers in context.

See page 108

Estrategia 5

Describing weather

Notice that you only use verbs in the third person singular for describing the weather.

The third person singular is the part of the verb you use for he, she or it.

Hace sol – it is sunny.
Llueve – it rains.
Nieva – it snows.

Look back at the grammar box and find out how to say these things in the past tense.

Enlace

5.2 Groundwork is available in the Foundation book.

5.2 H ¿Cómo es tu barrio?

■ Mi barrio

A

Mi barrio está en las afueras de la ciudad. Es residencial. Antes había mucha industria y fábricas pero ahora hay mucho paro. El barrio es feo y no está muy limpio. Hay mucho tráfico y ruido porque la autopista pasa por el medio del barrio por lo tanto hay bastante contaminación. Es un poco peligroso y hay cámaras de seguridad en algunas calles. No hay mucha diversión y por lo tanto no hay mucho que hacer para los jóvenes. Lo bueno es que van a construir un polideportivo el año que viene. Lo que me gusta de mi barrio es que hay un centro comercial donde hay un multi-cine. Pero lo que necesitamos también es una zona peatonal y lo más importante, lugares verdes.

B

Vivo en un pueblo muy bonito en la costa. Hay mucho turismo aquí en verano porque hay playas muy cerca y un puerto pesquero pintoresco. También hay un parque de atracciones. En el centro histórico las calles son estrechas con tiendas turísticas y una plaza donde hay un mercado de artesanía los jueves. Hay muchos restaurantes y bares animados pero lo malo de mi barrio es que no hay mucho para los jóvenes. En invierno es aburrido y no hay nada que hacer porque todo está cerrado. Hay diversión en la ciudad pero está lejos y no hay autobuses. Antes había una discoteca pero ahora está cerrada. Hacen falta instalaciones para los jóvenes como un club de jóvenes o una piscina. También necesitamos una red de transporte eficiente.

1a 📖 🎧 Read the descriptions, and for each district find words or phrases that explain:

1 where the area is.
2 what it is like.
3 any facilities.
4 what young people can do.
5 what it needs.

1b 📖 🎧 Read the descriptions again, then read the following statements. Find the three that are true for each district.

Barrio A:

1 It's in the suburbs.
2 There's lots for young people to do.
3 The motorway passes thorugh the centre of the district.
4 There's a huge train station, etc.
5 It's very ugly and not very clean.
6 They need more car parks.

Barrio B:

1 It's a small town in the mountains.
2 There's a theme park.
3 It's not very popular with tourists.
4 There's a night club and a swimming pool.
5 It's not so lively in winter.
6 They need a good transport network.

Estrategia 1a–1b

Recognising common patterns within Spanish

Here are some ways of understanding common patterns in families of words.

Change the following nouns to adjectives by adding -oso, -osa, e.g. *ruido – ruidoso*
peligro, espacio

Change the following verbs to nouns by adding -ión or -ción, e.g. *animar – animación*
habitar, participar

Add -ería endings to these nouns to change them into the names of shops, e.g. *zapato – zapatería*
pescado, pastel, libro

Find words in the descriptions of the *barrios* related to the following:
industrial, peatón, animar, historia, aburrirse

2 ⓖ Join each pair of sentences using *que*, *quien* or *lo que*.

Ejemplo: Van a construir una piscina. La piscina es olímpica.
La piscina <u>que</u> van a construir es olímpica.

1 Hay basura en las calles. No me gusta.
2 Invité a una chica. Es argentina.
3 Me gustan los monumentos. Me gusta lo más el castillo.
4 Necesitamos instalaciones deportivas. No hay canchas de tenis.
5 Hablé con un policía. El policía me dio la dirección.

3a 🎧 Listen to the report about San Bartolomé del Pino. Where can you do each of the things below: in the town centre (**C**), in the suburb of Altamira (**S**) or both (**C + S**)?

1 catch a train
2 go swimming
3 go to a restaurant
4 go to the market
5 go to the post office
6 ride a horse
7 see a film
8 use sports facilities

3b 🎧 Listen again and put the information each speaker gives into the order in which you hear it.

Señora Alcaraz
1 They built a car park on one of the parks.
2 There are things for young people to do.
3 There's everything you need like banks and the post office.

Soledad
1 You have to catch the bus to the centre if you want a livelier atmosphere in the evening.
2 The sporting facilities are excellent.
3 It's an ideal place to bring up children.

4 🗫 Prepare an interview with your partner about your neighbourhood. One of you plays the interviewer. Ask and answer questions on the points below. Add one extra question that your partner has not been able to prepare for, but which is related to the subject. Then swap roles.

- where it is
- what it's like
- what facilities it has
- what there is for young people to do
- what it used to be like
- what it needs

Gramática *página 179*

Using relative pronouns

Que (who / what / that / which) can refer to people or things.

Use *que*, *quien* (who) to give more information about someone or something.

La chica, que trabaja en el polideportivo, es muy simpática. – The girl who works in the sports centre is very friendly.

After a preposition, use *quien* to refer to a person.

No me gusta la chica con quien sale. – I don't like the girl he is going out with.

Use *lo que* (what) to refer to an idea.

Lo que me gusta de mi barrio es que es tranquilo. – What I like about my area is that it's quiet.

Also learn how to use *hay* and *había*.

See page 109

Estrategia 4

Saying what is needed

To say what is needed use:

necesita, necesitamos, se necesita, hace falta.

Hace falta un parque infantil. – It needs a children's playground.

Mi barrio necesita más aparcamientos. – My neighbourhood needs more car parks.

En mi región necesitamos más instalaciones deportivas. – In my region we need more sports facilities.

Se necesita un supermercado en este barrio. – A supermarket is needed in this neighbourhood.

5.3 F   ¿Cómo ayudas?

1 **V** Unscramble the anagrams. Use the vocabulary on page 111 to help you.

> rccnioa   nopre   triqua   grefra   chalpran
>
> miprali   ragrelra   crasra

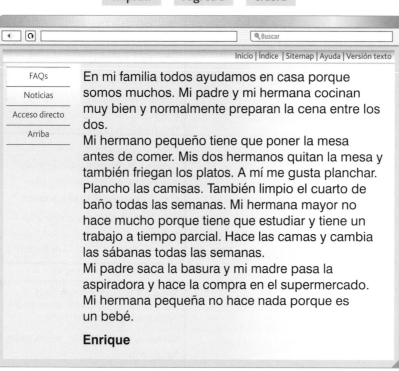

> ◀ | ↻ | [   ] | 🔍 Buscar
>
> Inicio | Índice | Sitemap | Ayuda | Versión texto
>
> FAQs / Noticias / Acceso directo / Arriba
>
> En mi familia todos ayudamos en casa porque somos muchos. Mi padre y mi hermana cocinan muy bien y normalmente preparan la cena entre los dos.
> Mi hermano pequeño tiene que poner la mesa antes de comer. Mis dos hermanos quitan la mesa y también friegan los platos. A mí me gusta planchar. Plancho las camisas. También limpio el cuarto de baño todas las semanas. Mi hermana mayor no hace mucho porque tiene que estudiar y tiene un trabajo a tiempo parcial. Hace las camas y cambia las sábanas todas las semanas.
> Mi padre saca la basura y mi madre pasa la aspiradora y hace la compra en el supermercado. Mi hermana pequeña no hace nada porque es un bebé.
>
> **Enrique**

2a 📖 🎧 Read Enrique's account and write the letters of the pictures in the order in which the household tasks are mentioned.

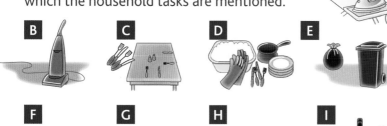

Using present and preterite tenses together

Use the present tense to talk about activities you do regularly and the preterite to talk about activities you have done. Remember the different endings:

Present	Preterite
arreglo	arreglé
cocino	cociné
friego	fregué
limpio	limpié
hago	hice
pongo	puse
saco	saqué

Also learn how to give opinions about the past.

See page 108

2b 📖 🎧 Read Enrique's account again and indicate who does each of the household tasks in the pictures: Enrique (**En**), father (**Fa**), mother (**M**), older sister (**OS**), younger brother (**YB**), other brothers (**OB**).

3 **G** Copy and complete Ramón's reply to Enrique with the correct form of the verbs in brackets.

¡Hola Enrique! El sábado pasado (**1**) _____ (hacer) mucho para ayudar. Primero (**2**) _____ (sacar) la basura y (**3**) _____ (pasar) la aspiradora. Luego (**4**) _____ (hacer) la cama y (**5**) _____ (arreglar) mi dormitorio. Después, (**6**) _____ (hacer) la compra, y (**7**) _____ (preparar) la cena. Finalmente, (**8**) _____ (fregar) los platos. ¡Uf! Estuve muy cansado. ¿Por qué (**9**) _____ (ayudar) tanto? ¡Era el cumpleaños de mi madre! Saludos **Ramón**

4a 🎧 Listen to Fátima, Jorge, Paula and Jordi. What are their opinions of the celebrations they talk about? Write **P** (positive), **N** (negative) or **P + N** (both).

4b 🎧 Listen again. Are these statements true (**T**) or false (**F**)?

1 Fátima helped her mother prepare the meal.
2 Fátima found it easy to fast during the day.
3 Jorge really enjoyed his little brother's birthday.
4 Jorge and his family went to a restaurant.
5 Paula had a great time at Christmas.
6 She went to bed really late.
7 Jordi received lots of presents on his saint's day.
8 Even Jordi's friends forgot to send him a text to say 'happy saint's day'.

5 🗣 Work with a partner. Have a conversation about how you help at home. Compare what you both do. Remember to ask and answer questions about:

■ the different jobs you normally do
■ what jobs you did yesterday / last weekend
■ how you helped out at a special occasion at home.

¿Cómo ayudas en casa?		
Normalmente	arreglo mi dormitorio / saco la basura / pongo la mesa / friego los platos / hago la compra.	
¿Cómo ayudaste	ayer / el fin de semana pasado?	
Ayer / El fin de semana pasado	arreglé mi dormitorio / saqué la basura / fregué los platos / puse la mesa / hice la compra.	
¿Ayudaste	para	las Navidades / el cumpleaños de tu hermano?
Ayudé a mi madre / Limpié la casa / Hice la compra / Preparé la cena con mi padre.		

Preparing for listening

You have to decide if the speakers liked the celebration or not. What might they say? Prepare a list, e.g. negative – *aburrido, ruidoso, no me gustó*, etc.

Estrategia 4a–4b

Using time expressions

These help you to understand and explain if something happened in the past, present or future.

Present
ahora — *de lunes a viernes*
hoy — *los domingos*
normalmente
Los sábados hago *la compra en el supermercado.*
Preterite
ayer — *la semana pasada*
anteayer — *hace dos días*
El sábado pasado hice *la compra en el mercado.*
Future
mañana — *la semana que viene*
el lunes que viene
El sábado que viene*, voy a hacer las compras con mi padre.*

Estrategia 5

⊖⊖⊖ Enlace
5.3 Groundwork is available in the Foundation book.

5.3 H — De fiesta

Objetivos

- Talking in detail about special occasions
- Using the imperfect tense
- Making use of social and cultural contexts

Nicolás tiene 15 años y vive en Madrid. Aquí describe lo que pasa durante las fiestas de Navidad.

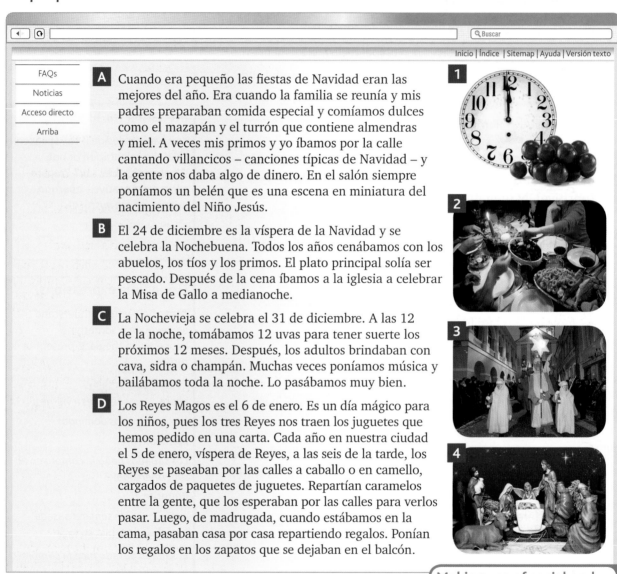

FAQs

Noticias

Acceso directo

Arriba

Inicio | Índice | Sitemap | Ayuda | Versión texto

A Cuando era pequeño las fiestas de Navidad eran las mejores del año. Era cuando la familia se reunía y mis padres preparaban comida especial y comíamos dulces como el mazapán y el turrón que contiene almendras y miel. A veces mis primos y yo íbamos por la calle cantando villancicos – canciones típicas de Navidad – y la gente nos daba algo de dinero. En el salón siempre poníamos un belén que es una escena en miniatura del nacimiento del Niño Jesús.

B El 24 de diciembre es la víspera de la Navidad y se celebra la Nochebuena. Todos los años cenábamos con los abuelos, los tíos y los primos. El plato principal solía ser pescado. Después de la cena íbamos a la iglesia a celebrar la Misa de Gallo a medianoche.

C La Nochevieja se celebra el 31 de diciembre. A las 12 de la noche, tomábamos 12 uvas para tener suerte los próximos 12 meses. Después, los adultos brindaban con cava, sidra o champán. Muchas veces poníamos música y bailábamos toda la noche. Lo pasábamos muy bien.

D Los Reyes Magos es el 6 de enero. Es un día mágico para los niños, pues los tres Reyes nos traen los juguetes que hemos pedido en una carta. Cada año en nuestra ciudad el 5 de enero, víspera de Reyes, a las seis de la tarde, los Reyes se paseaban por las calles a caballo o en camello, cargados de paquetes de juguetes. Repartían caramelos entre la gente, que los esperaban por las calles para verlos pasar. Luego, de madrugada, cuando estábamos en la cama, pasaban casa por casa repartiendo regalos. Ponían los regalos en los zapatos que se dejaban en el balcón.

1a 📖 🎧 Read Nicolás's description. Find the Spanish equivalents of these words and phrases. What differences do you notice in how certain things are said in Spanish?

1 the family got together
2 singing carols
3 Nativity scene
4 Midnight Mass
5 toasted with champagne
6 Twelfth Night
7 the three kings
8 very early in the morning

Making use of social and cultural contexts

Use what you know about Spanish-speaking countries to help you work out the meaning of unfamiliar words. For example, if you know that *Día de Reyes* is the 6th January, you can deduce from *día 5 de enero, víspera de Reyes* that *víspera* means 'the eve of' or 'the day before'.

Estrategia 1a–1c

1b 📖🎧 Match up each photo with the correct paragraph.

1c 📖🎧 Find out the following information from Nicolás's description.
1 Where did the family set up the Nativity scene?
2 At what time did the family go to church?
3 Why are 12 grapes eaten for each stroke of 12 midnight on *Nochevieja*?
4 When do Spanish children get their Christmas presents?
5 When do the Three Kings parade around the town?

2 Ⓖ Copy the sentences and fill in the gaps with the correct verb from the boxes below.
1 Mi familia _____ pescado en la cena de Nochebuena.
2 Mis hermanos _____ un belén.
3 ¿_____ vosotros a la Misa de Gallo?
4 Mi madre _____ los regalos en los zapatos.
5 ¿Tú _____ 12 uvas para tener suerte?
6 Ustedes _____ para ver la cabalgata.

| tomabas | esperaban | ibais | ponía | hacían | comía |

3a 🎧 In many parts of South and Central America, a girl's 15th birthday is an extremely important celebration. Listen to Guadalupe's account of her 15th birthday. Which of the following does she mention?

A   **B**   **C** **D**  **E**

3b 🎧 Listen again. Decide whether the following statements are true (**T**), false (**F**) or not mentioned (**?**). Correct the ones that are false.
1 Guadalupe had a *quinceañera* party in July.
2 She was woken up by a band of musicians.
3 She was given a camera as a present.
4 She wore a pink designer dress.
5 She sat at the top table with her friends.
6 The party finished at four in the morning.

4 ✏️ Write about how you celebrate a special occasion now, and how you used to when you were younger. Include:
■ how you prepare / used to prepare for the celebration
■ what clothes you wear / used to wear
■ what you eat / used to eat
■ what you do / used to do
■ what you think / used to think about it all.

Ⓖramática *página 182*

Using the imperfect tense

Use the imperfect tense for things that used to happen regularly in the past and to describe incomplete actions in the past.

The imperfect is formed by replacing the infinitive endings with the following:

-ar verbs: *-aba, -abas, -aba, -ábamos, -abais, -aban*

-er and *-ir* verbs: *-ía, -ías, -ía, -íamos, -íais, -ían*

Cenaba pescado. – I used to eat fish.

Comíamos dulces – We used to eat sweets.

The only irregular imperfects are *ir*, *ver* and *ser*.

ir – iba   ver – veía   ser – era

Also learn about when to use the imperfect and preterite tenses.
See page 109

Estrategia 4

When to use the imperfect tense

Use the imperfect to express habitual actions in the past, and the preterite to express an action completed at a definite time. These time expressions indicate habit and should be used with the imperfect tense:

siempre / con frecuencia

frecuentemente / a menudo

a veces / de vez en cuando

muchas veces

cada año / día / mes

todos los días (jueves)

Home and local area

1 Read these sentences. Are they using *ser* or *estar*? Why? Choose the correct reason from the list in the grammar box.

Ejemplo: **1 b** what is unlikely to change

1 Madrid es la capital de España.
2 Gerona está en Cataluña.
3 Mi padres están contentos.
4 Yo soy de Bilbao.
5 Las sillas son de plástico.
6 Nosotros estamos en la plaza.
7 En estos momentos, estoy en el museo.
8 Mi hermano está en la sala de estar.

Gramática página 187

> ### Recognising the uses of *ser* and *estar*
>
> As you saw on page 96, both these verbs in Spanish mean 'to be'. Remember that:
>
> *Ser* is used to describe:
> a what things and people are
> b what is unlikely to change:
>
> *Mi casa es antigua* – My house is old. (what it is, unlikely to change)
>
> *Estar* is used to describe:
> c where things are
> d things which are likely to change, for example moods:
>
> *Mi barrio está en las afueras de la ciudad.* – My neighbourhood is on the outskirts of the city. (where it is)
>
> *Estoy muy contento.* – I'm very happy. (mood, likely to change)

2 Copy the sentences and fill in the gaps with the correct number written in words, in Spanish.

1 En invierno la temperatura baja hasta (15) _____ grados bajo cero.
2 ¿La piscina? Pues, toma la (4) _____ calle a la derecha.
3 En (1984) _____ sus padres vivían en Menorca.
4 Mis padres tienen (3) _____ hijos y (4) _____ hijas. Soy la (2) _____ hija.
5 Vivo en un bloque moderno, en un apartamento en la (10) _____ planta.
6 El pueblo está a (750) _____ metros sobre el nivel del mar.

Gramática página 188

> ### Numbers in context
>
> You will find numbers in a wide variety of contexts, and it is important to be able to recognise and use them.
>
> For most purposes, use normal, or cardinal numbers: one, twenty-two, five hundred, four thousand six hundred and ninety-nine, etc. You also use these for ages – *Tengo quince años*, dates – *el tres de marzo*, times – *las ocho menos veinte*, and years – *dos mil trece*.
>
> Use ordinal numbers: first, fifth, fourteenth, to describe things or people – *la segunda hija, la quinta planta, la tercera calle a la derecha*.
>
> For a full list of ordinal numbers see page 188 in the grammar section at the back of the book.

3a Look at these opinions and categorise them into positive and negative. Use the glossary at the end of the book to help you.

cómico   aburrido   ruidoso   desastroso   estresante   agradable

increíble   raro   fatal   estupendo   horroroso   decepcionante   rico

3b Complete the sentences with a suitable opinion.

1 Cuando era niño siempre celebraba mi cumpleaños con una gran fiesta – ¡era _____!
2 Por Carnaval casi siempre llovía – ¡era _____!
3 Había veinte mil personas en el partido de fútbol en el estadio Camp Nou – ¡era _____!
4 Antes veía películas divertidas con mis amigos – ¡era _____!
5 En A level tenía exámenes de español cada semana – ¡era _____!

Gramática página 182

> ### Giving opinions about the past
>
> The easiest way to explain how you felt about something that happened is to use *era* + an opinion word, e.g. *era aburrido, era fantástico*.
>
> Remember, the *-o* ending changes when you are describing something feminine, e.g. *la fiesta era estupenda*.

4 Copy and complete the following sentences wth the correct form of the possessive pronoun.

1 Estos libros son ___ (*mine*).
2 Yo tengo mis billetes pero Carlos no tiene los ___ (*his*).
3 El piso de Fátima tiene más dormitorios que ___ (*ours*).
4 Aquellas bolsas son ___ (*hers*).
5 El jardín de mi abuelo es mucho más bonito que ___ (*theirs*).
6 La cocina de mi casa es más pequeña que la ___ (*yours, informal plural*).

Gramática (página 179)

Possessive pronouns – plural forms

Here are all the forms of the possessive pronouns, including all the plural forms.

mío, mía, míos, mías – mine

tuyo, tuya, tuyos, tuyas – yours (referring to a singular person)

suyo, suya, suyos, suyas – his / hers / its

nuestro, nuestra, nuestros, nuestras – ours

vuestro, vuestra, vuestros, vuestras – yours (referring to a plural person)

suyo, suya, suyos, suyas – theirs

Use them with *el / la / los / las* and remember to make them agree with the nouns they replace.

Estos zapatos *son* **los míos**. – These shoes are mine. (Plural shoes, so plural possessive pronoun)

Esta casa *es* **la vuestra**. – This house is yours. (Singular house, but referring to more than one 'you' that lives there)

Ese coche *es* **el suyo**. – That car is theirs.

Estos coches *son* **los suyos**. – These cars are theirs.

It will be clear from the context if, for example, *suyo*, refers to his, hers, its or theirs.

5 Translate the following sentences into English.

1 En invierno hay mucha nieve.
2 Siempre había mucho ruido en la calle.
3 Ahora hay una zona peatonal en el centro.
4 Hace diez años había una bolera en mi pueblo.
5 El fin de semana pasado había nieve en los Pirineos.

Gramática (página 184)

Hay and *había*

To say 'there is' and 'there are' use *hay*:

En mi barrio **hay** *una comisaría y dos bancos.*

To say 'there was' and 'there were' use *había*:

Antes **había** *un teatro.*

6a Choose the correct verb forms to complete the following text.

Nosotros siempre (**1**) comíamos / comimos pavo el día de Navidad pero el año pasado (**2**) íbamos / fuimos a casa de mis amigos vegetarianos y (**3**) probábamos / probamos los garbanzos por primera vez. Generalmente mis padres no (**4**) gastaban / gastaron mucho dinero en regalos pero hace dos años mis padres me (**5**) regalaban / regalaron una bicicleta de montaña. Con frecuencia (**6**) salíamos / salimos al centro a ver las luces en las calles principales. Generalmente (**7**) celebrábamos / celebramos la Nochevieja en casa pero un año (**8**) viajábamos / viajamos a Australia y lo (**9**) pasábamos / pasamos en la playa.

6b Write three sentences in the imperfect tense and three in the preterite tense, using the time expressions in the grammar box.

Gramática (páginas 181–182)

When to use the imperfect and preterite tenses

Time expressions like these indicate habit and should be used with the imperfect tense:

siempre / a veces / todos los días

e.g. *Cuando* **era** *pequeño, siempre* **iba** *a la escuela a pie.*

Time expressions like these indicate one-off actions and should be used with the preterite tense:

ayer / el otro día / hace tres años

e.g. *Ayer hizo sol.*

Home and local area

Topic 5.1 Home

5.1 F Mi casa y mi barrio ➡ *pages 96–97*

las	afueras	the suburbs
	al lado de	next to / beside
el	aparcamiento	car park
el	apartamento	flat
el	campo	the countryside
la	casa adosada	terraced house
la	casa	house
la	casa pareada	semi-detached house
el	centro	the centre
	cerca (de)	close (to)
el	chalet	detached house
la	comisaría	police station
la	nueva construcción	new development
la	costa	the coast
el	desván	loft
	lejos (de)	far (from)
	mudarse	to move house
el	patio	patio
el	piso	flat / floor
el	sótano	basement / cellar
la	torre / el bloque	tower block

5.1 H ¿Cómo es tu casa? ➡ *pages 98–99*

	acoger	to welcome
	alquilado/a	rented
el	ascensor	lift
el	ático	attic
la	bañera	bathtub
la	calefacción	central heating
el	césped	lawn
	compartir	to share
	dar a	to have a view of

la	ducha	shower
la	granja	farm
	grueso/a	thick
el	lavaplatos	dishwasher
	lujoso/a	luxurious
la	luz	light
el	microondas	microwave
la	nevera	fridge
el	palacio	palace
la	pared	wall
las	persianas	blinds

Topic 5.2 Local area and region

5.2 F Mi región ➡ *pages 100–101*

la	autopista	motorway
el	bosque	forest
la	catarata	waterfall
los	cielos despejados	clear skies
el	clima	climate
el	lago	lake
la	mezquita	mosque
la	montaña	mountain
	montar a caballo	to go horse riding
el	monumento	monument
	nevar	to snow
la	nieve	snow
el	nivel de mar	sea level
	nublado/a	cloudy
la	región	region
el	río	river
el	teatro	theatre
la	tienda	shop
la	tormenta	storm
el	valle	valley

5.2 H ¿Cómo es tu barrio? ➡ *pages 102–103*

el	club de jóvenes	youth club
	concurrido/a	busy
	construir	to build
la	diversión	entertainment
la	estación	station
	estrecho/a	narrow
	hacer falta	to need / to be needed
la	industria	industry
la	instalación	facility
el	lugar	place
	necesitar	to need
la	oficina de correos	post office
	peligroso/a	dangerous
	residencial	residential
el	ruido	noise
	seguro/a	safe / secure
	sucio/a	dirty
	tranquilo/a	peaceful
la	zona peatonal	pedestrian zone

Topic 5.3 Life at home and special occasions

5.3 F ¿Cómo ayudas? ➡ *pages 104–105*

	arreglar el dormitorio	to tidy the bedroom
	ayudar	to help
	cocinar	to cook food
	encantar	to really like something
las	felicidades	congratulations
	fregar los platos / el suelo	to wash the dishes / floor
	hacer la cama	to make the bed
	hacer la compra	to do the shopping
	invitar	to invite
	limpiar el cuarto de baño	to clean the bathroom
	mandar un texto	to send a text message

	no hacer nada	to do nothing
	pasar la aspiradora	to vacuum
	planchar	to do the ironing
	poner la mesa	to set the table
	preparar	to prepare (food)
	quitar la mesa	to clear the table
	recibir	to receive
	regalar	to give a present
	sacar la basura	to take out the rubbish

5.3 H De fiesta ➡ *pages 106–107*

el	banquete	feast
el	belén	nativity scene / crib
	brindar	to toast
el	camello	camel
	cumplir	to reach (a certain age)
	¡Feliz Navidad!	Happy Christmas!
la	fiesta de cumpleaños	birthday party
el	invitado	guest
la	madrugada	very early in the morning
la	Misa de Gallo	Midnight Mass
el	nacimiento	birth
la	Navidad	Christmas
la	Nochevieja	New Year's Eve
la	quinceañera	party for a girl's 15th birthday
	repartir	to give out
	reunirse	to meet / get together
los	Reyes Magos	the Three Kings / Wise Men
	sentarse	to sit
la	uva	grape
la	víspera	eve

6.1 F Los problemas del medio ambiente

1 ❶ Find the odd one out in each of these lists. Use the vocabulary list on pages 122–123 to help you.

1 la basura
la contaminación acústica
la luz excesiva
el aire puro

2 la basura
las pintadas
los edificios
el exceso de anuncios

3 tóxico
el vertido
la contaminación
la naturaleza

4 fastidiar
dormir
molestar
preocupar

1 La suciedad molesta más

Según la encuesta, lo que más molesta a los habitantes de Barcelona es la suciedad. El 20,9% se queja de los papeles, las bolsas y los envases de plástico que se encuentran en las calles. Unos comentan que no duermen bien, dicen que la luz excesiva durante la noche les impide dormir. Otros dicen que los edificios muy altos y mal diseñados y el exceso de anuncios, dañan el aspecto visual de la ciudad.

2 La contaminación acústica – noches de pesadilla

Los habitantes de los barrios alrededor del aeropuerto han presentado una denuncia por exceso de ruido. La apertura de la tercera pista del aeropuerto se ha convertido en una pesadilla para los vecinos de las urbanizaciones cercanas: los aviones pasan a poca altura de sus casas y el ruido no les deja dormir.

3 Más de la mitad de los españoles respiran aire contaminado

Un informe sobre la calidad del aire concluye que el 53% de los españoles respira aire contaminado. Por consiguiente, en Barcelona, el gobierno ha aprobado un paquete de 73 medidas para reducir la contaminación del aire, provocada especialmente por el tráfico. Una de las medidas más controvertidas es limitar la velocidad a 80 km/h.

4 Residuos químicos peligrosos

Este martes, a las 6.30 de la mañana, se ha producido una fuga en una fábrica al Río Ebro. Esta fuga estaba compuesta por una solución de 30 metros cúbicos, que contenía 12 gramos de mercurio por litro. La división de medio ambiente de la policía está investigando el vertido. En estos casos se suelen poner multas muy fuertes a los empresarios responsables.

1b 📖 Read the news stories again and answer the following questions in English.

1 Why did the US cancel a 25 million dollar debt owed by Peru?
   a to help victims of natural disasters
   b to protect the forests
   c to promote use of alternative energy sources

2 What is the Amazon area threatened by?
   a forest clearance and prospecting for oil and other resources
   b natural disasters such as floods and earthquakes
   c tourism

3 Why has the local government of Fuente Vaqueros decided to use renewable energy? (2)

4 Which public buildings in Fuente Vaqueros are mentioned? (3)

5 How can the children from Fuente Vaqueros help to protect the environment?

(**Total** = 8 marks)

2a 🎧 Listen to the interviews. What are they about?

1 better public transport
2 more people cycling
3 congestion charging

(**Total** = 1 mark)

2b 🎧 Listen again and note each person's point of view. Write **F** (for), **A** (against) or **N** (neither for nor against) for each interviewee: the young man, the girl and the older woman.

(**Total** = 3 marks)

3 🎧 Listen to Marcos telling his friend Carlos about his daily routine after a study visit in Colombia. Copy the grid and fill it in with the correct information in English. The first one has been done for you.

	Before the study visit	During the study visit
Washing the dishes	Used to wash the dishes after each meal	
Preparing food		
Ironing		
Making the bed		
Taking out the rubbish		

(**Total** = 9 marks)

(**Total for Reading and Listening** = 26 marks)

Listen out for tenses

Estrategia 3

It is important to listen carefully to the tenses when tackling a Higher Listening exercise. There may be a combination of them.

e.g. *Cuando vivía en París me preparaba la comida, pero ahora como siempre fuera.* – When I lived in Paris I prepared my own food, but now I always eat out. (past then present)

Also look for key words or expressions that will give you clues about the tenses, *normalmente, con frecuencia* > present tense, *antes, ahora, cuando vivía en* > past tense.

Higher – Speaking

El medio ambiente

A Spanish TV company is making a programme about young Europeans' views on the environment and they want to interview you. Plan for the interview by preparing the following points to mention:

1 A description of your region

2 Climate and weather

3 Pollution in your local area

4 Your views on the greatest environmental threats to the planet

5 Being eco-friendly at home and at school

6 How to reduce CO_2 emissions and combat climate change

7 !

! Remember you will have to respond to something that you have not yet prepared.

1 A description of your region.
  - say where you live and describe your area
  - say where your home town is in relation to the nearest well-known city
  - describe the main features of your region, now and in the past, and any future plans for the area
  - say which part of the country your region is in

> **Estrategia**
>
> Start your plan. Remember that the maximum number of words allowed in your plan is 40. Write a maximum of six words for each bullet point. Here are some suggested words for bullet point 1: *vivir, barrio, región, ciudad, pueblo*.
> Use the imperfect to say what the area used to be like, e.g. *En el pasado había mucha industria.*

2 Climate and weather.
  - describe the natural features near your town
  - describe the climate in your region and give details of summer and winter temperatures
  - say what the weather was like last summer or last winter and what you did as a result
  - mention any unusual or extreme weather conditions in your region in the last year

> **Estrategia**
>
> Note down useful terms linked to the climate and weather in your area such as: *estable, variable, despejado, nublado, tormenta, inundación*. Use the relevant Spanish numbers. *(40 / cuarenta) grados*
> Use the <u>imperfect</u> to describe past weather conditions and the **preterite** to say what you did, e.g. *<u>Nevaba</u> mucho e **hicimos** una guerra de nieve*

3 Pollution in your local area.
  - say what worries you about pollution in your area
  - say what other negative aspects of your local environment bother you, e.g. noise, litter, traffic
  - explain what kind of problems the negative factors cause, e.g. difficult to sleep, dangerous to cycle
  - mention any local plans to combat these issues in the future

> **Estrategia**
>
> Look at pages 112–119 and make a list of all the kinds of pollution mentioned such as *contaminación acústica* and *residuos químicos*.
> Use the appropriate verbs to give your opinions.
> *(lo que más) me molesta* = what bothers me most
> *(lo que más) me preocupa* = what worries me most

4 Your views on the greatest environmental threats to the planet.

- say which global environmental issues worry you
- say which of these issues most threaten the future of the planet
- explain the possible outcomes of these threats
- say what you think will happen in the future

Estrategia

Look at pages 112–119 and draw a spidergram showing key global environmental issues, their causes and likely outcomes.

Use a variety of verbs to introduce your opinions.
Creo que … Pienso que …
En mi opinión …. Me parece que …

Use the future to say what you think will happen, e.g.
Creo que en el futuro subirá la temperatura global y habrá muchas más catástrofes naturales.

5 Being eco-friendly at home and at school.

- say what you recycle, e.g. types of packaging, food, clothes, plastic bags, paper
- give your suggestions for saving energy, e.g. saving on heating, lighting, air conditioning, electricity
- give your suggestions for saving water
- say what you have done recently to be eco-friendly at home and at school

Estrategia

Write down no more than six words to do with being eco-friendly such as *ahorrar* and *apagar*.

Use verbs of obligation to say what we should do.
Debemos / Tenemos que. See page 186.

Use *hay que* or the third person impersonal forms with *se* to say what should be done.
Se debe
Se podría

6 How to reduce CO_2 emissions and combat climate change.

- talk about ways of reducing the number of cars in your area or city
- mention vehicles that are less polluting and more energy efficient
- say how ways of driving can help the environment
- say what you think individuals can do and what the government should do

Estrategia

Make a list of useful phrases for talking about ways to protect the environment. Make separate sections, e.g. things individuals can do and what the government should do.
Todos debemos …
elegir coches de bajo consumo y de baja emisión (coches híbridos).
El gobierno debe …
poner multas a las empresas que contaminan el agua o el aire con residuos químicos.

7 ! At this point, you may be asked …

- Which policies to protect the environment have been successful in your town or local area?
- What do you think about people who say climate change doesn't exist?
- How do you think climate change will affect your country or region?
- Do you think current measures to reduce climate change will be successful?

Estrategia

Show that you know different ways of referring to the past.

Use the perfect tense to talk about the recent past:
En mi región hemos reducido la cantidad de basura y hemos reciclado más.

Use the preterite to talk about events that happened in the past: *El año pasado los supermercados decidieron no dar bolsas de plástico a los clientes.*

Use the future to give predictions: *Los veranos serán más calurosos. Habrá más tormentas. Subirá el nivel del mar y tendremos inundaciones.*

 **Enlace**

Foundation sample assessment tasks for this Context can be found in the Foundation book.

Higher – Writing

El lugar donde vivo

Your Spanish friend Javier is coming to stay with you and your family for a holiday. He has asked you to write him an email in Spanish describing your house and local area to give him an idea of what to expect. Call the email 'Where I live'. You could include:

1 where you would like to live in the future
2 your current house
3 your current bedroom
4 comparing your neighbourhood now and in the past
5 things for young people to do
6 your region
7 a special occasion in your home.

(i)nfo

Important information:
This sample task is for practice purposes only and should not be used as an actual assessment task. Study it to find out how to plan your Controlled Assessment efficiently to gain maximum marks and / or work through it as a mock exam task before the actual Controlled Assessment.

---

1 **Where you would like to live in the future.**
- say what your ideal house would be like
- say what town, country or area you would like to live in and give reasons for your choice
- talk about what makes an area a good place to live
- mention what improvements you would make if you were mayor of a town

Estrategia

Start your plan. Remember that the maximum number of words allowed in your plan is 40. Write a maximum of six words for each bullet point.

Here are some suggested words first bullet point 1: *desván, césped, lavaplatos*. Use the conditional tense for saying what you would do: *sería, tendría, habría, viviría, compraría*. See page 184.

You could begin to describe what makes an area a good or bad place to live by using the following sentence as a model: *Un pueblo en el campo es un lugar ideal para las familias porque es tranquilo y no hay crimen.*

---

2 **Your current house.**
- say whether you live in a house or flat and what type of building it is
- mention the number and types of rooms and if it has a garden, garage, balcony, etc.
- say whether you like your house or not and why
- say how long you have lived there and compare it to your previous house

Estrategia

Now start your notes. Write down six words: *casa, dormitorios, cocina, arriba, jardín, balcón*
Think of a verb for each word:
vivir, ser, tener, haber, estar
To say how long you have lived somewhere use *desde hace*:
Vivo aquí desde hace diez años.
To give an opinion of your old house remember to use the imperfect tense:
No me gustaba mi antigua casa porque era pequeña.

---

3 **Your current bedroom.**
- say where it is in the house
- mention how it is decorated
- compare your bedroom to Javier's
- say what you do in your room

Estrategia

Write down six words to do with your home such as *alquilado/a, adosado/a, planta, lujoso/a, acogedor(a), espejo*.
To compare your house or bedroom with Javier's, use *el mío / la mía* to say 'mine' and *el tuyo / la tuya* to say 'yours', e.g. *Mi dormitorio es más grande que el tuyo.*

---

4 Comparing your neighbourhood now and in the past.
- say what your neighbourhood is like now and what it used to be like
- mention what it has and what it used to have
- say what you like about it and why
- say what you dislike about it and give a reason

Add six more words to your notes to help you describe things in your local area such as *centro comercial* and *zona peatonal*.

Use *lo que* to say 'the ... thing': *Lo malo es que no hay mucho para los jóvenes.*

Lo que me gusta de mi barrio es que es limpio.

Remember that *¿por qué?* means 'why?' and *porque* means 'because'.

5 Things for young people to do.
- mention what there is for young people to do
- say what you do there at weekends
- mention what you did last weekend and what you plan to do next weekend
- say what you think would improve your local area

To say what you do in your local area use phrases from pages 102–103, e.g. *De vez en cuando voy al cine.* Add another phrase of your own.

Using different tenses correctly will get you extra marks.

Use the preterite tense to say what you did last weekend: *El fin de semana pasado fui al polideportivo.*

Use the future or the simple future to say what you will do next weekend.

6 Your region.
- say where your region is
- write about what it has and what it is like
- talk about the weather and the seasons
- mention what the weather was like this time last year

Add six geographical words to describe your region: *bosque, río, montaña* and three others.

To say how far away something is use *está a*: *Está a unos 40 minutos de Londres. Está a 120 kilómetros al norte de Edimburgo.*

Use the preterite tense to talk about weather in the past and combine this with the imperfect to say what you could or couldn't do: *El año pasado hizo mucho frío en invierno así que el lago se congeló y patinábamos todos los días.* See page 183.

7 A special occasion in your home.
- say what the special occasion is and what you are celebrating
- say when the special occasion is
- mention how you celebrate the occasion
- compare how you used to celebrate the occasion when you were younger

Write down six words on bullet point 7 for your notes: *vestido, pastel, regalar, tarjeta, divertirse, pasarlo bien.*

Remember how to write dates: *el primero / uno de mayo, el quince de noviembre.*

Use the imperfect tense to talk about how you used to celebrate special occasions: *Cuando era pequeño/a comía muchos dulces.* See page 182.

 **Enlace**

Foundation sample assessment tasks for this Context can be found in the Foundation book.

Exam technique – Speaking

S7 Ideas for practising

Treat each bullet point as a mini-task. Practise your answer to one bullet point at a time. Look at one word on your plan and say aloud all the things that the word is reminding you to say. Repeat the process for each word on your plan. Next, try to account for two words, then for three words, etc. Time your answer for one whole bullet point. Repeat the process for each bullet point. Record yourself if possible.

You can also practise with a partner. Together, work out the questions that your teacher might ask you in the exam and practise your answers to these questions in turn.

S8 Info about Interaction and Fluency

Interaction is about your ability to contribute to the conversation. To gain good marks, you will need to show initiative (see Exam technique S10).

Fluency is your ability to speak without hesitation. Try to speak with fluency but not too fast. If you are likely to be nervous when performing the task, practise it and practise it again. Time your whole response. Make a point of slowing down if you feel that you are speaking too fast. Practise with your plan in front of you so that you know what you are going to say next and therefore do not hesitate in the exam itself.

S9 Info about Communication, Range of language, and Accuracy

The marks that you get for Communication are for getting the message over to the teacher who is examining you. The marks for Range of language are awarded if you have a good variety of vocabulary and grammatical structures in your responses. The marks that you get for Accuracy will be linked to how well you know and use the rules of Spanish grammar and pronunciation. These three are closely linked because if you get the grammar wrong, it can change the meaning of your message. If this happens, you lose both Communication / Range of language, and Accuracy marks.

Grade booster

To reach grade B, you need to …

- Give a good amount of information for every bullet point and answer generally without hesitation, e.g. for bullet point 1 of the sample Controlled Assessment on page 126. Give a lot of details about your region: where in the country, type of area, facilities available.
- Include some complex structures and a variety of tenses which clearly communicate, e.g. bullet point 6. Show that you know a range of tenses. Use present, future and conditional here.

To reach grade A, you need to …

- Develop nearly all your answers and sometimes show initiative, e.g. bullet point 7. Show initiative by developing the last point, i.e. comparing what you do to help the environment and what you could do in the future. You could also extend your answer by saying what you think of environmental initiatives in your local area.
- Have a good range of vocabulary and your pronunciation must generally be good, e.g. bullet point 3. Use different adjectives to describe different types of pollution. Vary your vocabulary including verbs and phrases. Do not over-rely on *es* + adjective.

To reach grade A*, you need to …

- Present your ideas and points of view with confidence and sustain a conversation at a reasonable speed, e.g. bullet point 4. Give your opinion of environmental threats: what is a problem locally, what is a problem globally, what will be the biggest problem in the future, how did we cause the problems, and explain your points of view by saying why (not) each time.
- Use a variety of verb tenses and other structures with accuracy, e.g. bullet point 2. By following the detailed plan, you will show that you can use the present, the preterite and the imperfect. Focus on accuracy.

Exam technique – Writing

W7 Marking of the tasks

AQA examiners will mark your work. A senior examiner will check the work of the examiner. This is to ensure that candidates are given the correct mark for their work.

The pair of Writing tasks count for 30% of the whole GCSE Spanish exam, so each of the Writing tasks is worth 15%. Your work will be marked in terms of Content, Range of language, and Accuracy. Each task will be marked out of 30. Fifteen of these marks are for Content, 10 are for Range of language and 5 are for Accuracy.

W8 Info about Range of language

If you are aiming at grade A, you must use a wide variety of vocabulary and structures. You must also include more complex sentences and use different verb tenses (see Exam technique W5).

W9 Info about Content

You will be awarded marks under the heading 'Content' for:

- the amount of relevant information you give
- expressing and explaining ideas and points of view
- developing the points you make
- producing a well-structured piece of work.

Refer to Exam technique W6 for the number of words you should aim to write.

Grade booster

To reach grade B, you need to …

- Have a good variety of vocabulary and structures, e.g. for bullet point 5 of the sample Controlled Assessment on page 129. Use a variety of ways to say what could or should be done. e.g. *se debe / se puede / hace falta / sería posible / sería esencial …*
- Convey a lot of information clearly, e.g. bullet point 2. Give many details about your house – location, size, rooms within it, additional items and descriptions, etc.

To reach grade A, you need to …

- Express and explain ideas and points of view with clarity, e.g. bullet point 5. Explain the available facilities and explain why these are adequate or not. Describe what the area needs to improve it.
- Develop the majority of the points you make, whilst being accurate, particularly with regard to verb and tense formations, e.g. bullet point 6. Use past, present and future in your answer to this bullet point. Focus on accuracy.

To reach grade A*, you need to …

- Give a fully relevant and detailed response to the task which is largely accurate, e.g. bullet point 7. Write at least 50 words to cover all the ideas included in this bullet point.
- Handle complex sentences with confidence, making very few errors in the process, e.g. bullet point 4. Include different tenses in your answer: what the area used to be like (imperfect), how it has changed (perfect), what it is like now (present), any plans to improve the area (future).

7.1 F   Bienvenidos al colegio

1 ⓥ 🎧 Copy the verbs and fill in the gaps with the missing vowels. Listen to the recording to check your answers. Then match up each Spanish verb with its English equivalent.

1 c_mpr_nd_r	a to learn
2 _pr_nd_r	b to teach
3 _ns_ñ_r	c to fail
4 ch_rl_ r	d to chat
5 c_st_g_r	e to punish
6 f_lt_r	f to understand
7 s_sp_nd_r	g to be missing / to lack

Bienvenidos al Instituto Cervantes

En el Instituto Cervantes, ofrecemos cursos de Educación Secundaria Obligatoria, de Bachillerato y de Formación Profesional. Nuestros alumnos consiguen un nivel muy alto en sus estudios en un ambiente feliz y amistoso.

Tenemos laboratorios de idiomas, informática y ciencias así como aulas específicas para las diferentes asignaturas. En sus clases de deporte los estudiantes disponen de piscina (exterior y climatizada), polideportivo, pistas de tenis, patinaje, atletismo, campos de fútbol y gimnasios.

Hay alrededor de novecientos cincuenta alumnos en el instituto, que actualmente tiene sesenta y cinco profesores. Estos profesores son expertos en la asignatura que enseñan.

La biblioteca del colegio ahora cuenta con más de 4.500 libros y los alumnos suelen utilizar su servicio de préstamo y consulta todos los días. Hay también más de treinta ordenadores allí.

Durante el año tienen lugar numerosos viajes de estudios y visitas extraescolares. Por ejemplo el febrero pasado un grupo de estudiantes de arte fue al museo de cerámica y otro grupo fue a ver un espectáculo de baile tradicional. Esas actividades y otras se repiten cada año.

En la hora de la comida muchos departamentos dan clases de apoyo no solamente para los que tienen problemas con el trabajo, sino también para los que quieren mejorar sus conocimientos.

2a 📖 🎧 Read the text then read the following sentences. Find the four that are correct according to the text.

1 The atmosphere in the school is friendly.
2 The outdoor pool is bigger than the indoor one.
3 There are about 950 students in the school.
4 There are 75 teachers in the school.
5 The computers in the library are available after school.
6 There was a visit to a traditional dance show last year.
7 Support lessons take place at lunchtime.
8 Support lessons are only for students with problems.

2b 📖 🗣 Read the text again. With your partner, ask and answer the questions below.

A ¿Cómo es el ambiente?
¿Qué instalaciones hay?
¿Cuántos alumnos hay?

B ¿Cuántos ordenadores hay en la biblioteca?
¿Adónde fue un grupo de estudiantes en febrero?
¿Qué hay en la hora de la comida?

3 **G** Copy the sentences and fill in the gaps with the missing pronoun or verb from the boxes below.

Ejemplo: *Me gusta la geografía.* I like geography.

1 ___ gusta el inglés.   You (sing.) like English.
2 Nos ___ las aulas.   We love the classrooms.
3 ___ interesan las matemáticas.   She is interested in maths.
4 Les ___ sus profesores.   They are bothered by their teachers.
5 ___ encanta el colegio.   You (pl.) love the school.
6 Me ___ la tecnología.   I like technology.

me	te	le	nos	os	les
gusta	interesa	molesta	encanta		
gustan	interesan	molestan	encantan		

4a 🎧 Listen to four students giving their opinions about their school. Note whether each student's opinion is positive (**P**), negative (**N**) or positive and negative (**P + N**).

1 Eva   2 Juan   3 Paula   4 Antonio

4b 🎧 Listen again and match up each person with the aspect of their school they are talking about from the list below.

a teachers   c subjects   e school food   g exams
b facilities   d timetable   f head teacher

5 🗣 Prepare a presentation about your school, to last about two minutes and covering the points below. Perform your presentation to a partner, a group and / or the whole class.

■ Say where your school is located.
■ Say what there is in your school (teachers, students, facilities …).
■ Say what type of school it is.
■ Say what type of activities the school offers (clubs, trips …).
■ Say what you can do at lunchtime.

Gramática   *página 186*

Revision of impersonal verbs

Remember that some verbs of opinion only have a singular and plural form but they need a pronoun before them.

Me gusta el dibujo. – I like art. (singular)

Me gustan las matemáticas. – I like maths. (plural)

The literal translations are 'Art pleases me' and 'Maths pleases me'. Remember that if the noun is plural you need to use *gustan*.

Interesar (to be interested), *encantar* (to love) and *molestar* (to bother) work in the same way.

me gusta(n)	I like
te gusta(n)	you like
le gusta(n)	he / she likes
nos gusta(n)	we like
os gusta(n)	you (pl.) like
les gusta(n)	they like

Also revise demonstrative adjectives.
See page 144

Estrategia 5

Developing spoken answers

When you prepare for your speaking Controlled Assessment, you will have bullet points similar to the ones in this activity. Try to develop the points you are going to make so that you have at least two elements to each response. Give your own opinions using the constructions in the grammar box, include adjectives to add interest and join short sentences together with connectives to make longer ones.

🔗 **Enlace**

7.1 Groundwork is available in the Foundation book.

7.1 H   Colegios británicos y españoles

◀ | ⟳ | [   ] | 🔍 Buscar

Inicio | Índice | Sitemap | Ayuda | Versión texto

Hola Juan

Estoy un poco estresado con todo el trabajo que tengo que hacer de momento. Los días parecen muy largos, ya que tengo que levantarme antes de las siete, desayunar y ponerme el uniforme, que incluso tenemos que llevar en colegios públicos como el mío. Pasan lista a las ocho y media, aunque la primera clase no empieza hasta las nueve menos diez. Las clases terminan a las tres, así que es duro.

La semana pasada perdí mi libro de historia y tuve que comprar otro, lo que me parece muy injusto.

La comida en el instituto es fatal y no podemos salir durante la hora que tenemos para comer. Por eso si no llevamos bocadillos de casa, tenemos que comer la basura que sirven en el comedor.

Espero con impaciencia el fin de los exámenes en junio y las nueve semanas de vacaciones que voy a tener – normalmente tengo seis.

Danny

◀ | ⟳ | [   ] | 🔍 Buscar

Inicio | Índice | Sitemap | Ayuda | Versión texto

Hola Danny

Como ya sabes, voy a un colegio privado y tenemos que llevar uniforme, a diferencia de los colegios públicos en mi ciudad.

Tienes suerte que solamente tienes que comprar los libros que pierdes, porque mis padres tienen que comprármelos todos. Y esto ocurre también en los colegios públicos.

Empiezo a las nueve y termino a las cinco o a las seis, dependiendo del día. Hay dos horas para la comida, cuando voy a la cafetería en el pueblo. Hoy fui allí y tomé una tortilla española.

En mi colegio pasan lista en todas las clases, y como consecuencia no hay una clase especial como en el tuyo. Sin embargo, cada estudiante tiene un tutor personal que fija objetivos académicos y que te ayuda con problemas personales. Hablamos con el tutor cada tres semanas y hay reuniones con los padres una vez cada trimestre.

Todavía no sé lo que voy a hacer durante los tres meses de vacaciones de verano, pero seguro que voy a visitarte otra vez.

Juan

1a 📖 🎧 Read the emails and find the Spanish equivalents of these words and phrases.

1 They take the register
2 unfair
3 I am looking forward to
4 state schools
5 however
6 meetings

1b 📖 🎧 Read the emails again and decide to which school each of the following statements applies. Write **D** (for Danny's school), **J** (for Juan's school) or **D + J** (for both schools).

1 Lunchtime lasts one hour.
2 The register is taken in every lesson.
3 Uniform is compulsory.
4 The students can go out of school at lunchtime.
5 The school is a state school.
6 They have to buy all the books.

2 **G** Choose the correct tense of the verb to complete these sentences.

1 Durante las próximas vacaciones fui / iré / voy de excursión con el colegio.
2 Actualmente comemos / comimos / comeremos en el comedor del instituto.
3 Anoche haré / hago / hice los deberes antes de cenar.
4 La semana pasada tuve / tengo / tendré una reunión con mi tutora.
5 El año que viene creo que mi amigo Pablo estudiaba / estudiará / estudió en la universidad.
6 Cuando vuelvo a casa, siempre leeré / leí / leo el periódico digital.

3a 🎧 Listen to four Spanish students speaking about the English schools they have visited during an exchange visit. Note whether each person's opinion is positive (**P**), negative (**N**) or positive and negative (**P + N**).

3b 🎧 Listen again and write down why you made each of these choices. Answer in English.

4 ✏ Write in Spanish what you have found to be some of the differences in Spanish schools compared to your own. Write an imaginative account, focusing on a Spanish student's school day, either in the present tense saying what normally happens, or in the past describing what was done yesterday.

Using different tenses

Gramática · **páginas 180–185**

As you already have seen, verbs in Spanish tell us the person (*yo, tú,* etc.) and the tense of the verb.

The **present tense** is used to talk about things that we normally do:
Como en el comedor todos los días.

The **preterite** is used to talk about a completed event in the past:
Ayer comí en el comedor con mis amigos.

The **future** is used to express what will happen:
Mañana comeré en el comedor.

The **imperfect** is used to describe something in the past or to talk about actions that used to happen in the past:
Antes, comía en el comedor todos los días pero ahora ya no.

Also learn about the present subjunctive.

See page 145

Writing verbs accurately

Estrategia 4

It is not enough to just use different tenses in your written work. If you want to access the higher grades, you need to use them accurately. Here are two ways to improve your verbs:

Every time you produce a piece of writing, go back through every verb and check it is correct, using the verb tables on pages 190–194 if you are not 100% sure.

Each time you have to look up a verb you didn't know, try to write it in different tenses, checking the endings in the verb tables. You can focus on the first person (I) first.

7.2 F Los problemas escolares

1 ❷ Find the odd word out in the following groups. Then make up one of your own using school vocabulary. Test it out on the rest of the class.

1 director   profesor   comedor   tutor
2 deberes   trabajo   tarea   estuche
3 castigar   apoyar   ayudar   enseñar
4 me gusta   me encanta   me enfada   me interesa

Foro de estudiantes – ¡Habla con Ana!

Problemas

1 Por una parte, me gustaría llevar uniforme y no tener que pensar en la ropa que me tengo que poner. Algunos chicos y chicas de mi clase llevan ropa de marca y me dan envidia. A mí también me gustaría llevar ropa de marca pero es muy cara. María 16

2 Muchas asignaturas me parecen aburridas. Es por eso que no presto atención en clase y saco muy malas notas. Carlos 14

3 En mi colegio no hay muchos ordenadores y por eso me gustaría usar mi ordenador portátil pero no se permite. Creo que es ridículo. Javier 15

4 No podemos llevar joyas en el colegio y me parece una tontería. Si llevo una pulsera o unos pendientes, ¿cuál es el problema? Raquel 14

Respuestas de Ana

A Estoy de acuerdo contigo. Creo que los profesores deberían permitirlo. Sin embargo, lo puedes usar para revisar y hacer los deberes después del colegio.

B Está bien seguir la moda y las tendencias pero no es lo más importante. Puedes tener una buena imagen sin gastar tanto dinero.

C No es realmente un problema. No entiendo porque prohíben llevarlas, pero te recomiendo que sigas las reglas. Llevar joyas no es necesario.

D Sé que es difícil pero tienes que hacer un esfuerzo. ¿Quieres tener un trabajo interesante en el futuro? Piensa en eso para motivarte. También puedes hablar con tus profesores.

2a 📖 🎧 Read the magazine problem page and match up each student's problem with the correct reply A–D.

2b 📖 🎧 Read the problem page again then read the following statements. Find the three that are true according to the text.

1 Ana says that laptops are not as good as school computers.
2 What to wear is an issue for María.
3 Ana suggests thinking of a future career to get more motivated.
4 Raquel finds it silly not being able to wear jewellery.
5 Ana agrees that jewellery should be banned.
6 Carlos finds his subjects far too easy.

Dealing with 'true or false' activities

When reading material that is not immediately understandable, focus on what a paragraph is dealing with before tackling activities on it. For a true or false activity, narrow down the area of a text to where you are likely to find the answer and concentrate on that section.

Estrategia 2a–2b

3 **G** Copy the sentences and fill in the gaps with the correct form of the comparative.

1 El uniforme es _____ _____ _____ la ropa normal. (*The uniform is less comfortable than normal clothes.*)

2 Las reglas son _____ _____ _____ los profesores. (*The rules are as silly as the teachers.*)

3 Las zapatillas de deporte son _____ _____ los zapatos. (*Trainers are better than shoes.*)

4 La chaqueta es _____ _____ _____ la falda. (*The jacket is nicer than the skirt.*)

4 🎧 Listen to the head teacher explaining the school rules. Complete the following sentences with the correct option.

1 All pupils should … **a** arrive on time **b** treat others considerately **c** hand in work to teachers on time.

2 If you are ill you should … **a** phone school to say you won't be in **b** catch up with all work **c** bring a letter from home.

3 Smoking is allowed … **a** nowhere in the school **b** in specially marked areas **c** for teachers only.

4 In class you must … **a** listen and be quiet **b** make notes and listen **c** have all your books and equipment.

5 The fifth rule concerns … **a** procedure at break time **b** school uniform **c** bullying.

5 🗨 Work with a partner. Take turns to compare the following things now with what they were like at primary school.

Ejemplo: ¿Cómo son las instalaciones?

Las instalaciones aquí son más modernas.

a las matemáticas	c la comida	e el inglés
b los profesores	d las reglas	f los deberes

6 ✏ Write an article for Ana's magazine about your school pressures and problems. Include opinions, connectives and give solutions wherever you can. Write about your views on:

- el uniforme
- las reglas principales
- los deberes.

Pienso que Me parece que Encuentro que	algunas asignaturas son aburridas / inútiles. hay demasiados deberes. los exámenes son muy / bastante / demasiado difíciles.
No se permite / está prohibido	llevar joyas / llevar maquillaje / fumar.
Hay que	llevar uniforme / ser puntual / ser educado.
No tenemos	(suficientes) ordenadores / pizarras interactivas / libros.

Gramática *página 175*

Revision of the comparative

You use comparatives to compare two things. The comparative is formed by using:

más + adjective + *que* (more … than)

Mi uniforme es más cómodo que el tuyo. – My uniform is more comfortable than yours.

menos + adjective + *que* (less … than)

Tu colegio es menos estricto que el mío. – Your school is less strict than mine.

tan + adjective + *como* (as … as)

Las clases son tan buenas como las instalaciones. – The lessons are as good as the facilities.

Irregular comparatives:

mejor que – better than

peor que – worse than

Also learn about the personal *a*.
See page 144

Enlace

7.2 Groundwork is available in the Foundation book.

7.2 H ¡Cuánto estrés!

1a 📖🎧 Read the text and find the Spanish equivalents of these words and phrases.

1 bullying
2 punishments
3 good marks
4 behaviour
5 pressure
6 although

Las preocupaciones de los estudiantes

Aquí están los resultados de un sondeo realizado con un grupo de estudiantes españoles entre 14 y 16 años:

Problema	Porcentaje afectado
Exámenes / evaluaciones	76%
Deberes	59%
Comportamiento de compañeros	42%
Acoso escolar	38%
Padres	31%
Profesores	29%
Ropa	23%
Castigos	11%
Falta de libertad	8%

Es evidente al observar este sondeo que a los estudiantes entrevistados les preocupan sobre todo los asuntos relacionados con el trabajo escolar. La necesidad de sacar buenas notas es cada vez más importante hoy en día tanto para los que buscan trabajo como para los que quieren seguir con los estudios. Había gran número de alumnos que estaban a favor de un sistema de evaluación continua como alternativa a los exámenes, porque éstos provocan demasiado estrés.

Con respecto al comportamiento había dos problemas para los encuestados. Primero, les enfadaba a muchos estudiantes que algunos de sus compañeros de clase se comportaran mal y eso hace el trabajo del profesor o de la profesora muy difícil. La consecuencia de esto es que a menudo los que quieren aprender no pueden. Segundo, había muchos que sufrían violencia física y verbal por parte de otros estudiantes. Algunos estudiantes sufrían desde hacía muchos años.

La presión por parte de los adultos (padres y profesores) afecta a ciertos estudiantes, aunque generalmente reconocen que esta presión puede ser beneficiosa cuando no es demasiado y cuando los castigos en casa y en el colegio no son graves.

La ropa es algo que causa problemas en colegios donde no hay uniforme, porque puede ser muy caro comprar cosas de última moda.

1b 📖🎧 Read the text again and answer the following questions in English.

1 Who took part in the survey?
2 What has become more important for those students who want to find a job?
3 Why were a lot of students in favour of continuous assessment?
4 What are the two consequences of bad behaviour by students?
5 What has been affecting some students for many years?
6 How can not having a uniform be a problem?

2 **G** Change the infinitive of the verb in brackets to the imperfect tense. Translate each sentence into English.

1 (Estudiar, ellos) en ese colegio desde hacía cuatro años.
2 (Sufrir, nosotros) acoso escolar desde hacía mucho tiempo.
3 (Esperar, ella) a su amigo en el patio desde hacía quince minutos.
4 (Vivir, él) en la casa de al lado de su víctima desde hacía un mes.

Gramática *página 187*

Using *desde hacía* and the imperfect tense

To say that something had been happening for a certain amount of time, use *desde hacía* + a time expression, with a verb in the imperfect tense.

Desde hacía tres años.

Desde hacía mucho tiempo.

Ana estudiaba español todos los martes desde hacía cinco meses. – Ana had been studying Spanish every Tuesday for five months.

Also learn about using the conditional.

See page 145

3 🎧 Listen to the three teenagers. For each person, decide which of the following statements are true.

María

1 a I have never been bullied.
   b I am bullied sometimes.
   c I have to admit that I am a bully sometimes.
2 a I find homework quite easy.
   b My teachers don't explain things well enough.
   c I spend a lot of time doing homework.

Carlos

3 a Some of my friends have been bullied.
   b My friends have a bad effect on my studies.
   c I am an unlucky person.
4 a I don't like sport of any description.
   b I don't have any problems at school.
   c Basketball is never played at my school.

Lucía

5 a My parents aren't interested in what I do at school.
   b My parents put a lot of pressure on me.
   c My parents always help me with my homework.
6 a My teachers sympathise with the problems I have at home.
   b I go out too often.
   c My parents don't mind me going out.

4 💬 Working with a partner, or in groups of three or four, answer the following questions. You could play the role of someone who is more or less affected by these problems than you are.

■ Dame ejemplos de comportamiento bueno y malo en clase.
■ ¿Cuál de los problemas mencionados en el sondeo te preocupa más? ¿Por qué?
■ ¿Es mejor tener exámenes o evaluación continua? ¿Por qué?
■ ¿Cuáles son los aspectos positivos y negativos de llevar uniforme?
■ ¿Cómo son las relaciones entre tu familia y tú con respecto al trabajo escolar?

Expanding your answers

Estrategia 4

For speaking and writing activities, where you have a series of bullet points, try to say or write something about all of them. Focus on the question word and the tense of the question. Answer the question and try to make links with another tense, for example you can use the present tense and the imperfect tense together. Also remember to join lots of ideas together with connectives.

7.3 F   ¿Qué vas a estudiar?

1 ⓥ Read the list of words below. Which ones refer to getting good grades (**A**), which to bad grades (**B**) and which are more generic words that apply to both (**A + B**)?

> sacar buenas notas   sacar malas notas   suspender
>
> el fracaso escolar   el resultado   la nota
>
> el sobresaliente   el examen   la prueba

2a 📖 🎧 Read the article. Then answer the following questions with the correct person: Ana (**A**), Pedro (**P**) or both (**A + P**).

Who …

1. likes their school?
2. likes PE?
3. had lots of support from the teachers?
4. wants to do a vocational course?
5. does not like to study that much?
6. is going to get good grades overall?

> **Tips for reading questions**
>
> With these types of activity, you will read the texts in a more focused way if you have read the questions first. Also, read both texts before you answer any of the questions.

Estrategia 2a–2b

¿Qué van a hacer nuestros estudiantes?

Llegué al instituto hace casi cuatro años.
El primer día estaba muy nerviosa. Todo era nuevo, las instalaciones, los profesores, las rutinas, los alumnos e incluso algunas asignaturas.
Me encantó la clase de tecnología y la de cocina desde el primer día. Los profesores me ayudaron mucho y he aprendido un montón de cosas en estos años. Sin embargo, no aguanto la educación física. Ahora tengo dieciséis años y estoy pensando en lo que voy a hacer en los dos próximos años. Mis profesores dicen que voy a sacar buenas notas. Creo que voy a continuar con la tecnología y el diseño en el bachillerato. Después tengo la intención de ir a la universidad. En el futuro me gustaría ser diseñadora de muebles. *Ana*

Empecé la enseñanza secundaria hace cuatro años también. Me encanta el instituto y he hecho muy buenos amigos. Soy bueno en educación física y siempre saco buenas notas en todas las pruebas. Sin embargo, encuentro las ciencias muy difíciles y no sé qué notas voy a sacar en los exámenes finales. No quiero ir a la universidad porque no me gusta demasiado estudiar. Así que creo que voy a hacer un curso de formación profesional el año que viene. Voy a estudiar integración social porque me gusta ayudar a otras personas. Además voy a seguir estudiando idiomas. Quiero trabajar y ganar dinero, eso es lo que interesa. *Pedro*

2b 📖🎧 Read the article again and answer the following questions in English.

1 How did Ana feel when she started high school?
2 Why did she feel like this?
3 What is she going to study at A level?
4 When did Pedro start high school?
5 Why does he want to study social care?
6 What is he interested in?

3 🅖 Copy the sentences and fill in the gaps with the correct infinitive from the boxes below.

1 Mi hermano tiene la intención de _____ todos los exámenes.
2 Quiero _____ buenas notas este año.
3 ¿Quieres _____ a la universidad?
4 Voy a _____ un curso de alemán.
5 Odio el inglés, creo que voy a _____.
6 Durante el verano, tengo la intención de _____ con mi padre.

suspender	sacar	aprobar
trabajar	ir	hacer

Gramática | página 183

Using different ways to express the future

You have seen different ways of expressing the future before. Use them to add variety to what you want to say about the future. They will help you to get a higher grade.

querer + infinitive (to want to …)

me gustaría + infinitive (I would like to …)

near future: *ir a* + infinitive (to be going to …)

tener la intención de + infinitive (to have the intention of …)

Quiero ir a la universidad.

Me gustaría ir a la universidad.

Voy a ir a la universidad.

Tengo la intención de ir a la universidad.

Also learn about 'if' sentences.

See page 144

4 🎧 Listen to Manolo talking about school subjects. Match up each subject with the correct comment.

1 History
2 English
3 Geography
4 Art

a I would like to change to another subject.
b My teacher for this subject is really boring.
c It's a shame I'm not good at the subject because I like it.
d We never have to take notes in the lessons.
e I'm enjoying the subject much more than in the past.
f I've not had any problems with this subject.

5 🗨 What are you going to study next year? Work with a partner. Partner A asks the questions and partner B replies. Then swap roles.

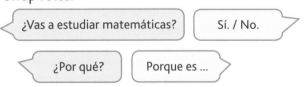

¿Vas a estudiar matemáticas? Sí. / No.

¿Por qué? Porque es …

6 🗨 Do a class survey. Interview five classmates about what they are going to do in the future. Then prepare a brief presentation with your findings.

- ¿Qué vas a estudiar el año que viene?
- ¿Vas a ir a la universidad? ¿Qué quieres estudiar?
- ¿Qué te gustaría hacer después de terminar los estudios?

Enlace

7.3 Groundwork is available in the Foundation book.

7.3 H   Después de los exámenes

1a 📖 🎧 Read the article and find the Spanish equivalents of these words and phrases.

| compulsory | to think | next year | advice | to earn | training |
| qualification | the world of work | electrician | to continue | university |

Instituto San Jaime – ¿Qué vas a hacer el año que viene?

Tienes quince o dieciséis años y estás empezando el último curso obligatorio en el instituto. Este año es cuando tienes que empezar a pensar en las posibilidades para el futuro y tus planes para el año próximo.

Aquí, los profesores del Instituto San Jaime te ofrecemos algunos consejos …

Puedes **buscar trabajo**. La gran ventaja es comenzar a ganar un poco de dinero y a tener algo más de libertad. Si es posible, es mejor buscar trabajos que ofrezcan formación como parte del empleo. Muchos aprendizajes incluyen la oportunidad de obtener un certificado académico además de experiencia laboral.

Puedes hacer **formación profesional.** Aquí en el instituto ofrecemos cursos de uno o dos años en los que aprenderás todo lo que necesitas para entrar en el mundo laboral. Hay clases para los electricistas, los peluqueros y los mecánicos del futuro … ¡y muchas más!

Puedes hacer **el bachillerato.** Esta opción es ideal si te han gustado tus asignaturas en el instituto y simplemente quieres estudiar un poco más, o si estás pensando en seguir tus estudios en la universidad. Estudiarás una variedad de asignaturas comunes a todos pero también escogerás otras que correspondan con tus planes para el futuro.

1b 📖 🎧 Read the article again and answer the following questions in English.

1. Who is this article written for?
2. What must the reader start to do this year?
3. Who has written the article?
4. According to the article, what are the two main advantages of getting a job?
5. Why are apprenticeships particularly recommended?
6. How long do vocational courses last?
7. What type of jobs could these courses lead to? Give two examples.
8. Give one reason why someone might opt to do the *bachillerato*.
9. Which of these statements is true?
   a. In the *bachillerato* you have a completely free choice of subjects.
   b. In the *bachillerato* there is a mixture of compulsory subjects.

2 **G** You are giving advice to some of your friends about what not to do. Copy the sentences, changing the infinitive in brackets to the correct form of the imperative (*tú* form). Then make up more sentences giving advice to people on what not to do.

Ejemplo: ¡No (mencionar) ese incidente!
                    ¡No menciones ese incidente!

1   ¡No (buscar) trabajo en esa región!
2   ¡No (ser) perezosa!
3   ¡No (escuchar) a Ramón!
4   ¡No (escribir) a esa empresa!

Gramática   *página 184*

Using imperatives in the negative

Imperatives are used to give instructions to people on what to do or what not to do.

Negative commands always use the subjunctive of the verb:

¡No escribas eso! – Don't write that!

Revise endings for the subjunctive in the grammar section at the end of the book.

Also learn about the imperfect subjunctive.   *See page 145*

3 Listen to the interview with Julia and choose the correct option to complete each sentence.

1   Of the three possible options, Julia immediately rejected:
    a   getting a job.
    b   vocational training.
    c   continuing academic studies.

2   One disadvantage of continuing with her studies is:
    a   it can be boring.
    b   she has no friends at school.
    c   she hasn't got much money.

3   The big advantage is that:
    a   she likes what she is doing.
    b   she can be with her friends.
    c   she can work at weekends.

4   She criticises her school for:
    a   giving too much homework.
    b   not organising work experience.
    c   not leaving her enough time for a Saturday job.

5   Julia does **not** express an interest in the work of:
    a   a lawyer.
    b   a doctor.
    c   an accountant.

6   Julia thinks that university graduates:
    a   get better job opportunities.
    b   earn more money.
    c   are less likely to be unemployed.

4 Write an email to your Spanish friend, Cristina, telling her about your plans for next year.

La ventaja	es que	ganas dinero.
		obtienes más calificaciones.
El aspecto negativo		hay que estudiar mucho más.
		las horas son largas.
Puedes	hacer	formación profesional.
		otras cosas.
	continuar	con tus estudios.
		estudiando lo que te gusta.
	empezar	a trabajar / a ser independiente.
Sería	fenomenal / útil	ir a la universidad / buscar trabajo.
	posible / perfecto	estudiar la química / tener más libertad.
Por un lado / por otro lado / aunque / también / además		

Estrategia 3

Finding techniques for listening tasks

Be careful with this type of activity, as the incorrect answers could have subtle differences from what the speaker says, so don't jump to conclusions and always listen twice before you write your answer.

(G) School, college and future plans

1 Translate the following words into Spanish. Use the nouns in the box below and check in a dictionary if you are unsure of the gender.

1 this exam
2 those classrooms
3 these bags
4 that word
5 this term
6 those teachers
7 that test
8 this uniform
9 these pupils
10 that vocabulary

uniforme
aulas
prueba
alumnos
mochilas
profesores
trimestre
examen
palabra
vocabulario

Revision of demonstrative adjectives
Remember that demonstrative adjectives are the words for 'this', 'these', 'that' and 'those'. They will agree with the noun that comes after them.

	Masc. sing.	Fem. sing.	Masc. pl.	Fem. pl.
This / these	Este	Esta	Estos	Estas
That / those	Ese	Esa	Esos	Esas

Gramática · página 176

2 Copy the sentences and fill in the gaps with *a* if you think it is needed.

1 Busco _____ mi cuaderno.
2 ¿Has visto _____ Mónica?
3 Voy a terminar _____ los deberes.
4 Manolo compró _____ un nuevo estuche.
5 Tuve que ver _____ la directora.

The personal a
When the **object** of a verb is a person, you have to write *a* before that person, as in these examples:

Vi a Elena en el patio. – I saw Elena in the yard.

Escuchamos a la profesora. – We listened to the teacher.

Gramática · página 187

3 Copy the sentences and fill in the gaps with the correct form of the verb in brackets (present, immediate future or simple future).

1 Si _____, voy a ir a la universidad. (aprobar)
2 Si trabajo mucho, _____ mucho dinero. (ganar)
3 Si mi hermano va a la universidad, _____ medicina. (estudiar)
4 Si no saco buenas notas, _____ un curso de formación profesional. (hacer)

'If' sentences
Use 'if' clauses to talk about possibilities in the future:

Si + present + immediate future

Si estudio mucho, voy a aprobar todo. – If I study a lot, I am going to pass everything.

You can also use the **simple future**. This is important if you are aiming for the higher grades.

Si + present + simple future

Si estudio mucho, lo aprobaré todo. – If I study a lot, I will pass everything.

Gramática · página 183

Gramática página 184

4 Copy the sentences and fill in the gaps with the correct form of the subjunctive of the verb in brackets.

1 Es importante que _____ todos los días. (estudiar, yo)

2 Es necesario que los colegios _____ clases de apoyo. (dar)

3 Es probable que mi amigo _____ en el comedor mañana. (comer)

4 Es posible que la biblioteca _____ más libros en septiembre. (tener)

5 Es necesario que _____ un gimnasio en tu colegio. (haber)

6 Es importante que las aulas _____ grandes y cómodas. (ser)

The present subjunctive

The subjunctive is used to express wishes, doubt, uncertainty, possibility and also feelings. The following expressions take the subjunctive.

Es + adjective + que   Es importante que

Es posible que   Es probable que

Es necesario que

Es importante que estudie más. – It is important that I study more.

To form the present subjunctive, take the yo form of the present tense and replace the -o ending with the following endings:

-ar verbs: -e, -es, -e, -emos, -éis, -en

-er and -ir verbs: -a, -as, -a, -amos, -áis, -an

Some verbs are irregular but the endings follow the same pattern. Here are some in the 'I' (yo) form:

ser (to be) – sea

ir (to go) – vaya

haber (there is / are) – haya

dar (to give) – dé

Gramática página 184

5 Choose the correct part of the conditional to complete these sentences.

1 En mi opinión, el colegio sería / serían / seríamos mejor con una piscina.

2 Me gusta / gustaría / gustarían tener más laboratorios de ciencias.

3 Mis amigos y yo recomendarían / recomienda / recomendaríamos un cambio de director.

4 Creo que los profesores deberían / deben / debería hacer más para ayudar a los alumnos menos inteligentes.

Using the conditional

This is used to say what **would** happen or what someone **would** do:

Me gustaría tener un horario diferente. – I would like to have a different timetable.

Gramática página 185

6 Read the following sentences and say whether they are using the present subjunctive (**P**) or imperfect subjunctive (**I**).

1 Es imposible que lo apruebe todo.

2 No era cierto que estudiara arquitectura.

3 Mi padre me dijo que hiciera el bachillerato.

4 A mi madre le gusta que estudie tecnología.

5 Es importante que apruebe todo en junio.

The imperfect subjunctive

The imperfect form of the subjunctive is used in the same expressions as the present subjunctive, but when the main verb is in the past tense. It is formed by taking the third person plural (ellos) form of the preterite past tense, dropping the ending -ron and then adding the appropriate imperfect subjunctive ending (-ra / -ras / -ra / -ramos / -rais / -ran).

Mi madre **quiere** que **vaya** a la universidad. – My mother wants me to go to university.

Mi madre **quería** que **fuera** a la universidad. – My mother wanted me to go to university.

School, college and future plans

Topic 7.1 Describing and comparing schools

7.1 F Bienvenidos al colegio ➡ *pages 132–133*

el	ambiente	atmosphere
el	apoyo	support
	aprender	to learn
la	asignatura	subject
el	bachillerato	equivalent of an A-level course
el	campo de deporte	sports field
	castigar	to punish
	charlar	to chat
	comprender	to understand
el	conocimiento	knowledge
el	curso	course / academic year
	enseñar	to teach
	explicar	to explain
	faltar	to miss / lack
el	horario	timetable
(el / la)	mejor	better / best
	mixto/a	mixed
	moderno/a	modern
el	nivel	level
	secundario/a	secondary

7.1 H Colegios británicos y españoles
➡ *pages 134–135*

los	apuntes	notes
	comenzar	to begin
el	director	head teacher
	duro/a	hard
	empezar	to begin
	entregar	to hand in
	pasar lista	to take the register
	perder	to lose
	ponerse a	to begin to
	privado/a	private

	público/a	public ('state' when referring to schools)
el	recreo	break
la	reunión	meeting
	salir	to go out
	severo/a	strict
	suspender	to fail
el	trabajo	work
el	trimestre	term
el / la	tutor(a)	tutor
el	vocabulario	vocabulary
	volver	to go back

Topic 7.2 School pressure and problems

7.2 F Los problemas escolares ➡ *pages 136–137*

	asistir	to attend
la	carta	letter
	divertirse	to have fun
la	envidia	jealousy
el	esfuerzo	effort
	estar de acuerdo	to agree
	estar de moda	to be fashionable
	fumar	to smoke
	intimidar	to intimidate / threaten
	obligatorio/a	compulsory
los	pendientes	ear-rings
	pensar	to think
el	portátil	laptop
	prohibir	to forbid
la	pulsera	bracelet
la	regla	rule
	respetar	to respect
	revisar	to revise
la	ropa de marca	designer clothes
	sin embargo	however
la	tontería	silliness, nonsense

7.2 H ¡Cuánto estrés! ➡ *pages 138–139*

el	acoso escolar	bullying
	apoyar	to support
el	asunto	matter / topic
	atacar	to attack
	ausente	absent
la	ayuda	help
	castigar	to punish
el	castigo	punishment
el	comportamiento	behaviour
la	conducta	behaviour
	enfadarse	to get angry
	entender	to understand
el	equilibrio	balance
	estar a favor	to be in favour
	estar en contra	to be against
	estar harto de	to be fed up with
la	evaluación	assessment
	golpear	to hit
	insultar	to insult
la	presión	pressure
el	sondeo	survey

Topic 7.3 Present and future studies

7.3 F ¿Qué vas a estudiar? ➡ *pages 140–141*

	aprobar	to pass
	ayudar	to help
	cambiar	to change
	concentrarse	to concentrate
	conseguir	to get
el	diseño	design
el	examen	exam
la	formación profesional	vocational course
el	fracaso escolar	failure
el	instituto	high school
la	nota	grade
	optativo/a	optional
la	prueba	test
el	resultado	result

	sacar buenas notas	to get good grades
	sacar malas notas	to get bad grades
	ser bueno en	to be good at
el	sobresaliente	outstanding / A*
	suspender	to fail
la	universidad	university

7.3 H Después de los exámenes
➡ *pages 142–143*

el	aprendizaje	apprenticeship learning
la	calificación	qualification
el / la	contable	accountant
	criticar	criticise
los	derechos	rights
la	desventaja	disadvantage
el	empleo	job
	encontrar	to find
	escoger	to choose
el	futuro	future
	ganar	to earn
el / la	mecánico/a	mechanic
	obtener	to obtain
	ofrecer	to offer
	organizar	to organise
la	preocupación	worry
	seguir	to carry on
	tomar decisiones	to make decisions
	tomar un año libre / sabático	to have a gap year
la	ventaja	advantage

8.1 F El trabajo a tiempo parcial

1 🅥 🎧 Read the speech bubbles. Are the students talking about their past work experience (**P**) or about their current part-time job (**C**)?

1 Trabajo de once a dos cuidando a niños.

2 Di clases de apoyo durante tres semanas.

3 Vendo periódicos por la mañana.

4 Lavo coches los fines de semana.

5 Archivé todos los documentos de la oficina.

6 Vigilo a la gente en una piscina.

2a 📖 🎧 Read the descriptions the teenagers have written about their part-time jobs. Answer the following questions with the correct name: Laura (**L**), Ramón (**R**) or Sara (**S**).

Who ...
1. gets along with his / her work colleagues?
2. works at weekends?
3. used to work as a babysitter?
4. has a better timetable now?
5. likes her / his boss?
6. is going to work full time this summer?

Laura

Tengo un trabajo a tiempo parcial desde hace tres meses. Antes hacía de canguro los viernes y cuidaba a mis primas pequeñas pero mis tíos no me pagaban mucho dinero. Ahora soy camarera en un restaurante japonés, que está cerca de mi casa. Nunca había pensado en ser camarera pero me gusta el trabajo. Trabajo todos los viernes y sábados por la noche y también de vez en cuando durante las vacaciones del colegio. Tengo que servir a los clientes y limpiar las mesas. Lo bueno es que no está mal pagado. No me llevo muy bien con mis compañeros pero mi jefe es muy simpático.

Ramón

Empecé a trabajar de cajero el año pasado. Hice las prácticas de trabajo en un supermercado de mi barrio y me gustó mucho. Cuando terminé las prácticas me ofrecieron un trabajo de tres días a la semana. Trabajo por las tardes después del colegio. El sueldo es bastante bueno y ahora tengo más dinero para salir. Además, me llevo muy bien con mis compañeros. En el pasado había repartido periódicos por la mañana pero este trabajo me gusta mucho más porque el horario es mejor.

Sara

Mi madre es dentista y trabajo en su clínica los lunes por la tarde. No gano mucho porque trabajo solo un día pero tengo suficiente para mis gastos. Trabajo como recepcionista. Tengo que contestar el teléfono, recibir a los clientes y hacer café. Me gusta mi trabajo porque me gusta hablar con la gente. Este verano voy a trabajar todo el mes de agosto.

2b 📖 🎧 Read the descriptions again and decide if the following statements are true (**T**), false (**F**) or not mentioned (**?**).

1 Laura works in a restaurant near her house.
2 Laura had thought about being a waitress before.
3 Ramón thinks his salary is not that good.
4 Ramón did his work experience at the same place.
5 Sara finds it easy to work with her mum.
6 Sara is a sociable person.

3 🄖 Read the following sentences and identify the verbs in the pluperfect tense. Then translate the sentences into English.

1 En el pasado había trabajado sin contrato.
2 Hasta ahora siempre había tenido trabajos de media jornada.
3 Nunca había mandado tantos correos electrónicos.
4 Cuando mi madre llamó, ya había salido de la oficina.

4a 🎧 Listen to three people talking about their part-time jobs. Which aspect do they mention? Write the correct letter a–f for each person 1–3.

a duties   c uniform   e boss
b working hours d salary   f colleagues

4b 🎧 Listen again. Write down the job they do and where they work. Answer in English.

5 🗨 Prepare a two-minute presentation about your current part-time job. Include the following points:

■ what you do and where you work
■ your working hours and your salary
■ whether you get along with your colleagues / boss
■ your opinion about your work.

Trabajo como	cocinero/a	en un hotel / restaurante.
	dependiente	en una clínica / empresa / compañía.
	camarero/a	
Trabajo		todos los días / los fines de semana / tres días por semana / de … a …
Gano		mucho / poco / bastante.
Mando correos electrónicos. / Sirvo comida. / Corto el césped.		
Me llevo bien / mal con		mi jefe / mis compañeros porque es / son …
(No) Me gusta mi trabajo porque …		el ambiente es guay.
		el día es muy largo.
		tengo mucha responsabilidad.

Learning vocabulary

Make sure you note vocabulary as you go along and revise it little and often – about 10 words at a time works well. Remember that you can't use a dictionary in the Reading exam so you need to have the vocabulary in your head!

Estrategia 2a–2b

Recognising the pluperfect tense

The pluperfect tense says what **had** happened or what someone **had** done. It is formed with the imperfect tense of *haber* and the past participle.

Antes había trabajado como camarera. – I had worked as a waitress before.

Había terminado cuando mi jefe llegó. – I had finished when my boss arrived.

Also learn about using *lo* in the past to extend your paragraphs.

See page 160

Gramática   página 183

🔗 **Enlace**
8.1 Groundwork is available in the Foundation book.

8.1 H Hacer prácticas

This extract from a problem page in a teenage magazine concerns Elena's problems with her parents over her part-time job.

Consultorio de Rosario

Problema

Querida Rosario

Soy una alumna de dieciséis años y te escribo para pedirte consejo acerca de un problema que tengo con mis padres.

Siempre había pensado que era muy importante ganar dinero mientras estudiaba, y por eso hace un mes empecé a trabajar en un restaurante en mi barrio tres noches por semana. Mis padres me dan dinero cada semana y en el pasado ha sido bastante para comprar revistas y maquillaje. Sin embargo, ahora tengo novio y salimos a cafeterías o al cine y es bastante caro.

No quiero pedir más dinero a mis padres, porque a mi juicio no sería justo. Por otro lado, necesito más dinero para salir.

Ayer mi madre me dijo que no podía continuar con mi trabajo porque está afectando mis notas en el colegio. No obstante, dejar el trabajo posiblemente sería el fin de la relación con mi novio, puesto que ya no podría salir con él.

¿Qué puedo hacer?

Elena

Respuesta

Querida Elena

Lo que está pasando contigo es común entre la gente de tu edad y no tienes que preocuparte. Tienes que encontrar un compromiso con tu madre y hablar también con tu padre, cuya opinión también será importante.

¿Por qué no sugieres a tus padres que trabajes una noche o dos noches solamente y que te den un poco más de dinero para que puedas seguir saliendo con tu novio? Estoy segura de que van a entender tu problema y ayudarte a disfrutar de tu tiempo libre y estudiar al mismo tiempo. Se puede hacer las dos cosas, pero tú tienes que ser responsable y no olvidar que el futuro dependerá de tus estudios.

Rosario

1a 📖 🎧 Read the problem page extract and find the Spanish equivalents of these words and phrases.

1 ask you for advice
2 I had thought
3 earn money
4 in my opinion
5 leave the job
6 to forget

1b 📖 🎧 Read the extract again and answer the following questions in English.

1 What had Elena always thought that it was important to do?
2 What two things has Elena usually spent her money on?
3 Why has life become more expensive for Elena?
4 Why did her mother tell her that she could no longer work in the restaurant?
5 Why does Elena think that giving up her job would be a bad idea?
6 Why does Rosario think that Elena has no need to worry?
7 What two things does Rosario suggest that Elena should do?
8 How does Rosario tell Elena to behave and why?

2 **G** Copy the sentences, changing the infinitive in brackets into the correct part of the pluperfect tense. Those with a '!' have an irregular past participle.

1 Yo siempre _____ (pensar) que era fácil trabajar en una tienda.
2 Marta _____ (dejar) su paraguas en la oficina y tuvo que volver a recogerlo.
3 Los chicos _____ (comer) demasiados caramelos y se sentían un poco enfermos.
4 Paula y yo _____ (volver !) muy tarde la noche anterior.
5 ¿Tú _____ (beber) sangría antes?
6 El Señor García, mi jefe, _____ (hacer !) planes para comprar una compañía en Madrid.

3 🎧 Listen to three students talking about their work experience. Copy and complete the table.

	Where they worked	How long for	Overall opinion
1			
2			
3			

4 🖊 You want to find out your friends' thoughts about their part-time jobs. Plan and write a questionnaire in Spanish which will ask for people's opinions. Look at the examples below.

- ¿De qué trabajas?
- ¿Qué es lo peor de tu trabajo?
- ¿Te llevas bien con tu jefe?

5 💬 In groups of three or four ask the questions you have devised in Activity 4 and make notes in Spanish on the answers given. Report your findings to the class in Spanish.

X trabaja como …

Le gusta su trabajo porque …

X (no) ha tenido problemas con sus padres porque …

X se lleva bien / mal con su jefe / sus compañeros porque …

Gramática página 183

Using the pluperfect tense

The pluperfect tense is used to indicate an action in the past that occurred before another action in the past. The pluperfect is formed with the imperfect of the auxiliary verb *haber* + the past participle of the main verb.

había	
habías	
había	+ past participle
habíamos	(*-ado* / *-ido*)
habíais	
habían	

Mi madre había terminado de trabajar cuando mi padre llegó. – My mother had finished work when my father arrived.

¿Habías trabajado de camarero antes? – Had you worked as a waiter before?

Also learn how to use the relative adjective *cuyo* to improve your sentences.

See page 161

Estrategia 4

Including a range of tenses

To get the best grade, make sure you include a range of tenses in your work: past, present and future.

*Me **gustan** los niños así que **hice** las prácticas de trabajo en una escuela. Cuando **termine** mis estudios, **iré** a la universidad porque me **gustaría** ser profesora de primaria.*

8.2 F Buscando trabajo

1 ⓥ Write down as many Spanish words as you can think of which are associated with the following jobs.

| cocinero/a | socorrista | camarero/a | recepcionista | guía |

Ejemplo: cocinero/a – comida, cocina, plato, etc.

2a 📖 🎧 Read the adverts (A–F). Which one mentions each of the following aspects? Write the letter of the correct advert.

1 experience is essential
2 training is offered
3 good appearance is required
4 first aid knowledge is useful

A

Se busca cocinero para preparar platos regionales e internacionales. Experiencia esencial.

B

Buscamos a jóvenes para ayudar a cuidar niños en el club infantil. Organizarás juegos y excursiones. Conocimiento de primeros auxilios útil.

Nuevo complejo turístico en Mariroca.

Se necesitan personas para trabajar este verano.

C

Se necesita socorrista para la seguridad en la playa. Ofrecemos formación.

D

Queremos camareros para los tres restaurantes. Imprescindible tener buenas relaciones con los clientes y buen aspecto personal.

E

Se busca recepcionista para el Hotel Solimar. El candidato ideal tendrá conocimientos de informática y hablará más de un idioma.

F

¿Quieres trabajar de guía? Este verano buscamos a alguien que acompañe a los veraneantes en sus excursiones en autobús. Conocimiento de la región sería útil.

2b 📖 🎧 These students are looking for work in Spain. Which job would suit each of them? Read the adverts and write the correct letter for each person.

1 I'd really love to work here. I spent a year in this area as part of my Spanish degree so I know all the local beauty spots.

2 My main qualities are my extrovert personality and my ability to get on with people. I don't mind hard work and I'm often complimented on my smart appearance.

3 It would be great to work here to practise my Spanish, and I could probably use my German as well, as it's a popular area with tourists. Hopefully my IT skills will impress!

4 I'm looking for outdoor work hopefully. I haven't got any particular qualifications but I love sport and I'm very fit because I swim every day. I'm also prepared to learn!

3a ⓖ Ask for the following items, using *quisiera*.

1 The phone number
2 The new job
3 An appointment

3b ⓖ Say that you would like to do these things, using *quisiera* followed by the infinitive.

1 Leave a message
2 Send an email
3 Phone the office

4 🎧 Listen to three phone messages and complete the missing information in the table below.

Name	Contact details	When to call back
		After 5
	dieterh@aol.de	
Xanti Ansotegi		

5 💬 Work with a partner. Your partner is preparing for an interview for one of the jobs advertised on page 152. Ask him / her questions like the ones below: note that these questions use the formal (*usted*) form of the verb in a formal situation. Then swap roles.

- ¿Por qué le interesa este trabajo?
- ¿Cuándo puede empezar?
- Su personalidad, ¿cómo va a ayudarle en el trabajo?
- ¿Cuántas horas puede trabajar por día / semana?
- Hábleme de su experiencia de trabajo.

¿?
¿?

Me interesa el trabajo porque	me gusta trabajar con …	
Además, creo que el trabajo	será	fascinante / emocionante / ideal.
	tendrá	muchas ventajas / buen sueldo.
Soy Creo que soy	una persona	fiable / trabajadora / honesta / entusiasta.
Puedo Quisiera	trabajar	todos los días / veinticinco horas a la semana / los fines de semana.
	empezar	en junio / en verano / después de las vacaciones.
He trabajado / ayudado Trabajé	en una panadería / como peluquera / en una empresa.	

Gramática *página 185*

Using *quisiera*

Quisiera can be used to say that you would like a particular item or to say that you would like to do a particular thing, in which case it is followed by the infinitive of the verb:

Quisiera un café.

Quisiera mandar un fax.

Also learn how to use *usted / ustedes*.

See page 160

Estrategia 4

Recognising numbers when spoken

Make sure you can recognise numbers in Spanish – they often come up in listening activities. Challenge a partner! Ask them to say 10 numbers between 1 and 100, write them down and check how many you got correct. Then you say 10 numbers for your partner. Who got most right? Keep going with different numbers until you can both get 10 out of 10!

🔗 **Enlace**

8.2 Groundwork is available in the Foundation book.

8.2 H Conocer los procedimientos de trabajo

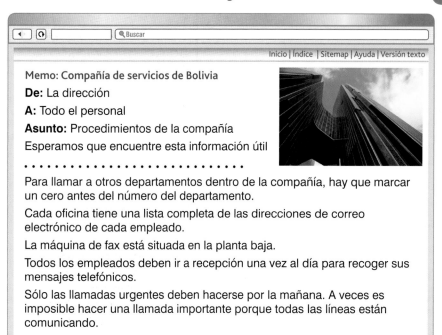

◀ | ⟳ | | 🔍 Buscar

Inicio | Índice | Sitemap | Ayuda | Versión texto

Memo: Compañía de servicios de Bolivia

De: La dirección

A: Todo el personal

Asunto: Procedimientos de la compañía

Esperamos que encuentre esta información útil

· ·

Para llamar a otros departamentos dentro de la compañía, hay que marcar un cero antes del número del departamento.

Cada oficina tiene una lista completa de las direcciones de correo electrónico de cada empleado.

La máquina de fax está situada en la planta baja.

Todos los empleados deben ir a recepción una vez al día para recoger sus mensajes telefónicos.

Sólo las llamadas urgentes deben hacerse por la mañana. A veces es imposible hacer una llamada importante porque todas las líneas están comunicando.

1a 📖 🎧 Read the memo and find the Spanish equivalents of these words and phrases.

1 you have to
2 dial zero
3 email addresses
4 employee
5 fax machine
6 the ground floor
7 telephone messages
8 all lines are engaged

1b 📖 🎧 Read the memo again. What is said about the aspects below? Answer in English.

1 making internal phone calls
2 what can be found in each office
3 where the fax machine is
4 collecting telephone messages
5 what type of phone calls should be made in the mornings

2 **G**  Work with a partner, changing the verbs from the infinitive into the *tú* form of the preterite tense. Answer each question with a sentence that includes a preterite verb in the first person. Take turns to ask and answer the questions.

1 ¿(Trabajar) el sábado?
2 ¿(Ganar) mucho dinero?
3 ¿Por qué (decidir) trabajar allí?
4 ¿(Hablar) con los clientes?
5 ¿(Recibir) muchas llamadas?
6 ¿(Volver) tarde a casa?

3a 📹 Watch the video clip about summer jobs. Answer the questions in English.

1 a How many different shifts are available in the restaurant?
   b What bonus is offered to waiters?
2 a What does the restaurant specialise in?
   b What experience does Fátima have?

3b 📹 Watch again. Which question words do you hear in the dialogues? Translate them into English. How many other question words do you know? Write a list.

4 ✏️ You and your partner are in charge of putting together a guide giving information needed by someone starting a new job in an office – but with a twist! Make it as silly as you can! You could include some of the following aspects or add new ones of your own.

- office opening hours
- how to make a phone call
- where to find an internal phone directory
- where to find the postroom
- where to collect deliveries
- what the work involves

El horario es de … a …
Para llamar …
La lista de teléfonos está …
Para enviar cartas …
Para recoger entregas / pedidos …
El trabajo conlleva …

Gramática *página 181*

Asking questions using the preterite tense

To ask a person if they did something, simply tell them that they did it (using the preterite tense) and raise the pitch of your voice to sound like a question:

¿Fuiste a la oficina? – Did you go to the office? / You went to the office?

Also learn about asking questions using prepositions.

See page 161

Estrategia 3a–3b

Using question words to focus on key information

Make sure you know all the question words so you know what information is being asked for. This will help you to pick out the answer as you will know what type of information you need to focus on, e.g. where → a place, when → a day, date or time.

8.3 F Comparando empleos diferentes

1 **V** Look at these adjectives and expressions that could be used to describe work, and categorise them into two separate lists: positive and negative. Then try to add at least three more entries to each list.

| aburrido | bien pagado | mal pagado | difícil | interesante |
| entretenido | seguro | estupendo | inseguro | divertido |

2a 📖 🎧 The three people below have written about their jobs. Read the descriptions and select the correct person, Luisa (**L**), Susana (**S**) or José (**J**).

Who ...

1 doesn't have to study?
2 talks about the pressure of the job?
3 is going against parental wishes?

4 attends a training course once a week?
5 worries about losing their job?

Luisa

Yo trabajo como contable para una gran empresa en la ciudad. Nunca pensé que trabajaría con números porque, de niña, no era muy buena en matemáticas. El trabajo puede ser aburrido, a veces, pero está muy bien pagado. Lo peor es que hay muchos exámenes al principio y hay que aprobarlos o perderás el empleo. Por eso, como te puedes imaginar, es muy estresante porque tengo que estudiar muchísimo. La empresa donde trabajo está en el centro de la ciudad, bastante cerca de mi piso – ¡menos mal!

Susana

Estoy muy contenta porque empecé mi nuevo trabajo el mes pasado y me encanta. Estoy haciendo un aprendizaje para ser peluquera y lo bueno es que es muy variado. Creo que siempre aprendes mejor cuando tienes la experiencia práctica del trabajo. También voy a un colegio un día a la semana para estudiar – es parte de la formación profesional. Las clases son muy interesantes porque son útiles en mi trabajo y puedo charlar con los otros alumnos para compartir ideas y hablar de problemas.

José

De momento, trabajo en una tienda de muebles en la ciudad. No está mal pero sólo tengo este trabajo hasta encontrar algo mejor. Mis padres tienen una granja y pensaban que yo iba a trabajar allí con ellos. Tuve que explicarles que no tenía ganas de quedarme en el campo y vivir la vida de un granjero. Trabajas muchas horas, el trabajo es sucio y te pagan peor que en la ciudad. Sé que el aire es puro, el trabajo es físico y te ayuda a mantenerte en forma, pero no es para mí. No me gusta la vida rural, la vida urbana es más divertida.

2b 📖 🎧 Read the three people's texts again and answer the following questions in English.

1   Who do you think is happiest in their job? Give a reason for your answer.
2   Who did not expect to be doing their current job? Give a reason for your answer.

3 **G** Read the following sentences and pick out the intensifiers / quantifiers. Then translate the sentences into English.

1   Mi jefe es muy simpático.
2   El trabajo es bastante aburrido.
3   Trabajo muchas horas.
4   Mi madre trabaja pocos días a la semana.
5   Hay bastante trabajo en la oficina.

Gramática *página 178*

Using quantifiers and intensifiers

Quantifiers and intensifiers are used in front of nouns or adjectives to tell us how much, or to intensify the words they precede.

mucho/a/os/as – much / many / a lot of (with nouns)
muchísimo/a/os/as – a large amount of (with nouns)
poco/a/os/as – few (with nouns)
bastante – enough / quite a lot of (with nouns)
bastante – quite (with adjectives)
muy – very (with adjectives)
demasiado/a/os/as – too much / many (with nouns)
demasiado – too (with adjectives)
Also learn about the superlative.   *See page 160*

---

4 🎧 Listen to three students talking about their work experience. Write down the numbers of the three statements from the list below that are correct.

1   María worked in a hotel reception.
2   María would have preferred to work in a shop.
3   Luis worked as an electrician.
4   Luis would like to work as a carpenter.
5   Juan worked as a receptionist.
6   In the future, Juan would like to do something more active.

5 💬 Choose a job and imagine it's your own job. Prepare a short presentation to explain to school leavers what your job entails. Make sure you include: your opinions; all three tenses; at least one superlative adverb (*lo mejor / lo peor*); at least two quantifiers / intensifiers. When you present it to your partner or to the class, they must check that you have included everything on the list.

Estrategia 4

Listening for different tenses

You know that it is important to listen out for key words when listening, but make sure you also listen carefully for the tense. Are they talking about something they have done (past), do now (present) or plan to do (future / conditional)? It can make a big difference!

Trabajé en una tienda.
Trabajo en una tienda.
Voy a trabajar en una tienda.
Me gustaría trabajar en una tienda.

El trabajo de	camarero / periodista / profesora / arquitecto es …
En mi trabajo tengo que	escribir artículos cada día / preparar clases / diseñar edificios …
En este trabajo necesitas ser	(bastante / muy) responsable / puntual / creativo.
Lo mejor es … Lo peor es …	porque …

🔗 **Enlace**

8.3 Groundwork is available in the Foundation book.

8.3 H | Trabajos ideales para estudiantes

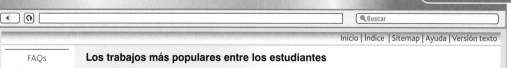

Objetivos

Talking about what job you would like to do

Using the conditional tense

Using *que* and *quien* to extend sentences

◀ ↻ [   ] 🔍 Buscar

Inicio | Índice | Sitemap | Ayuda | Versión texto

FAQs

Noticias

Acceso directo

Arriba

Los trabajos más populares entre los estudiantes

Una de las principales razones de ir a la universidad es obviamente conseguir un buen trabajo. Sin embargo, todos sabemos que no sólo es cuestión de títulos. La competencia es fuerte, así que es importante mostrar algo de experiencia laboral en el currículum vitae. Como las empresas buscan a jóvenes emprendedores, es recomendable compaginar los estudios con algún trabajo que no quite mucho tiempo.

Hemos entrevistado alrededor de cien estudiantes universitarios que trabajan. Aquí abajo encontrarás algunos de sus comentarios. Tú también podrías encontrar un trabajo al mismo tiempo que estudias.

• •

Estoy estudiando magisterio para ser profesora de primaria y hago de canguro por las tardes y los fines de semana. Está bien pagado y puedes estudiar mientras cuidas a los niños. Además, está relacionado con lo que estoy estudiando. Sin embargo, si pudiera trabajaría en una escuela. **Verónica, Barcelona**

• •

Mi vida gira alrededor de los ordenadores. Estudio informática ya que tengo la intención de ser programador. Por las mañanas trabajo en la sección de ventas de una tienda de informática. Cuando no hay muchos clientes ayudo a reparar ordenadores que es lo que realmente me interesa. Las horas no están muy bien pagadas pero tengo mucha flexibilidad. Además, si tengo exámenes puedo pedir días libres. Es un trabajo ideal porque no interfiere con mis estudios. **Manuel, Valencia**

• •

Soy estudiante de filología inglesa. Para ganar un poco de dinero extra, doy clases de español a los estudiantes extranjeros que vienen a mi universidad. Es genial porque los estudiantes vienen a mi casa o doy las clases online. Además, esto también me ayuda a mejorar el inglés. **Ana, Salamanca**

• •

Estoy en el último curso de turismo. Llevo dos años trabajando para una agencia de traductores, ya que hablo árabe, español y francés. Mi familia se trasladó a España cuando tenía nueve años. Es un trabajo muy bueno ya que trabajo desde casa. Además, los idiomas poco comunes tienen mucha demanda. No me importaría hacer esto en el futuro. **Amín, Zaragoza**

• •

Me queda un año para terminar la carrera de arquitectura. Desde que empecé la universidad trabajo en un bar los fines de semana. Aunque este no sería el trabajo ideal de muchos jóvenes porque no tienes tiempo para salir, a mí me permite estudiar durante la semana. Es entretenido y además las propinas son muy buenas, de lo contrario, tendría que pedir dinero a mis padres. **Marta, Alicante**

1a 📖🎧 Read the blog. Find the Spanish equivalents of these words and phrases.

1 to combine

2 job that does not take up much of your time

3 we have interviewed

4 I babysit

5 revolves around

6 foreigners

7 demand

8 tips (money)

1b 📖 🎧 Read the blog again and answer the following questions in English.

1 According to the blog, why is it important that students work while they study?
2 What type of students did they interview?
3 Who receives very good tips?
4 Who has a well paid job?
5 Which aspect of Marta's job puts other students off?
6 Other than earning money, how is Ana benefiting from tutoring?

2 🄖 Read the sentences and fill the gaps with the appropriate form of the conditional tense of the verb in brackets.

1 _____ trabajar por las tardes. (poder, yo)
2 Nosotros _____ más horas pero no podemos. (trabajar)
3 Con más ventas, la compañía _____ más éxito. (tener)
4 ¿_____ con el cliente en inglés? (hablar, ellos)
5 Mi hermana y yo _____ nuestro propio negocio, pero no tenemos dinero. (abrir)

3 🎧 Listen to the interview with a bullfighter, Emilio Gutiérrez. Copy the table and fill in the missing information in English.

a	Location of first experience of 'bullfighting'.	
	Age at that time.	
	Where he first got used to animals.	
b	Where he started to learn the job of a *matador*.	
	Two problems when he started to be a *matador*.	
c	What gave him his 'big break'.	
	The cost of a *traje de luces*.	
	His overall view of the job of a *matador*.	

4 ✎ Write an entry for a blog on ideal jobs. Where would you like to be in 10 years' time? Use the conditional tense and use *que / quien* to develop your sentences at least once. Talk about:

■ your ideal job
■ the workplace
■ the working hours
■ work colleagues / your boss
■ holidays
■ job responsibilities.

Using the conditional tense

Gramática *página 184*

Use the conditional tense to talk about what could or would happen. To form the conditional, add the appropriate ending to the infinitive:

I	trabajar-**ía**
you (singular)	trabajar-**ías**
he / she / it	trabajar -**ía**
we	trabajar -**íamos**
you (plural)	trabajar -**íais**
they	trabajar -**ían**

The irregular verbs are the same as in the future tense. Have a look at some of them:

Tendría – I would have
Haría – I would do
Podría – I would be able to
Pondría – I would put
Saldría – I would go out

Also learn about verbs with prepositions.

See page 161

Using *que* and *quien* to extend sentences

Estrategia 4

Que and *quien* are used to add extra information about an object or a person in an explanatory way. Remember that a variety of vocabulary and structures will get you extra marks.

*Mi amigo, **quien** trabaja en un bar, es muy responsable.* – My friend, who works in a bar, is very responsible.

*El bar **que** está en la plaza busca un camarero.* – The bar which is in the square is looking for a waiter.

G ## Jobs and employment

1 Copy the sentences and fill in the gaps to give your opinion about some aspects of work experience, using an appropriate adjective from the boxes below.

1 _____ fue el horario, trabajé diez horas cada día.

2 _____ fue limpiar.

3 _____ fue que tuve que levantarme muy temprano.

4 _____ fue conocer a gente famosa.

5 _____ fue que no hice nada.

| Lo mejor | Lo peor | Lo bueno | Lo malo |

| Lo difícil | Lo interesante | Lo aburrido |

> **Gramática** página 174
>
> **Using *lo* + adjective in the past**
>
> Remember that you can put *lo* in front of an adjective to mean 'the … thing'. It can be followed by a noun or an infinitive.
>
> *Lo interesante **fue el trabajo**.* – The interesting thing **was the work**.
>
> *Lo interesante **fue hablar** con los clientes.* – The interesting thing **was talking** to the clients.
>
> You can also use *lo* + adjective + *fue que* to talk about the past:
>
> *Lo bueno **fue que** conocí a mucha gente.* – The good thing **was that** I met lots of people.
>
> Remember, *lo mejor* and *lo peor* mean 'the best thing' and 'the worst thing'.

2a An interviewer gives feedback to someone who has recently been for an interview. Copy the following text, replacing the English words with the correct verb from the boxes below. The verbs are in the preterite, in the *usted* form.

Durante la entrevista, usted (1) *spoke* muy bien y siempre (2) *listened* con atención. Sin duda, (3) *read* el anuncio y (4) *wrote* su solicitud con mucho cuidado. Es evidente que (5) *thought* antes de contestar y siempre me (6) *asked* si algo no estaba claro.

| preguntó | escribió | bailó | habló |

| pensó | vio | escuchó | leyó |

> **Gramática** página 178
>
> ***Usted* and *ustedes***
>
> When you are addressing someone as 'you', if you do not know them or if they are older than you are, you should address them as *usted*, or *ustedes* if you are speaking to more than one person. When using a verb, use the third person singular form for *usted* or the third person plural form for *ustedes*.

2b Choose the correct form of the verb to match the person to whom the question is addressed.

1 ¿Cuánto dinero tiene / tienes? (*your best friend*)

2 ¿Puedes / Puede decirme dónde están los servicios, por favor? (*an elderly lady at the station*)

3 ¿Eres / Es español? (*a boy of your age whom you have just met*)

3 Choose the correct option to complete these sentences. Then translate the sentences into English.

1 El horario es el / la mejor parte del trabajo.

2 Mi jefe es el / la mejor del mundo.

3 Mis compañeros son el / la / los / las más divertidos.

4 Cuidar de niños es el / la peor trabajo que he hecho.

5 María es el / la empleada más eficiente de la oficina.

> **Gramática** página 175
>
> **The superlative**
>
> The superlative construction is similar to the comparative:
>
> *el / la* + (noun) + *más* + adjective – the most …
>
> *el / la* + (noun) + *menos* + adjective – the least …
>
> *el / la* + *mejor* – the best   *el / la* + *peor* – the worst
>
> *Tomás es el chico más simpático de la oficina.* – Tomás is the nicest boy in the office.
>
> *Tomás es el más simpático de la oficina.* – Tomás is the nicest in the office.
>
> As in English, the noun can be omitted.

4 Copy the sentences and fill in the gaps with *cuyo, cuya, cuyos* or *cuyas*.

1 Mi amigo, _____ padre es periodista, dice que hay oportunidades de trabajo en su periódico.

2 Éste es Esteban, _____ oficina está al lado de la mía.

3 Le voy a presentar a Ángela, _____ ideas siempre son interesantes.

4 Trabajarás con José, _____ hijos van a tu instituto.

> **Gramática** · página 176
>
> **The relative adjective *cuyo***
>
> *Cuyo* translates into English as 'whose' and must agree with the noun that follows it, as in these examples:
>
> *Éste es Manuel, **cuya** hermana es mi mejor amiga.* – This is Manuel, whose sister is my best friend.
>
> *Es la mujer **cuyas** fotos están en la pared.* – It's the woman whose photos are on the wall.

5 Translate these sentences into English.

1 ¿En qué consiste el trabajo?

2 ¿De quién es este libro?

3 ¿A quién vas a mandar la carta?

4 ¿Para cuándo tengo que terminar el trabajo?

5 ¿Con quién tengo que hablar en inglés?

6 ¿Para qué quieres ver al director?

> **Gramática** · páginas 186–187
>
> **Interrogatives with prepositions**
>
> When you ask a question which requires a preposition (*a, de, en, con, por, para, sin,* etc.) with the verb, the preposition will generally appear at the start of the sentence.
>
> *¿Con quién saliste anoche?* – Who did you go out with last night? / With whom did you go out last night?
>
> *¿A qué ciudad vas?* – Which town are you going to? / To which town are you going?

6a Copy the sentences and fill in the gaps with the correct preposition from the boxes below. You won't need them all, but you will need some more than once.

1 Mi compañero se disculpó _____ llegar tarde.

2 Me olvidé _____ llamar al cliente ayer.

3 Mi hermano me animó _____ solicitar el trabajo.

4 Mis compañeros me ayudaron _____ terminar con la limpieza.

5 He empezado _____ trabajar a las siete.

a	por	de	con	en

6b Pick three verbs from the list in the grammar box and write a sentence using each of them.

> **Gramática** · página 187
>
> **Verbs with prepositions**
>
> As in English, in Spanish there are some verbs that are followed by a particular preposition – but not necessarily the same one in both languages. Some of the most common ones are listed below:
>
> *animar **a*** – to encourage to
>
> *ayudar **a** alguien* – to help someone
>
> *cuidar **a** alguien* – to look after someone
>
> *empezar **a*** – to begin to
>
> *negarse **a*** – to refuse to
>
> *acabar **con*** – to put an end to
>
> *hablar **con*** – to speak to
>
> *cansarse **de*** – to get tired of
>
> *olvidarse **de*** – to forget to
>
> *terminar **de*** – to stop
>
> *confiar **en*** – to trust
>
> *quedar **en*** – to agree to
>
> *disculparse **por*** – to apologise for

Jobs and employment

Topic 8.1 Part-time and casual work

8.1 F El trabajo a tiempo parcial
➡ pages 148–149

	bien pagado	well paid
	cobrar	to earn
	cuidar	to look after
el / la	dentista	dentist
el / la	dependiente	shop assistant
el	gasto	expense
	hacer de canguro	to do babysitting
el / la	jardinero/a	gardener
el / la	jefe/a	boss
	lavar	to wash
	mal pagado	badly paid
el	periódico	newspaper
el / la	recepcionista	receptionist
	repartir	to deliver
la	responsabilidad	responsibility
el	sueldo	salary
la	tarea	task
	tiempo parcial	part-time
el	trabajo	job
	vender	to sell
	vigilar	to keep an eye on

8.1 H Hacer prácticas ➡ pages 150–151

	a tiempo completo	full-time
	al mismo tiempo	at the same time
el / la	aprendiz	apprentice
el / la	camionero/a	lorry driver
el	consejo	advice
el	día festivo	(bank) holiday
el / la	encargado/a de	person in charge
	encargarse de	to be in charge of
la	entrevista	interview

el / la	entusiasta	enthusiast
	ganar	to earn
	hacer un aprendizaje	to do an apprenticeship
el	horario de trabajo	working hours
las	horas flexibles	flexible hours
la	intención	intention
	llegar a ser	to become
la	participación	participation
	probar	to have a go / try
el	taller	workshop
	trabajador(a)	hard-working

Topic 8.2 Looking for and getting a job

8.2 F Buscando trabajo ➡ pages 152–153

	arroba	@
la	barra	slash
la	cita	appointment
las	condiciones de trabajo	working conditions
	contactar	to contact
	contratar	to take on / hire
el	contrato	contract
la	desventaja	disadvantage
el / la	electricista	electrician
la	entrevista	interview
el	entusiasmo	enthusiasm
el	número de contacto	contact number
	obtener	to get
la	preocupación	worry
el	propósito	aim
el	punto	dot
	solicitar	to apply
la	solicitud	application
el	título	university degree
	tomar un año sabático	to take a gap year

8.2 H Conocer los procedimientos de trabajo
➡ *pages 154–155*

el	anuncio	advert
	buscar	to look for
la	cita	appointment
	conllevar	to entitle
	consistir	to consist
el	correo	mail
el	correo electrónico	email
la	correspondencia	mail
el	departamento	department
el / la	empleado/a	employee
la	entrega	delivery
	especializarse	to specialise
	estar comunicando	to be engaged (phone)
la	fotocopiadora	copy machine
la	impresora	printer
la	línea	line
la	máquina de fax	fax machine
	marcar	to dial
el	mensaje	message
	recoger	to collect

Topic 8.3 Advantages and disadvantages of different jobs

8.3 F Comparando empleos diferentes
➡ *pages 156–157*

	activo/a	active
el / la	aprendiz	apprentice
el / la	bombero/a	firefighter
el / la	cajero/a	cashier
el	contrato	contract
	decepcionante	disappointing
	desagradable	unpleasant
la	dificultad	difficulty
	duro/a	hard

el	empleo	employment
	entretenido/a	entertaining
	estar estresado/a	to be stressed
	estresante	stressful
	fascinante	fascinating
	inseguro/a	insecure
	quitar	to take up (time)
	seguro/a	secure
	sencillo/a	easy
	variado/a	varied
la	vida rural	country life

8.3 H Trabajos ideales para estudiantes
➡ *pages 158–159*

	adjuntar	to attach
	compaginar	to combine
	común	common
	dedicar	to dedicate
la	demanda	demand
	emprendedor	enterprising
	en línea	online
la	encuesta	survey
	enfrentarse	to face
la	falta de	lack of
la	ganancia	earning
el	idioma	language
las	redes sociales	social networks
	rellenar	to fill in
	sugerir	to suggest
el	teletrabajo	teleworking
	torear	to fight bulls
el	traje de luces	bullfighter's suit
el	triunfo	triumph / success
la	venta	sale

Higher – Exam practice

ℹnfo

These pages give you the chance to try GCSE-style practice exam questions at grades B–A*, based on the AQA Context of Work and education.

Enlace

Foundation practice exam questions (grades D–C) are available at the end of this Context in the Foundation book.

Los días escolares de Carmen

Empecé a ir a la escuela primaria cuando tenía seis años y estaba muy contenta allí. Los profesores eran simpáticos y amables. La vida era fácil porque los estudios consistían en jugar con los amigos, bailar y escuchar historias.

A los doce años empecé la enseñanza secundaria. No tenía miedo de ir al instituto porque mi hermano mayor ya era alumno allí, pero hay que admitir que estaba nerviosa. Un gran cambio fue que tenía que coger el autobús en lugar de ir andando y por eso era necesario levantarme más temprano. Me acuerdo de mi primer día: todo era tan grande, y los otros alumnos parecían muy maduros y mayores.

Llevo ya casi cuatro años en el instituto y lo conozco muy bien. En realidad, no es tan grande como pensé – sólo tiene unos quinientos alumnos – y está en las afueras de la ciudad. Los profesores son bastante estrictos pero muy trabajadores y las reglas son justas. Lo que parece molestar al director más que cualquier otra cosa es el chicle … ¡lo odia!

Las instalaciones son bastante buenas, sobre todo para deportes y ciencias, pero hay muy poco espacio para relajarse durante el recreo por ejemplo. También es necesario que haya una cafetería para comprar un bocadillo o algo para beber. Lo mejor

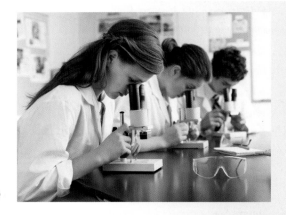

son las actividades extraescolares porque hay un montón de clubes y excursiones. ¡Incluso hay un intercambio con un instituto de Inglaterra!

Ahora, tengo dieciséis años y estoy pensando en lo que quiero hacer en los dos próximos años. Me ha gustado el tiempo que he pasado aquí en el instituto y mis profesores dicen que voy a sacar buenas notas. Puede ser que haga el bachillerato de tecnología; se me dan bien estas asignaturas. ¿O sería mejor hacer formación profesional? Pase lo que pase, no creo que busque trabajo, hay muy pocos empleos para los jóvenes de mi edad y además, es posible que vaya a la universidad …

---

1 📖 Read Carmen's account about her school life and answer the following questions in English.

1 How did Carmen feel when she was at primary school?

2 What were her teachers like at primary school?

3 Why didn't Carmen feel frightened on her first day at secondary school?

4 How many pupils are there at the school?

5 What does she think about the teachers? (2)

6 What is the head teacher's pet hate?

7 Which subjects have the best facilities? (2)

8 What aspect does Carmen criticise? (2)

9 What school trip does Carmen mention?

10 What decision is Carmen trying to make? (2)

Total = 14 marks

Answer questions completely

Always make sure you answer every bit of the question; if there is a (2) you have to give two bits of information. Look at question 5, for example. If you just say one thing about teachers, e.g. they are strict, you will get one of the marks. The (2) tells you that you need to look further and find out what else Carmen thinks about teachers to get the other mark.

No marks will be given for writing complete sentences or perfect English, just for getting all the facts down accurately.

Estrategia 1

2 📖 Read paragraphs 1–3 which give tips about searching for and applying for jobs. Then match up each paragraph with the correct summary a–e below. (There are two more summaries than you need.)

a Writing a CV
b Writing a letter of application
c Where to look for jobs
d Deciding what sort of job to look for
e Preparing for an interview

Total = 3 marks

3 🎧 Listen to five people describing their jobs and match up each person with the correct job from the list below.

a Translator
b Police officer
c Firefighter
d Postal worker
e Flight attendant
f Vet
g Chef

Total = 5 marks

4a 🎧 Listen to Domingo giving his opinion about different aspects of his job. Decide whether his comments about each aspect are positive (**P**), negative (**N**) or positive and negative (**P + N**).

1 job itself
2 salary
3 working shifts
4 colleagues
5 place of work

Total = 5 marks

4b 🎧 Listen again and answer the following questions in English.

1 Has he always worked in the same place? How do you know? (2)
2 What does Domingo suggest doing to make sure of a good salary?
3 Does he work long shifts? How do you know?
4 Do Domingo and his colleagues normally argue at work? How do you know? (2)
5 Would he like to work for another hotel? How do you know?

Total = 7 marks

Total for Reading and Listening = 34 marks

Buscando empleo

1 Es normal sentirse nervioso en el momento de hacer la entrevista. Sin embargo, piensa que estarás más tranquilo si te preparas bien y llegas con tiempo. Debes tener claro el motivo por el que has solicitado el trabajo y demostrar seguridad. Para ello, es buena idea escribir algunas preguntas, por ejemplo, sobre el horario o tus responsabilidades.

2 Hay que buscar los mejores sitios para los anuncios de empleos – el periódico o una página web. Si conoces a alguien que trabaje para una empresa que te interese, podrías preguntarle si hay trabajo en su compañía.

3 A la hora de buscar trabajo es muy importante estar preparado y tener todo listo. El primer paso debe ser organizar tus calificaciones y tu formación, así como la experiencia de trabajo con las fechas correspondientes. Por último, destacarás tus cualidades e intereses personales.

Score well in positive / negative questions

This type of question occurs in most exam papers, so it is worth learning a few pointers that will help you to make sure you spot the examples where both positive and negative opinions are mentioned. The pointers are various types of connectives such as *pero* (but), *por otro lado* (on the other hand), *a pesar de esto* (in spite of this), and *sin embargo* (nevertheless).

Estrategia 4a

Higher – Speaking

Las prácticas laborales

You are going to have a conversation with your teacher about work experience and your plans for next year. Your teacher will ask you the following:

1 If you think it is a good idea to do work experience and why (not)

2 Where you did your work experience

3 What you had to do there

4 What was your opinion of your work experience

5 What plans you have for your holidays now that your work experience has finished

6 What you intend to do in September

7 !

! Remember you will have to respond to something that you have not yet prepared.

info

Important information:
This sample task is for practice purposes only and should not be used as an actual assessment task. Study it to find out how to plan your Controlled Assessment efficiently to gain maximum marks and / or work through it as a mock exam task before the actual Controlled Assessment.

1 If you think it is a good idea to do work experience and why (not).
  - describe the positive aspects of doing work experience
  - describe one negative aspect
  - explain how it can help you get to know what work is all about
  - explain what your expectations of work experience are

Estrategia

Start your plan. Remember that the maximum number of words allowed in your plan is 40. Write a maximum of six words for each bullet point. Read through what is expected of you and think about what you are going to say. The whole task lasts between four and six minutes, so it is important that you expand on your answers as much as you can. You cannot use any symbols or codes or any visuals (drawings etc.) in addition to the 30–40 words.

Choose the six words you will use for this part of the plan, for example: *distinto/a, emocionante, gente nueva*.

2 Where you did your work experience.
  - describe what type of place it was (an office, a school, etc.)
  - describe if it was near to or far from your house, and how you got there every day
  - describe what the place was like
  - say how you got on with your work colleagues

Estrategia

Suggested words for this bullet point: *taller, empresa, lejos, viajar, disfrutar, aprender*.

Say where you did your work experience, but go beyond merely saying such things as *Trabajé en una oficina en el centro*. Describe the place of work, say how you felt and so on.

You can use both preterite and imperfect tenses here.

3 What you had to do there.
  - say how and at what time your day began
  - describe the jobs you had to do
  - say how well you could do those jobs and what you thought of them
  - explain how it was different from your school routine

Estrategia

Suggested words for this bullet point: *empezar, rellenar, correspondencia*; think of two more of your own.

You will be using past tenses here and you should use the imperfect tense to say what you did every day: *Me levantaba a las seis y media y salía de casa a las siete y cuarto.* See page 182.

Use *más … que …* and *menos … que …* to compare work experience with your normal school day.

4 What was your opinion of your work experience.

- say what your first impressions were
- say what you think makes a good boss, and if your boss was one
- say how you felt when it was time to leave, and what you thought of your time there overall
- say if it persuaded you to follow a similar career in the future and why / why not

Suggested words for this bullet point: *aburrido/a, difícil, estresante*; think of three positive descriptions of your own.

Say what the work was like. Your opinion may have changed over the time you were there as you became more comfortable, so use expressions such as *al principio … pero más tarde … después de unos días*.

Again you will be using past tenses; check when to use the preterite and imperfect if you are not sure.

Use the conditional to say what type of job you would like to do in the future.

5 What plans you have for your holidays now that your work experience has finished.

- describe where you plan to go
- describe the things you will do there
- give several reasons why it is going to be good
- say who you are going with and why they are good companions on holiday

Suggested words for this bullet point: *veranear, senderismo*; add four more words of your own.

A chance to use future tenses: *iré a / voy a* + infinitive. See page 183.

Again you should be developing your response, so if you will not be going away for the holidays either say what you will be doing at home, or make up a holiday you will go on (or both!).

Extend your sentences when giving reasons: *Será muy divertido porque me encanta broncearme y salir con mis amigos a restaurantes típicos.*

6 What you intend to do in September.

- explain what options are available to you
- say what you intend to do and why
- explain what your choice will lead to in the more distant future, and why you want to do that
- say what sort of qualifications / training you might need, and where you will go to get them

Write down six words for this bullet point.

Future and conditional tenses can both be used here. See pages 183–184.

Give several reasons as to why you want to pursue a particular career path to extend your answer.

7 ! At this point, you may be asked …

- Would you like to do the same job as you did for work experience in the future? Why (not)?
- Do you prefer school or work experience? Why?
- Would you like to go to university? Why (not)?
- What are the positive aspects of starting work? Are there any disadvantages to starting work at once?

For this part of the task you will not have prepared an answer and you will have to listen carefully to what your teacher asks and reply to the question. Prepare answers for all the possibilities and in your plan write a few different points for each possibility.

Try to give a reason to back up any statements you make, e.g. *Me gustaría ir a la universidad porque quiero tener un título.*

Enlace

Foundation sample assessment tasks for this Context can be found in the Foundation book.

Higher – Writing

Mi colegio

Your Spanish friend, Blanca, has emailed you, asking for your views on your school. Reply to her email. You could include:

1 details of what your school is like
2 what happens on a typical day at school
3 your subjects and your opinions of them
4 the quality of food in the dining room
5 extra-curricular activities you did last week
6 homework – how much you get and your opinions
7 what you would like to change and why.

> **ⓘnfo**
>
> **Important information:**
> This sample task is for practice purposes only and should not be used as an actual assessment task. Study it to find out how to plan your Controlled Assessment efficiently to gain maximum marks and / or work through it as a mock exam task before the actual Controlled Assessment.

1 Details of what your school is like.

- mention how many pupils and teachers there are
- say whether it is mixed or single sex, state or private, whether you have a uniform, etc.
- describe the buildings and facilities – how modern they are
- say what the atmosphere is like, and what you think of it as a place to study

> **Estrategia**
>
> Start your plan. Remember that the maximum number of words allowed in your plan is 40. Write a maximum of six words for each bullet point.
>
> Here are some suggested words that you might use: *estudiantes, profesores, mixto/a, laboratorios, amistoso/a, severo/a.*
>
> You will be using the present tense for this bullet point – give opinions as well as descriptions, and vary the words you use.

2 What happens on a typical day at school.

- describe how you get there, with whom, and how long it takes
- say at what time you arrive and explain if classes start immediately or not
- mention the length of lessons and how many there are each day
- say when you have breaks and what you do then

> **Estrategia**
>
> Suggested words for this bullet point: *transporte público, andar, pasar lista, comedor.*
>
> Try to form longer sentences by using linking words. For instance, the first two sub-divisions can be combined: *Voy al instituto en el autobús que llega al colegio a las ocho y veinte.*
>
> Use *lo que* to express opinions and extend your sentences, e.g. *Normalmente tomo un bocadillo en el comedor con mis amigos, lo que me gusta mucho.*

3 Your subjects and your opinions of them.

- say which subjects you study
- explain which you like and dislike and why
- mention subjects that you chose not to opt for and why not
- mention any plans you have for studying particular subjects next year

> **Estrategia**
>
> Suggested words for this bullet point: *decidir, odiar, trabajador(a)*; think of three others of your own.
>
> The third sub-division requires you to use the preterite tense and the fourth one to use the future or conditional. Revise those tenses if you are not sure how to use them. See pages 181, 183–184.
>
> Think of lots of different reasons for studying / not studying certain subjects: difficult, easy, interesting teacher, failed last year's exam, friends doing the same, etc.
>
> You can give lots of different opinions here.

▉ Glossary of terms

Adjectives *los adjetivos*

Words that describe somebody or something:

| *pequeño* | small |
| *tímido* | shy |

Adverbs *los adverbios*

Words that complement (add meaning to) verbs, adjectives or other adverbs:

| *mal* | badly |
| *lentamente* | slowly |

Articles *los artículos*

Short words used to introduce nouns:

un / una	a, an
unos / unas	some, any
el / la / los / las	the

The infinitive *el infinitivo*

The verb form given in the dictionary:

| *ir* | to go |
| *tener* | to have |

Nouns *los nombres*

Words that identify a person, a place or a thing:

| *madre* mother | *casa* house |

Prepositions *las preposiciones*

Words used in front of nouns to give information about when, how, where, etc.:

con	with
de	of, from
en	in

Pronouns *los pronombres*

Words used to replace nouns. For example, subject pronouns:

yo	I
tú	you
él	he
ella	she

Verbs *los verbos*

Words used to express an action or a state:

| *trabajo* | I **work** |
| *vive* | he **lives** |

A Nouns

Masculine and feminine nouns

All Spanish nouns are either masculine or feminine.

- In the singular, masculine nouns are introduced with *el* or *un*:

el padre	**the** father
un libro	**a** book

- Feminine singular nouns are introduced with *la* or *una*:

la madre	**the** mother
una mesa	**a** table

- Some nouns have two different forms, masculine and feminine:

un amigo	a male friend
una amiga	a female friend
un peluquero	a male hairdresser
una peluquera	a female hairdresser

- Some nouns stay the same for masculine and feminine:

el estudiante	the male student
la estudiante	the female student

Singular and plural forms

As in English, Spanish nouns can either be singular (one) or plural (more than one).

- Nouns ending in a vowel add *-s* for the plural.

un perro > dos perros	one dog > two dogs

- Nouns ending in a consonant add *-es* for the plural.

un ordenador > dos ordenadores	one computer > two computers

- For nouns ending in *-z*, change the *z* to *c* and add *-es*:

un lápiz > dos lápices	one pencil > two pencils

- If a noun ends in *-ión*, drop the accent and add *-es*:

una invitación > dos invitaciones	one invitation > two invitations

B Articles

Definite articles: *el, la, los, las* (the)

The word for 'the' depends on whether the noun it goes with is masculine, feminine, singular or plural.

masculine singular	feminine singular	masculine plural	feminine plural
el	*la*	*los*	*las*

el abuelo	**the** grandfather
la fruta	**the** fruit
los billetes	**the** tickets
las palabras	**the** words

Indefinite articles: *un, una, unos, unas* (a, an, some)

- The word for 'a / an' and 'some' also depends on whether the noun it goes with is masculine or feminine, singular or plural.

masculine singular	feminine singular	masculine plural	feminine plural
un	*una*	*unos*	*unas*

un autobús, *una* moto, *unos* coches	**a** coach, **a** motorbike, (**some**) cars

- When talking about jobs, *un* and *una* are not used in Spanish where 'a' or 'an' is used in English.

Mi padre es electricista.	My father's an electrician.

The neuter article: *lo*

- Use *lo* with an adjective to mean 'the … thing'. The adjective after *lo* is always masculine and singular.

lo importante	the important thing

- Use it with an adjective + *es que*:

Lo bueno es que hay fruta fresca.	The good thing is that there is fresh fruit.

- Use it with an adjective + *es* + an infinitive:

  Lo importante es comer comida sana.
  The important thing is to eat healthy food.

C Adjectives

Feminine and masculine, singular and plural adjectives

In Spanish, adjectives have different endings depending on whether they describe masculine, feminine, singular or plural nouns:

– the masculine singular form usually ends in *-o*:

El barco es blanco.	The boat is white.

– if the noun is feminine singular, the adjective will usually end in -*a*:

*Mi hermana es tími**da**.*   My sister is shy.

– add -*s* to the masculine adjective if the noun is masculine plural:

*Los barcos son blanc**os**.*   The boats are white.

– add -*s* to the feminine adjective if the noun is feminine plural:

*Mis hermanas son tími**das**.*   My sisters are shy.

– when an adjective describes a group of both masculine and feminine nouns, it has to be in the masculine plural form:

*Mis padres son alt**os**.*   My parents are tall.

■ There are exceptions:

– adjectives that already end in -*e* don't change in the feminine:

un chico inteligente   an intelligent boy

una chica inteligente   an intelligent girl

to form the plural, simply add an -*s*:

*unos chicos inteligente**s***   some intelligent boys

*unas chicas inteligente**s***   some intelligent girls

– adjectives that end in a consonant (except *r*) do not change in the feminine:

un bolígrafo azul   a blue pen

una regla azul   a blue ruler

to form the plural, add -*es*:

*unos bolígrafos azul**es***   some blue pens

*unas reglas azul**es***   some blue rulers

– adjectives of nationality often end in -*o* and follow the same rules as other adjectives ending in -*o*:

*un chico mexican**o***   a Mexican boy

*una chica mexican**a***   a Mexican girl

*unos chicos mexican**os***   some Mexican boys

*unas chicas mexican**as***   some Mexican girls

– for adjectives of nationality that end in a consonant, add -*a* for the feminine singular form, -*es* for the masculine plural form and -*as* for the feminine plural form:

un chico español   a Spanish boy

*una chica español**a***   a Spanish girl

*unos chicos español**es***   some Spanish boys

*unas chicas español**as***   some Spanish girls

– note that adjectives of nationality do not begin with a capital letter.

The position of adjectives

■ Most adjectives follow the noun they describe:

una dieta sana   a healthy diet

■ However, a few adjectives, such as *alguno, malo, ninguno, primero* and *tercero* come in front of the noun and lose their final -*o* when the following noun is masculine singular. Notice that an accent is sometimes needed the keep the stress on the correct syllable:

ningún deporte   no sport

ninguna idea   no idea

Comparatives and superlatives

■ To make comparisons, use:

– *más ... que*   more ... than, ...er than

*Mi casa es **más pequeña que** la tuya.*
My house is **smaller than** yours.

*El alcohol es **más caro** en Inglaterra **que** en España.*
Alcohol is **more expensive** in England **than** in Spain.

– *menos ... que*   less... than

*Mi hermano es **menos alto que** mi padre.*
My brother is **less tall than** my father.

– *tan* + adjective + *como*   as ... as

*Los tomates son **tan sanos como** las naranjas.*
Tomatoes are **as healthy as** oranges.

■ For superlatives, use:

– *el / la / los / las* + *más*   the most, the ...est

*Esta casa es **la más vieja** de la región.*
This house is **the oldest** in the area.

– *el / la / los / las* + *menos*   the least

*Este hotel es **el menos caro** de la región.*
This hotel is **the least expensive** in the area.

■ For 'as much ... as', use *tan* + adjective + *como*:

*El alcohol es **tan peligroso como** el tabaco.*
Alcohol is **as dangerous as** tobacco.

■ For 'as many ... as', use *tantos(as)* + plural noun + *como*:

*Las chicas practican **tantos** deportes **como** los chicos.*
Girls take part in **as many** sports **as** boys.

■ For 'better than', use *mejor que*:

*Es **mejor** estudiar **que** trabajar.*
Studying is **better than** working.

- For 'worse than', use *peor que*:

  *Te pagan **peor que** en la ciudad.*
  They pay **worse than** in the city.

- Note also two other irregular comparative adjectives:

  – *mayor* is a special comparative of *grande* used to refer to **older** brothers and sisters

  – *menor* is a special comparative of *pequeño* used to refer to **younger** brothers and sisters

  *Mi hermana **mayor** es más tímida que mis hermanos **menores**.*
  My **big** sister is more shy than my **little** brothers.

Demonstrative adjectives: *este, esta, estos, estas; ese, esa, esos, esas; aquel, aquella, aquellos, aquellas* (this, that, these, those)

- Spanish has three groups of demonstrative adjectives: one group for 'this' and 'these' (*este, esta, estos, estas*), one for 'that' and 'those' (*ese, esa, esos, esas*), and one to indicate more distant things ('that / those over there' – *aquel, aquella, aquellos, aquellas*).

this		these	
este	esta	estos	estas
that (not very distant)		**those (not very distant)**	
ese	esa	esos	esas
that (more distant)		**those (more distant)**	
aquel	aquella	aquellos	aquellas

este cine	**this** cinema
esa estrella	**that** star
aquellas películas	**those** films

Indefinite adjectives: *cada, otro, todo, mismo, alguno*

- Although *cada* is an adjective, it never changes:

cada sección	**each** section
cada resultado	**each** result

- *Otro, todo* and *mismo* must agree with the noun they describe:

otra ciudad	**another** city
la **misma** idea	the **same** idea
todo el mundo	**all** the world (= everyone)
todas las chicas	**all** the girls
los **mismos** libros	the **same** books

- *Alguno* means 'some' and must agree with its noun. It drops the -o ending and gains an accent when it is placed before a masculine singular noun:

algunas chicas	**some** girls
algún pan	**some** bread
algunos estudiantes	**some** students

Relative adjectives: *cuyo, cuya, cuyos, cuyas*

- *Cuyo* means 'whose' and agrees in number and gender with the noun that follows it.

  *Ésta es Paulina **cuya hermana** está casada desde hace seis meses.*
  This is Paulina **whose sister** has been married for six months.

Possessive adjectives, one 'owner'

mi / mis	my
tu / tus	your
su / sus	his / her / its

A possessive adjective must agree with the noun that follows it:

mi padre	**my** father
mi madre	**my** mother
mis padres	**my** parents
tu padre	**your** father
tu madre	**your** mother
tus padres	**your** parents
su pie	**his / her / its** foot
su puerta	**his / her / its** door
sus ventanas	**his / her / its** windows

Possessive adjectives, several 'owners'

nuestro / nuestra / nuestros / nuestras	our
vuestro / vuestra / vuestros / vuestras	your
su / sus	their
nuestro padre	**our** father
nuestra madre	**our** mother
nuestros padres	**our** parents
vuestro padre	**your** father
vuestra madre	**your** mother
vuestros amigos	**your** friends
su hermano	**their** brother
su hermana	**their** sister
sus profesores	**their** teachers

■ Spanish doesn't have three different words for 'his', 'her' and 'its'. With a Spanish possessive adjective, what counts is whether the noun it describes is masculine, feminine, singular or plural. Like other adjectives, they agree with their noun.

■ Possessive adjectives also have a 'long' form which is used just in certain expressions:

hijo **mío**	my son
Muy señora **mía**	Dear Madam (in a letter)

Interrogative adjectives: *qué, cuánto, cuántos, cuántas, cuál, cuáles*

■ To ask 'what?', use *qué*:

¿Qué bebida quieres?	What drink would you like?

■ To ask 'which?', use *cuál*. It must agree with the noun that follows it, but it does not change for the feminine, only for the plural:

¿Cuál coche prefieres?	Which car do you prefer?
¿Cuáles prefieres?	Which (ones) do you prefer?

■ To ask 'how much?', use *cuánto*. It must agree with the noun that follows it: masculine / feminine, singular / plural.

¿Cuánto dinero tienes?	How much money do you have?
¿Cuántos libros hay?	How many books are there?
¿Cuántas hermanas tienes?	How many sisters do you have?

■ Remember that all interrogative adjectives must have an accent.

D Adverbs

Adverbs are used with a verb, an adjective or another adverb to express how, when, where, or to what extent something happens.

■ Many Spanish adverbs are formed by adding *-mente* (the equivalent of '-ly' in English) to the feminine form of the adjective:

masculine adjective	feminine adjective	adverb
rápido	rápida	rápidamente – quickly

■ Some common adverbs are completely irregular:

bien	well
Habla **bien**.	He / She speaks well.
mal	badly
Come **mal**.	He / She eats badly.

■ As with adjectives, you can make some comparisons using *más / menos ... que*:

*Se puede estar en contacto **más fácilmente que** antes.*
It's possible to stay in touch **more easily than** before.

*Como **menos rápidamente que** mi hermana.*
I eat **less quickly than** my sister.

■ You can also use superlative adverbs. Use the definite article + *más* + adverb:

*El fútbol es **el** deporte que practico **más frecuentemente**.*
Football is the sport I do **most often**.

Adverbs of time

hoy	today
mañana	tomorrow
ayer	yesterday
pasado mañana	the day after tomorrow
ahora	now
ya	already

Adverbs of frequency

a veces	sometimes
frecuentemente / a menudo	often
siempre	always
raramente	rarely, not very often

Adverbs of sequence

después	then, afterwards
luego	next
por último	finally

Adverbs of place

dentro de	inside
fuera de	outside
aquí	here
allí	(over) there
lejos	far

Quantifiers and intensifiers

- This group of adverbs (qualifying words) enables you to indicate intensity and quantity when you use an adjective or adverb:

bastante	enough
demasiado	too (much)
mucho	a lot
un poco	a little
muy	very

*La gramática es **un poco** complicada, pero es **bastante** interesante.*
Grammar is **a bit** complicated, but it's **quite** interesting.

Interrogative adverbs

Note that these words all have an accent when they are used as an interrogative.

¿cómo?	how?
¿cuándo?	when?
¿dónde?	where?

E Pronouns

Subject pronouns: *yo, tú, él, ella, usted, nosotros, nosotras, vosotros, vosotras, ellos, ellas, ustedes* (I, you, he, she, it, we, they)

In Spanish, subject pronouns are usually only used with the verb to emphasise who or what performs the action.

yo – I	*nosotros* – we (m) *nosotras* – we (f)
tú – you	*vosotros* – you (m) *vosotras* – you (f)
él – he / it	*ellos* – they (m)
ella – she / it	*ellas* – they (f)
usted – you (formal)	*ustedes* – you (formal pl)

Ella es estudiante, pero **él** ha acabado de estudiar.
She is a student, but **he** has finished studying.

- In Spanish there are two ways to translate 'you': *tú* (plural: *vosotros*) and *usted* (plural: *ustedes*).

  – Use *tú* when talking to someone (one person) of your own age or to someone in your family.

  – Use *vosotros* when talking to more than one person of your own age or to your relatives.

  – Use *usted* when talking to an adult not in your family (e.g. your teacher). *Usted* can be shortened to *Ud.* or *Vd.*

  – Use *ustedes* when talking to more than one adult not in your family. It can be shortened to *Uds.* or *Vds.*

Direct object pronouns: *me, te, lo / la, nos, os, los / las*

Direct object pronouns replace a noun that is not the subject of the verb.

singular	plural
me – me	*nos* – us
te – you	*os* – you
lo – him / it (masculine)	*los, las* – them
la – her / it (feminine)	

- These pronouns come in front of the verb, unlike in English:

  Los compré en Barcelona. I bought **them** in Barcelona.

Indirect object pronouns: *me, te, le, nos, os, les*

Indirect object pronouns are used to replace a noun which is not the direct object of the verb.

singular	plural
me – (to) me	*nos* – (to) us
te – (to) you	*os* – (to) you
le – (to) him / her / it	*les* – (to) them

Les dio mil euros. **Le** escribieron para dar**le** las gracias.
He gave **them** a thousand euros. They wrote **to him** to thank **him**.

- Note that when two pronouns are used together in the same sentence, the indirect object pronoun always comes before the direct object pronoun.

  *Tengo un móvil. Mis padres **me lo** regalaron por mi cumpleaños.*
  I have a mobile. My parents gave **it to me** for my birthday.

  me – indirect object pronoun, *lo* – direct object pronoun

Reflexive pronouns: *me, te, se, nos, os, se*

Reflexive pronouns are used in Spanish when the subject and object of the verb are the same. They come before the verb.

singular	plural
me – myself	*nos* – ourselves
te – yourself (informal)	*os* – yourselves (informal)
se – himself, herself, itself, yourself (formal)	*se* – themselves, yourselves (formal)

Me lavo. I am washing myself.

Disjunctive pronouns: *mí, ti, él, ella, usted, nosotros, nosotras, vosotros, vosotras, ellos, ellas, ustedes*

These are also called emphatic pronouns.

- Use them for emphasis:

  Para mí, las vacaciones de invierno son las más divertidas.
  For me, winter holidays are the most fun.

- Use them after a preposition:

  A mí, no me gusta el pescado. **Me**, I don't like fish.

- To say 'with me', 'with you (*tú*)' there is a special form:

conmigo	with me
contigo	with you
Mi hermano viene **conmigo**.	My brother is coming **with me**.

Possessive pronouns

A possessive pronoun is used to replace a possessive adjective and its noun.

> *¿Ese es su perro? No, no es el suyo.*
> Is that **their dog**? No, it isn't **theirs**.

masculine singular	feminine singular	masculine plural	feminine plural	
mío	*mía*	*míos*	*mías*	mine
tuyo	*tuya*	*tuyos*	*tuyas*	yours
suyo	*suya*	*suyos*	*suyas*	his / hers / its
nuestro	*nuestra*	*nuestros*	*nuestras*	ours
vuestro	*vuestra*	*vuestros*	*vuestras*	yours
suyo	*suya*	*suyos*	*suyas*	theirs

Use possessive pronouns with the definite article *el / la / los / las* and remember that they must agree with the noun they replace.

> *Me gusta más la casa de Julia que la **mía**.*
> I like Julia's house more than **mine**.

Relative pronouns: *que, quien, lo que*

Relative pronouns are used to link phrases together.

- *Que* is used as the subject of the relative clause. It can refer to people and things, and means 'who', 'that' or 'which':

  *el amigo **que** vive en Barcelona*
  the friend **who** lives in Barcelona

  – Remember that *que* is not optional. Although it is often not translated in English, you cannot leave it out in Spanish.

*La película **que** veía era muy divertida.*
The film **(that)** I was watching was very funny.

- *Quien* and its plural form *quienes* is only used to refer to people:

  *No sé **quién** dijo eso.*
  I don't know **who** said that.

- Use *lo que* to refer to a general idea:

  ***Lo que** me gusta de mi barrio es que hay un centro comercial.*
  What I like about my neighbourhood is that there is a shopping centre.

- The pronouns *el que, la que, los que, las que* (note the necessary agreement with singular, plural, masculine and feminine nouns) are used after prepositions, to refer to both people and things:

  *Mi hermana, **la que** es peluquera, vive en Madrid.*
  My sister, **the one who** is a hairdresser, lives in Madrid.

- *El cual, la cual, los cuales, las cuales* are relative pronouns that can be used in place of *el que, la que, los que* and *las que*. They are not used in everyday conversation and tend to be used more in formal written Spanish:

  *Me queda un poco de dinero, **el cual** no quiero gastar.*
  I have a little money left, **which** I don't want to spend.

Demonstrative pronouns: *éste, ésta, éstos, éstas; ése, ésa, ésos, ésas; aquél, aquélla, aquéllos, aquéllas*

- Demonstrative pronouns replace the noun, to avoid repeating it:

this one		these	
éste	*ésta*	*éstos*	*éstas*
that one		those	
ése	*ésa*	*ésos*	*ésas*
aquél	*aquélla*	*aquéllos*	*aquéllas*

*¿Te gusta **ese** vestido?*	Do you like **that** dress?
*Prefiero **ése**.*	I prefer **that one**.

- Each demonstrative pronoun also has a neuter form: *esto, eso* and *aquello*. These do not agree in number or gender with a noun because they represent an idea rather than a person or a thing:

  ***Eso** es cierto.*   **That**'s true.

  *Martina es demasiado habladora. No me gusta **eso**.*
  Martina is too talkative. I don't like **that**.

Indefinite pronouns: *algo, alguien*

- The Spanish for 'something' is *algo*:

  *¿Quieres **algo** de comer?* Do you want **something** to eat?

- The Spanish for 'someone' is *alguien*:

  *Busco a **alguien**.* I'm looking for **someone**.

Interrogative pronouns: *cuál, cuáles; qué; quién, quiénes* (which one; what; who)

- As in English, interrogative pronouns usually come at the beginning of a sentence:

  *¿**Cuál** de estas preguntas es más difícil?*
  Which one of these questions is harder?

  *¿**Cuáles** prefieres?* **Which** ones do you prefer?

  *¿**Qué** quieres?* **What** do you want?

  *¿**Quién** habla?* **Who** is speaking?

  *¿**Quiénes** son?* **Who** are they?

However, if a preposition is used with the interrogative, it is the preposition which comes first:

  *¿**Con quién** vas a la fiesta?* **Who** are you going to the party **with**?

  *¿**Por qué** estás triste?* **Why** are you sad?

F Verbs

- Spanish verbs have different endings depending on who is doing the action and whether the action takes place in the past, the present or the future. The verb tables on pages 190–194 set out the patterns of endings for some useful verbs.

- When using a name or a singular noun instead of a pronoun, use the same form of the verb as for *él / ella*:

  *Jamie **habla** español.* Jamie **speaks** Spanish.

- When using two names or a plural noun, use the same form of the verb as for *ellos / ellas*:

  *Laura y Javier **viven** en Sevilla.* Laura and Javier **live** in Seville.

- When referring to yourself and someone else, use the same form of the verb as for *nosotros*:

  *Laura y yo **vamos** a Madrid.* Laura and I **are going** to Madrid.

The infinitive

The infinitive is the form of the verb you find in a dictionary, e.g. *hablar, comer, vivir*. It never changes.

- When two verbs follow each other, the second one is always in the infinitive. That is what happens in the following sentences:

  Me gusta dormir bien. I like to sleep well.

  Prefiero salir con mis amigos. I prefer to go out with my friends.

- *Ir a* + infinitive is a useful expression meaning 'to be going to do something' in the immediate future. The verb *ir* is conjugated, but the second verb will remain in the infinitive. The preposition *a* is always used:

  Voy a visitar España.
  I am going to visit Spain.

- *Volver a* + infinitive means to do something again.

  Volveré a leer ese libro. I will read that book again.

- *Acabar de* + infinitive means to have just done something very recently. Note that the preposition *de* is needed in this expression.

  Acabas de invitar a muchos amigos.
  You have just invited many friends.

G Verb tenses

The present indicative

- Use the present tense to describe:

  – something that is taking place now:

  Como una manzana. I am eating an apple.

  – something that happens regularly:

  Voy mucho al cine. I go to the cinema a lot.

- Verb endings change depending on who is doing the action:

  *Mi amigo **habla** español.* My friend **speaks** Spanish.

  ***Hablamos** inglés.* We **speak** English.

- Most verbs follow a regular pattern, as in the paradigms (lists) shown here. See the verb tables on pages 190–194 for irregular verb forms.

	-ar verbs	-er verbs	-ir verbs
	hablar – to speak	*comer* – to eat	*vivir* – to live
(yo)	hablo	como	vivo
(tú)	hablas	comes	vives
(él / ella)	habla	come	vive
(nosotros)	hablamos	comemos	vivimos
(vosotros)	habláis	coméis	vivís
(ellos / ellas)	hablan	comen	viven

Other *-ar* verbs:

aceptar	to accept
ganar	to win
invitar	to invite
tocar	to play

Other *-er* verbs:

deber	to owe
proteger	to protect

Other *-ir* verbs:

producir	to produce
salir	to go out

A few common verbs have an irregular first person in the present tense:

dar > doy

decir > digo

estar > estoy

hacer > hago

oír > oigo

poner > pongo

saber > sé

salir > salgo

ser > soy

tener > tengo

venir > vengo

Radical-changing verbs

- The biggest group of Spanish irregular verbs is called radical-changing, or stem-changing verbs.

The first part of the verb changes when stressed:

In one type, *u* changes to *ue*

jugar – to play

*ju**e**go*	*jugamos*
*ju**e**gas*	*jugáis*
*ju**e**ga*	*ju**e**gan*

In another type, *o* changes to *ue*

poder – to be able to

*p**ue**do*	*podemos*
*p**ue**des*	*podéis*
*p**ue**de*	*p**ue**den*

In another type, *e* changes to *ie*

preferir – to prefer

*pref**ie**ro*	*preferimos*
*pref**ie**res*	*preferís*
*pref**ie**re*	*pref**ie**ren*

The changes do not happen in the *nosotros* and *vosotros* parts of the verb, because the stress is not on the stem.

The gerund

- The gerund (or present participle) is formed by replacing the infinitive verb ending *-ar* with *-ando,* and the *-er and -ir* verb endings with *-iendo:*

  – *hablar > habl**ando***

Estoy hablando.	I am talking.

  – *comer > com**iendo***

¿Qué estás comiendo?	What are you eating?

  – *salir > sal**iendo***

Ana está saliendo.	Ana is going out.

- Some irregular gerunds are:

  dormir > durmiendo

  leer > leyendo

  oír > oyendo

  preferir > prefiriendo

  sentir > sintiendo

  vestir > vistiendo

  Note that where in English we often use the gerund of a verb in sentences like:
  I love swimming. My brother prefers going on bike rides.
  Spanish uses the infinitive.
  *Me gusta **nadar**. Mi hermano prefiere **dar** paseos en bici.*

The present continuous

- The present continuous tense is the Spanish equivalent of the English form 'I am …ing, you are …ing' etc. It indicates something that is happening at the time of speaking. It is formed by adding the gerund to the present tense of *estar*:

*¿Qué **estás leyendo**?*	What **are you reading**?

  ***Estoy leyendo** un libro estupendo.*
  I'm reading a fantastic book.

The preterite

- Use the preterite tense to talk about a single, completed event in the past.
  *Por la tarde **recibí** un mensaje de mi amiga.*
  In the afternoon **I got** a message from my friend.

- Regular verbs:

  – To form the preterite tense, remove the infinitive endings, *-ar, -er* or *-ir* to leave the stem, then add the following endings:

	-*ar* verbs	-*er* verbs	-*ir* verbs
	hablar – to speak	*comer* – to eat	*vivir* – to live
(yo)	*hablé*	*comí*	*viví*
(tú)	*hablaste*	*comiste*	*viviste*
(él / ella)	*habló*	*comió*	*vivió*
(nosotros)	*hablamos*	*comimos*	*vivimos*
(vosotros)	*hablasteis*	*comisteis*	*vivisteis*
(ellos / ellas)	*hablaron*	*comieron*	*vivieron*

Note that the endings for *-er* and *-ir* verbs are the same.

  – Some regular verbs have spelling changes in the first person in the preterite tense. These changes are there in order to keep the consonant sounds the same:

empezar	to begin
empecé	I began
jugar	to play
jugué	I played
sacar	to take
saqué	I took out
tocar	to play (instrument)
toqué	I played

- Irregular verbs:

  – Some common Spanish verbs are irregular in the preterite tense: *ser* and *estar, hacer, ir, poner, tener* and *ver*. The verb tables on pages 190–194 set out the patterns for these. The verbs *ser* (to be) and *ir* (to go) are the same in the preterite and you have to use the context to work out which verb is being used:

fui	I was / went
fuiste	you were / went
fue	he, she, it, you was / were / went
fuimos	we were / went
fuisteis	you were / went
fueron	they, you were / went

*Por la mañana **fuimos** al partido.*
We went to the match in the morning.

*El ambiente en el estadio **fue** fantástico.*
The atmosphere in the stadium **was** fantastic.

The perfect

- Use the perfect tense to say what you **have** done recently:

  He comprado un móvil.   **I've bought** a mobile phone.

- The perfect tense is formed with the present tense of *haber* (to have) plus the past participle:

  haber – to have
  he
  has
  ha
  hemos
  habéis
  han

  – to form the past participle add *-ado* to the stem of *-ar* verbs and *-ido* to the stem of *-er* and *-ir* verbs.

hablar	to speak	> *hablado*	spoken
comer	to eat	> *comido*	eaten
vivir	to live	> *vivido*	lived

*Este marzo **he ido** a Valencia a ver la fiesta.*
This March **I went** to Valencia to see the fiesta.

  – some Spanish verbs have irregular past participles. Here are some common ones:

decir	to say	> *dicho*	said
hacer	to make	> *hecho*	made
volver	to come back	> *vuelto*	came back
poner	to put	> *puesto*	put
ver	to see	> *visto*	saw / seen

Ya hemos visto esta película.   We have already seen this film.

The imperfect

- Use the imperfect tense:

  – to describe what something or someone was like in the past:

  *Cuando **era** pequeño las fiestas de Navidad **eran** las mejores del año.*
  When **I was** young, the Christmas festivities **were** the best of the year.

  – to say what was happening at a certain time in the past:

  Trabajaba entonces en Madrid.
  At that time **I was working** in Madrid.

– to describe something that used to happen regularly in the past:

Iba *al cine todos los sábados.*
I used to go to the cinema every Saturday.

▨ To form the imperfect tense of regular verbs, add the following endings to the stem of the verb:

	-ar verbs	*-er* verbs	*-ir* verbs
	hablar – to speak	*comer* – to eat	*vivir* – to live
(yo)	hablaba	comía	vivía
(tú)	hablabas	comías	vivías
(él / ella)	hablaba	comía	vivía
(nosotros)	hablábamos	comíamos	vivíamos
(vosotros)	hablabais	comíais	vivíais
(ellos / ellas)	hablaban	comían	vivían

Para los cumpleaños siempre **preparábamos** *una cena especial.*
We always **used to prepare** a special meal for birthdays.

▨ Three common Spanish verbs are irregular in the imperfect tense: *ser, ir* and *ver*:

	ser – to be	*ir* – to go	*ver* – to see
(yo)	era	iba	veía
(tú)	eras	ibas	veías
(él / ella)	era	iba	veía
(nosotros)	éramos	íbamos	veíamos
(vosotros)	erais	ibais	veíais
(ellos / ellas)	eran	iban	veían

Después de la cena **íbamos** *a la iglesia a celebrar le Misa de Gallo a medianoche.*
After the meal we **used to go** to church to celebrate Midnight Mass.

▨ You need the imperfect tense of *hacer* and *estar* to describe the weather in the past:

No **hacía** *frío pero* **estaba** *nublado.*
It **was**n't cold but it **was** cloudy.

The imperfect continuous

▨ The imperfect continuous tense is used to describe an ongoing action more vividly. It is formed using the imperfect of *estar* and the gerund:

Estaba comiendo *cuando llegó mi hermano.*
I was eating when my brother arrived.

Preterite or imperfect?

▨ To help you decide between the preterite and the imperfect:

– remember that the following time expressions describe a single, completed action and should be used with the preterite:

ayer	yesterday
el otro día	the other day
la semana pasada	last week
hace tres años	three years ago

– these time expressions indicate a repeated action and are used with the imperfect:

siempre	always
frecuentemente	frequently
a veces	sometimes
todos los días	every day

The pluperfect

▨ This tense is used to refer to something further back in the past than the perfect or the imperfect, to say what someone had done or had been doing. You use the imperfect tense of *haber* and the past participle:

Ya **habíamos visto** *aquella película.*
We had already **seen** that film.

The immediate future

▨ Use the present tense of *ir + a* followed by an infinitive to say what you are going to do or what is going to happen:

Hasta los 65 años **voy a continuar** *trabajando.*
I'm going to carry on working until the age of 65.

The future

▨ The future tense expresses what will happen or will be happening in the future:

Si no reducimos las emisiones de CO_2, la situación **será** *irreversible.*
If we don't reduce carbon emissions, the situation **will be** irreversible.

Las especies en peligro de extinción **desaparecerán** *por completo.*
Endangered species **will disappear** completely.

- To form the future tense, add the correct ending to the infinitive of the verb:

	-ar verbs	-er verbs	-ir verbs
	hablar – to speak	comer – to eat	vivir – to live
(yo)	hablaré	comeré	viviré
(tú)	hablarás	comerás	vivirás
(él / ella)	hablará	comerá	vivirá
(nosotros)	hablaremos	comeremos	viviremos
(vosotros)	hablaréis	comeréis	viviréis
(ellos / ellas)	hablarán	comerán	vivirán

- A few verbs have an irregular stem in the future (see the verb tables on pages 190–194), but all have the same future endings:

hacer – to do	haré, harás, hará, haremos, haréis, harán
poder – to be able	podré, etc.
poner – to put	pondré, etc.
tener – to have	tendré, tendrás, tendrá, tendremos, tendréis, tendrán
haber (hay) there is / are	habrá

The conditional

- You use the conditional in Spanish when 'would' is used in English:

Me gustaría ir a Perú.   **I would like** to go to Peru.

Sería una oportunidad fantástica. **It would be** a fantastic opportunity.

- The conditional has the same stem as the future tense and the same endings as the imperfect tense of -er and -ir verbs:

	-ar verbs	-er verbs	-ir verbs
	hablar – to speak	comer – to eat	vivir – to live
(yo)	hablaría	comería	viviría
(tú)	hablarías	comerías	vivirías
(él / ella)	hablaría	comería	viviría
(nosotros)	hablaríamos	comeríamos	viviríamos
(vosotros)	hablaríais	comeríais	viviríais
(ellos / ellas)	hablarían	comerían	vivirían

As the conditional tense uses the same stem as the future tense, the irregular stems are exactly the same as the future tense irregulars.

The imperative

- Use the imperative to give advice or instructions. Commands are either positive (**do** something) or negative (**don't** do something). They are also either informal (*tú / vosotros*) or formal (*usted / ustedes*).

- To form positive commands:

– For *tú*, simply use the *tú* form of the verb, but without the final -s:

Come muchas frutas.   **Eat** a lot of fruit.

Compra aquel vestido.   **Buy** that dress.

– For the *vosotros* form, remove the -r from the end of the infinitive and replace it with -d:

Escuchad con atención.   **Listen** carefully.

Escribid la carta.   **Write** the letter.

– *Usted* and *ustedes* use the third person of the present subjunctive:

Hable inglés.   **Speak** English.

Coman las patatas fritas. **Eat** the chips.

- To form negative commands, always use the negative word plus the present subjunctive:

	tú	vosotros	usted	ustedes
hablar	no hables	no habléis	no hable	no hablen
comer	no comas	no comáis	no coma	no coman
vivir	no vivas	no viváis	no viva	no vivan

No escuches a Nuria.   **Don't listen** to Nuria.

The subjunctive

- The subjunctive is a form of the verb that is used when there is an element of wishing or doubt. It is used in certain set expressions of surprise or exclamation:

¡Viva la Reina!   Long live the Queen!

¡Que aproveche!   Enjoy your meal!

- Some verbal expressions are followed by the subjunctive:

– wishes, advice and requests such as *querer que, pedir que, decir que*

*Mi madre no quiere que **salga** con eso chico.*
My mother doesn't want me to **go out** with that boy.

– emotional reactions: joy, hope, sorrow, anger, fear such as *me gusta que, siento que*:

*Tengo miedo que me **estén buscando**.*
I'm afraid that they **are looking for** me.

– doubt, uncertainty, possibility such as *es posible que, es probable que, no es cierto que*:

No es posible que **vengan** *ahora.*
It's not possible that **they will come** now.

– expressions of purpose: *para que, a menos que, a condición que*:

Te prestaré dinero para que **puedas** *ir de vacaciones.*
I'll lend you some money so **you can** go on holiday.

– conjunctions of time – *cuando, hasta que* – when they refer to the future:

Cuando **vengáis** *vamos a hacer la fiesta.*
When **you come** we'll have a party.

■ To form the present subjunctive, take the *yo* form of the present tense of the verb and replace the *-o* ending with the following endings:

	-ar verbs	-er verbs	-ir verbs
	hablar – to speak	comer – to eat	vivir – to live
(yo)	hable	coma	viva
(tú)	hables	comas	vivas
(él / ella)	hable	coma	viva
(nosotros)	hablemos	comamos	vivamos
(vosotros)	habléis	comáis	viváis
(ellos / ellas)	hablen	coman	vivan

■ The imperfect subjunctive is used in the same expressions as the present subjunctive, but in past tense sentences. It has two forms: one ending in *-ra* and one ending in *-se*. Either can be used, but the *-ra* form is more common than the *-se* form. The stem is always taken from the third person singular of the preterite form:

hablar		comer		vivir	
-ra form	-se form	-ra form	-se form	-ra form	-se form
hablara	hablase	comiera	comiese	viviera	viviese
hablaras	hablases	comieras	comieses	vivieras	vivieses
hablara	hablase	comiera	comiese	viviera	viviese
habláramos	hablásemos	comiéramos	comiésemos	viviéramos	viviésemos
hablarais	hablaseis	comierais	comieseis	vivierais	vivieseis
hablaran	hablasen	comieran	comiesen	vivieran	viviesen

■ The imperfect subjunctive form of *querer* (*quisiera*) is used to say what someone would like:

Quisiera *llamar a su amigo.*   **He'd like** to call his friend.

Quisiera *un café.*   **I'd like** a coffee.

H Reflexive verbs

■ Reflexive verbs have a reflexive pronoun in front of the verb:

(yo)	**me** quejo	I complain
(tú)	**te** quejas	**you** complain
(él / ella)	**se** queja	**he / she** complains
(usted)	**se** queja	**you** (formal) complain
(nosotros)	**nos** quejamos	**we** complain
(vosotros)	**os** quejáis	**you** complain
(ellos / ellas)	**se** quejan	**they** complain
(ustedes)	**se** quejan	**you** (formal plural) complain

■ Common impersonal expressions using reflexive phrases are:

– *se puede* + infinitive   you can

Se puede *cambiar las actitudes racistas.*
You can change racist attitudes.

– *se debe* + infinitive   you must

Se debe *leer más para comprender mejor la situación.*
You must read more in order to understand the situation better.

– *se habla de* + noun   people talk about

Se habla de *la violencia.*
People talk about violence.

Se habla *español.*   Spanish **spoken**.

– *se necesita* + noun   … is needed

Se necesita *un programa de acción.*
An action programme **is needed**.

– se dice que   it is said that

***Se dice que** hay mucho racismo contra los inmigrantes.*
It is said that there is a lot of racism towards immigrants.

I Negatives

- To make a sentence negative, you normally put *no* before the verb:

  No tengo dinero.   I haven't any money.

- Other common negative expressions: *nunca, nadie, nada, ni … ni*; never, no one, nothing, neither … nor.

There are two ways of using *nunca, nadie, nada*. They can go at the start of the sentence or *no* can go before the verb with *nunca, nadie, nada* after the verb.

    – nunca / jamás   never

  No voy nunca a Madrid. / Nunca voy a Madrid.
  I never go to Madrid.

    – nadie   no one

  No habla nadie. / Nadie habla.
  No one talks.

    – nada   nothing

  No me preocupa nada. / Nada me preocupa.
  I am not worried about anything.

    – ni …ni   neither … nor

  No soy ni guapo ni feo.
  I'm neither good-looking nor ugly.

    – no ningún(o/a)   no / not any

  No tengo ningún problema.
  I don't have a problem.

J Questions (Interrogatives)

- Forming questions in Spanish is easy. You can turn statements into questions by adding an inverted question mark at the beginning and a question mark at the end:

  Nati habla español.   Nati speaks Spanish.

  ¿Nati habla español?   **Does** Nati speak Spanish?

- These are common question words – note that they all have an accent:

¿Adónde?	Where (to)?
¿Dónde?	Where?
¿Cómo?	How?
¿Cuál(es)?	What? (Which?)
¿Cuándo?	When?
¿Cuánto?	How much?
¿Qué?	What?
¿Quién(es)?	Who?
¿Por qué?	Why?

K The passive

- The passive is used to say what is done to someone or something. It is formed from *ser* and a past participle:

  active form: *Los habitantes construyeron el castillo.*
  The inhabitants built the castle.

  passive form: *El castillo **fue construido**.*
  The castle **was built**.

- The passive is quite rare in Spanish – it is very formal. To avoid using the passive, Spanish speakers often use the pronoun *se* and the third person of the verb:

  ***Se venden** caramelos aquí.*   Sweets **are sold** here.

L Impersonal verbs

- The most common impersonal verbs in Spanish are *gustar* (to like) and *encantar* (to love).

  Me gusta esta isla.

This sentence means 'I like this island.' Its literal translation, however, is 'This island pleases me.'

Note that you need to include the indirect object pronoun to show who is doing the liking:

  *¿**Te** gusta esta isla? Sí, **me** encanta.*
  Do **you** like this island? Yes, **I** love it.

  ***Me** preocupan las emisiones de CO_2.*
  I worry about CO_2 emissions.

M Verbs + infinitive constructions

- There are many common verbs in Spanish that can be used with a second verb which appears in the infinitive. For example:
  Quiero pasar el verano en España.
  I want to spend the summer in Spain.

The following are ones you are most likely to use: *poder* (to be able to), *querer* (to want to), *soler* (to 'usually' do something), *necesitar* (to need), *deber* and *tener que* (both mean 'to have to').

N Expressions with *tener*

- *Tener* is a useful verb in Spanish. As well as its basic meaning 'to have', it is used in a range of expressions:

tener que — to have to

tener sed / hambre / sueño / miedo / frío / calor / suerte
to be thirsty / hungry / tired / afraid / cold / hot / lucky

tener prisa — to be in a hurry

tener éxito — to be successful

O Uses of *ser* and *estar*

- *Ser* and *estar* both mean 'to be'.

  – *Ser* describes who someone is, or what something is.

  Es mi hermana. — She **is** my sister.

  Es una revista. — It **is** a magazine.

  It describes something that is unlikely to change.

  Madrid es grande. — Madrid **is** big.

  Mi madre es habladora. — My mother **is** chatty.

  – *Estar* describes the location of someone or something.

  Mis padres están en Barcelona.
  My parents **are** in Barcelona.

  It is used with the past participle to describe a condition that might change. In such expressions the past participle works like an adjective, agreeing with its noun.

  Estamos preocupados. — **We are** worried.

P Prepositions

- Prepositions of place, with *estar*

  Because *estar* is the verb for 'to be' when you want to state where something is, the following prepositions are often seen after *estar*.

arriba	upstairs, above
debajo de	under
delante de	in front of
detrás de	behind
encima de	on top of
enfrente de	opposite
a la derecha de	to the right of
a la izquierda de	to the left of
al lado de	next to

personal *a*

- When the object of a verb is a person, you need to include personal *a* before that person:

  *Vi **a** María en el cine.* — I saw Maria in the cinema.

por, para

- *Por* and *para* both mean 'for'.

  – *Por* means 'per', 'because of', 'through', 'along':

  *30 kilómetros **por** hora* — 30 kilometres **per** hour

  ***por** exceso de ruido* — **because of** too much noise

  ***por** el parque, **por** el camino* — **through** the park, **along** the road

  – *Para* means 'in order to', 'for the purpose of', 'intended for':

  ***para** reducir la contaminación* — **to** reduce pollution

  *Esta carta es **para** ti.* — This letter is **for** you.

Q Expressions of time

desde hace and *desde hacía*

- To say how long you **have been doing** something which you are still doing, use the present tense with *desde hace*:

  *Vivo en Madrid **desde hace** diez años.*
  I have been living in Madrid **for** ten years.

- To say how long you **had** been doing something in the past, use the imperfect tense with *desde hacía*:

  *Vivía en Madrid **desde hacía** ocho años.*
  I had been living in Madrid **for** eight years.

R Conjunctions

The following words are used to link parts of sentences together:

y	and	*María **y** su hermana*	Maria **and** her sister
pero	but	*Hace frío **pero** no me importa.*	It's cold **but** I don't mind.
o	or	*el veinte de agosto **o** el seis de junio*	the 20th August **or** the 6th June
porque	because	*Estoy viendo la tele **porque** está nevando.*	I'm watching television **because** it's snowing.
como	as	***Como** soy atleta, bebo mucha agua.*	**As** I'm an athlete, I drink a lot of water.
cuando	when	*Empecé a ir a la escuela primaria **cuando** tenía seis años.*	I started primary school **when** I was six years old.

S Numbers, days, dates and time

1	*uno*	11	*once*	21	*veintiuno*
2	*dos*	12	*doce*	22	*veintidós*
3	*tres*	13	*trece*	23	*veintitrés*
4	*cuatro*	14	*catorce*	24	*veinticuatro*
5	*cinco*	15	*quince*	25	*veinticinco*
6	*seis*	16	*dieciséis*	26	*veintiséis*
7	*siete*	17	*diecisiete*	27	*veintisiete*
8	*ocho*	18	*dieciocho*	28	*veintiocho*
9	*nueve*	19	*diecinueve*	29	*veintinueve*
10	*diez*	20	*veinte*	30	*treinta*

31	*treinta y uno*	82	*ochenta y dos*
32	*treinta y dos*	90	*noventa*
40	*cuarenta*	91	*noventa y uno*
41	*cuarenta y uno*	92	*noventa y dos*
42	*cuarenta y dos*	100	*cien*
50	*cincuenta*	101	*ciento uno*
51	*cincuenta y uno*	102	*ciento dos*
52	*cincuenta y dos*	200	*doscientos*
60	*sesenta*	201	*doscientos uno*
61	*sesenta y uno*	300	*trescientos*
62	*sesenta y dos*	301	*trescientos uno*
70	*setenta*	1000	*mil*
71	*setenta y uno*	1001	*mil uno*
72	*setenta y dos*	1002	*mil dos*
80	*ochenta*	2000	*dos mil*
81	*ochenta y uno*		

Ordinal numbers: *primero, segundo,* etc.

■ The Spanish for 'first' is *primero* in the masculine and *primera* in the feminine:

– use *primer* before a masculine singular noun:

*mi **primer** niño*	my **first** child

■ To say 'second', 'third', etc:

segundo	second
tercero	third
cuarto	fourth
quinto	fifth
sexto	sixth
séptimo	seventh
octavo	eighth
noveno	ninth
décimo	tenth

Days and dates

lunes	Monday
martes	Tuesday
miércoles	Wednesday
jueves	Thursday
viernes	Friday
sábado	Saturday
domingo	Sunday
enero	January
febrero	February
marzo	March
abril	April
mayo	May
junio	June
julio	July
agosto	August
septiembre	September
octubre	October
noviembre	November
diciembre	December

■ Use normal numbers for dates:

*Mi cumpleaños es **el 27 de diciembre**.*
My birthday is **on the 27th of December**.

But *el primero* can be used, as well as *el uno* for 'the 1st': *El primero de mayo tenemos una fiesta.*
On the 1st of May we have a party.

- Days of the week and months do not start with a capital letter in Spanish (unless they are at the beginning of a sentence):

  *El cumpleaños de mi madre es el 13 de **abril**.*
  My mother's birthday is on the 13th of **April**.

- Use *el + lunes / martes*, etc. to say '**on** Monday / Tuesday', etc.:

  ***El domingo** un amigo me regaló dos entradas para un partido entre Villareal y Valencia.*

  On Sunday a friend gave me two tickets for the match between Villareal and Valencia.

- Use *los + lunes / martes*, etc. to say '**on** Monday**s** / Tuesday**s**' etc.:

  *Normalmente **los sábados** voy a una clase de música.*

  On Saturdays I normally go to a music lesson.

Time

- The 12-hour clock goes as follows:

Es la una.	It's one o'clock.
Son las dos.	It's two o'clock.
Es la una y cinco.	It's five past one.
Son las dos y diez.	It's ten past two.
Son las dos y cuarto.	It's a quarter past two.
Son las dos y media.	It's half past two.
Son las tres menos veinte.	It's twenty to three.
Son las tres menos cuarto.	It's a quarter to three.
A mediodía.	At midday.
A medianoche.	At midnight.

- As in English, when using the 24-hour clock, use numbers such as *trece, dieciocho,* etc:

  *a las **veinte** diez* at 20.10

- To ask the time:

  ¿Qué hora es? What time is it? / What's the time?

Verb tables

> **info**
>
> Verb tables help you to use verbs, particularly irregular verbs, correctly. If you're not sure how to use them, check out the grammar spread at the end of Topic 6 (see page 121) for two activities to help.
>
> The first column in the table shows the infinitive in Spanish and English, and then the participles for the verb. The **present participle** (or **gerund**) ends in -ando or -iendo and is used to translate the -**ing** form of the English verb (e.g. to speak → speaking; find out more on page 181 in *Gramática*). The **past participle** is used to form the perfect tense (e.g. to speak → I have spoken; find out more on page 182 in *Gramática*).

Regular -ar verbs

infinitive + participles	present	preterite	imperfect	future
hablar **to speak**	hablo	hablé	hablaba	hablaré
	hablas	hablaste	hablabas	hablarás
	habla	habló	hablaba	hablará
hablando	hablamos	hablamos	hablábamos	hablaremos
hablado	habláis	hablasteis	hablabais	hablaréis
	hablan	hablaron	hablaban	hablarán

Regular -er verbs

comer **to eat**	como	comí	comía	comeré
	comes	comiste	comías	comerás
	come	comió	comía	comerá
comiendo	comemos	comimos	comíamos	comeremos
comido	coméis	comisteis	comíais	comeréis
	comen	comieron	comían	comerán

Regular -ir verbs

vivir **to live**	vivo	viví	vivía	viviré
	vives	viviste	vivías	vivirás
	vive	vivió	vivía	vivirá
viviendo	vivimos	vivimos	vivíamos	viviremos
vivido	vivís	vivisteis	vivíais	viviréis
	viven	vivieron	vivían	vivirán

Irregular verbs

infinitive + participles	present	preterite	imperfect	future
dar to give	doy	di	daba	daré
	das	diste	dabas	darás
	da	dio	daba	dará
dando	damos	dimos	dábamos	daremos
dado	dais	disteis	dabais	daréis
	dan	dieron	daban	darán
decir to say	digo	dije	decía	diré
	dices	dijiste	decías	dirás
	dice	dijo	decía	dirá
diciendo	decimos	dijimos	decíamos	diremos
dicho	decís	dijisteis	decíais	diréis
	dicen	dijeron	decían	dirán
empezar to begin	empiezo	empecé	empezaba	empezaré
	empiezas	empezaste	empezabas	empezarás
	empieza	empezó	empezaba	empezará
empezando	empezamos	empezamos	empezábamos	empezaremos
empezado	empezáis	empezasteis	empezabais	empezaréis
	empiezan	empezaron	empezaban	empezarán
escribir to write	escribo	escribí	escribía	escribiré
	escribes	escribiste	escribías	escribirás
	escribe	escribió	escribía	escribirá
escribiendo	escribimos	escribimos	escribíamos	escribiremos
escrito	escribís	escribisteis	escribíais	escribiréis
	escriben	escribieron	escribían	escribirán
estar to be	estoy	estuve	estaba	estaré
	estás	estuviste	estabas	estarás
	está	estuvo	estaba	estará
estando	estamos	estuvimos	estábamos	estaremos
estado	estáis	estuvisteis	estabais	estaréis
	están	estuvieron	estaban	estarán

infinitive + participles	present	preterite	imperfect	future
haber to have	he	hube	había	habré
	has	hubiste	habías	habrás
	ha	hubo	había	habrá
habiendo	hemos	hubimos	habíamos	habremos
habido	habéis	hubisteis	habíais	habréis
	han	hubieron	habían	habrán
hacer to do, to make	hago	hice	hacía	haré
	haces	hiciste	hacías	harás
	hace	hizo	hacía	hará
haciendo	hacemos	hicimos	hacíamos	haremos
hecho	hacéis	hicisteis	hacíais	haréis
	hacen	hicieron	hacían	harán
ir to go	voy	fui	iba	iré
	vas	fuiste	ibas	irás
	va	fue	iba	irá
yendo	vamos	fuimos	íbamos	iremos
ido	vais	fuisteis	ibais	iréis
	van	fueron	iban	irán
jugar to play	juego	jugué	jugaba	jugaré
	juegas	jugaste	jugabas	jugarás
	juega	jugó	jugaba	jugará
jugando	jugamos	jugamos	jugábamos	jugaremos
jugado	jugáis	jugasteis	jugabais	jugaréis
	juegan	jugaron	jugaban	jugarán
poder to be able to	puedo	pude	podía	podré
	puedes	pudiste	podías	podrás
	puede	pudo	podía	podrá
pudiendo	podemos	pudimos	podíamos	podremos
podido	podéis	pudisteis	podíais	podréis
	pueden	pudieron	podían	podrán

infinitive + participles	present	preterite	imperfect	future
poner to put	*pongo*	*puse*	*ponía*	*pondré*
	pones	*pusiste*	*ponías*	*pondrás*
	pone	*puso*	*ponía*	*pondrá*
poniendo	*ponemos*	*pusimos*	*poníamos*	*pondremos*
puesto	*ponéis*	*pusisteis*	*poníais*	*pondréis*
	ponen	*pusieron*	*ponían*	*pondrán*
querer to want	*quiero*	*quise*	*quería*	*querré*
	quieres	*quisiste*	*querías*	*querrás*
	quiere	*quiso*	*quería*	*querrá*
queriendo	*queremos*	*quisimos*	*queríamos*	*querremos*
querido	*queréis*	*quisisteis*	*queríais*	*querréis*
	quieren	*quisieron*	*querían*	*querrán*
saber to know	*sé*	*supe*	*sabía*	*sabré*
	sabes	*supiste*	*sabías*	*sabrás*
	sabe	*supo*	*sabía*	*sabrá*
sabiendo	*sabemos*	*supimos*	*sabíamos*	*sabremos*
sabido	*sabéis*	*supisteis*	*sabíais*	*sabréis*
	saben	*supieron*	*sabían*	*sabrán*
sacar to get, take out	*saco*	*saqué*	*sacaba*	*sacaré*
	sacas	*sacaste*	*sacabas*	*sacarás*
	saca	*sacó*	*sacaba*	*sacará*
sacando	*sacamos*	*sacamos*	*sacábamos*	*sacaremos*
sacado	*sacáis*	*sacasteis*	*sacabais*	*sacaréis*
	sacan	*sacaron*	*sacaban*	*sacarán*
ser to be	*soy*	*fui*	*era*	*seré*
	eres	*fuiste*	*eras*	*serás*
	es	*fue*	*era*	*será*
siendo	*somos*	*fuimos*	*éramos*	*seremos*
sido	*sois*	*fuisteis*	*erais*	*seréis*
	son	*fueron*	*eran*	*serán*

infinitive + participles	present	preterite	imperfect	future
tener to have	tengo	tuve	tenía	tendré
	tienes	tuviste	tenías	tendrás
	tiene	tuvo	tenía	tendrá
teniendo	tenemos	tuvimos	teníamos	tendremos
tenido	tenéis	tuvisteis	teníais	tendréis
	tienen	tuvieron	tenían	tendrán
tocar to touch	toco	toqué	tocaba	tocaré
	tocas	tocaste	tocabas	tocarás
	toca	tocó	tocaba	tocará
tocando	tocamos	tocamos	tocábamos	tocaremos
tocado	tocáis	tocasteis	tocabais	tocaréis
	tocan	tocaron	tocaban	tocarán
venir to come	vengo	vine	venía	vendré
	vienes	viniste	venías	vendrás
	viene	vino	venía	vendrá
viniendo	venimos	vinimos	veníamos	vendremos
venido	venís	vinisteis	veníais	vendréis
	vienen	vinieron	venían	vendrán
ver to see	veo	vi	veía	veré
	ves	viste	veías	verás
	ve	vio	veía	verá
viendo	vemos	vimos	veíamos	veremos
visto	veis	visteis	veíais	veréis
	ven	vieron	veían	verán
volver to return	vuelvo	volví	volvía	volveré
	vuelves	volviste	volvías	volverás
	vuelve	volvió	volvía	volverá
volviendo	volvemos	volvimos	volvíamos	volveremos
vuelto	volvéis	volvisteis	volvíais	volveréis
	vuelven	volvieron	volvían	volverán

Glosario

A

abandonar to leave / abandon
abiertamente openly
el / la abogado/a lawyer
abril April
la abuela grandmother
el abuelo grandfather
aburrido/a boring
aburrir(se) to get bored
acabar to finish
el acceso access
el accidente accident
la acción política political action
el acento accent
acoger to welcome
el acoso escolar bullying
acostarse to go to bed
acostumbrado/a accustomed to / used to
la actitud attitude
la actividad activity
activo/a active / energetic
el acuario aquarium
me acuesto I go to bed
adecuado/a appropriate / suitable
además also
adictivo/a addictive
el / la adicto/a addict
adjuntar to attach / enclose
admirar to admire
el / la adolescente teenager
el / la adulto adult
el aeropuerto airport
afectar to affect
las afueras suburbs / outskirts
agosto August
agradable pleasant
el agua (f) corriente running water
el agua (f) mineral mineral water
aguantar to tolerate / put up with
ahora now
ahorrar to save
el aire air
el aire acondicionado air conditioning

el aire libre open air
aislado/a isolated
el albañil bricklayer
el albergue juvenil youth hostel
la alcantarilla drain
el alcohol alcohol
alcohólico/a alcoholic
el alcoholismo alcoholism
alegrarse to be pleased
alegre happy / cheerful
el alemán German (language)
Alemania Germany
la alfombra rug
algo something
alguno/a some
la alimentación food
el alimento food
allá over there
al lado de next to / beside
allí there
el almuerzo lunch
el almuerzo frío cold / packed lunch
alojarse to stay
alquilado/a rented
alquilar to hire
el alquiler hire
alrededor around
los altavoces speakers
alto/a tall
el / la alumno/a pupil
a menudo often
amable nice / pleasant
el / la amante lover
amarillo/a yellow
la ambición ambition
el ambiente atmosphere / environment
la amistad friendship
el / la amo/a de casa househusband / housewife
el amor love
el andén platform
animado/a lively
el año year
anoche last night
antes before
antiguo/a old
antipático/a unpleasant
el anuncio advert
apagar to turn off

el aparato machine / device
el aparcamiento parking
el apartamento flat
el apellido surname
apoyar to support
el apoyo support
aprender to learn
el / la aprendiz apprentice
el aprendizaje apprenticeship / learning
aprobar to pass
aprovechar to make the most of
apuntarse to sign up
los apuntes notes
el árbol tree
la arena sand
el armario wardrobe
arreglar to tidy
arreglarse to get ready
me arreglo I get myself ready
arriba up
arroba @
el arroz rice
arruinar to ruin
el arte dramático drama
el artículo article
el ascensor lift
asegurar to ensure
el aseo toilet
así que so
el asiento seat
la asignatura subject
la asistenta maid
asistir to attend / go to
asqueroso/a awful
el asunto matter / topic
atacar to attack
el ático attic
el atletismo athletics
atrás back
el atún tuna
el aula (f) classroom
aumentar to increase
aunque although
ausente absent
el autobús bus
el autocar coach
la autopista motorway
el AVE high-speed train
la aventura adventure
el avión plane
ayer yesterday

la ayuda   help
ayudar   to help
el ayuntamiento   town hall
la azafata   air stewardess
el azúcar   sugar
azul   blue

B

el bachillerato   equivalent of an A-level course
bailar   to dance
el baile   dance
bajar   to drop / go down
bajo/a   short (not tall)
el balcón   balcony
el baloncesto   basketball
el bañador   swimsuit
bañarse   to swim
el banco   bank
la banda ancha   broadband
la bañera   bathtub
el banquete   feast
barato/a   cheap
la barba   beard
el barco   boat
la barra   slash
la barrera generacional   generation gap
el barrio   district / area / neighbourhood
bastante   quite
bastar   to be enough
la basura   rubbish
la batería   drums
beber   to drink
la bebida (con gas)   (fizzy) drink
bebo   I drink
el belén   nativity scene / crib
el beneficio   benefit
la biblioteca   library
la bicicleta   bicycle
bien   well
el bigote   moustache
el billete   ticket
la biología   biology
el bistec   steak
blanco/a   white
la blusa   blouse
la boca   mouth
el bocadillo   sandwich
la bolera   bowling alley
el bolígrafo   pen
la bolsa de plástico   plastic bag
el bolso   handbag

el / la bombero/a   firefighter
bonito/a   pretty
borracho/a   drunk
el bosque   forest
las botas   boots
la botella   bottle
el botellón   binge drinking
el brazo   arm
brindar   to toast
broncearse   to sunbathe
el buceo   diving
hacer buen tiempo   to be nice weather
bueno/a   good
lo bueno   the good thing
buscar   to look for
la butaca   armchair
el buzón   postbox / mailbox

C

el caballo   horse
la cabeza   head
cada   every
caerse   to fall
el café   coffee
el / la cajero/a   cashier
los calcetines   socks
la calculadora   calculator
la calefacción   heating
el calentamiento global   global warming
la calidad   quality
de buena calidad   good quality
la calificación   qualification
calificado/a   qualified
callado/a   quiet
callarse   to be quiet
la calle   street
hacer calor   to be hot
caluroso/a   hot
calvo/a   bald
la cama de matrimonio   double bed
la cámara digital   digital camera
el / la camarero/a   waiter / waitress
cambiar   to change
el cambio climático   climate change
a cambio de   in exchange for
el camello   camel
caminar   to walk
el / la camionero/a   lorry driver

la camisa   shirt
la camiseta   t-shirt
el campamento   camp
la campaña   campaign
el campeonato   championship
el camping   campsite
el campo   field / countryside
el campo de deporte   sports field
el canabis   cannabis
el cáncer   cancer
la cancha (de baloncesto)   (basketball) court
la canción   song
el / la candidato/a   candidate
cansado/a   tired
el / la cantante   singer
la cantidad   quantity
la cantina   canteen
canto   I sing
capaz   capable
la capital   capital
la cara   face
el caramelo   sweet
la caravana   caravan
la cárcel   prison
cargar   to load
cariñoso/a   affectionate
la carne   meat
el carné joven   student card
el carnet de conducir   driving licence
el carnet / documento de identidad (DNI)   ID
el / la carnicero/a   butcher
caro/a   expensive
la carpeta   folder / file
el carpintero   joiner
la carrera   profession / race
la carretera   road
la carta   letter
el/ la cartero/a   postman / postwoman
el cartón   cardboard
la casa   house
una casa adosada   semi-detached / terraced house
casado/a   married
casarse   to get married
casi   almost
castaño/a   brown
castigar   to punish
el castigo   punishment
el castillo   castle
la catarata   waterfall

la *catástrofe natural* natural disaster
la *catedral* cathedral
catorce fourteen
causar to cause
el *CD (el disco compacto)* CD (compact disc)
celebrar to celebrate
celoso/a jealous
la *cena* evening meal
cenar to have dinner / supper
el *centro* the centre
el *centro comercial* shopping centre
cerca (de) close (to)
cercano/a near
los *cereales* cereal
cero zero
la *cerveza* beer
el *césped* lawn
un *chalet* detached house
la *chaqueta* jacket
charlar to chat
chatear to chat (online)
el *cheque de viaje* traveller's cheque
la *chica* girl
el *chicle* chewing gum
el *chico* boy
la *chimenea* fireplace / chimney
el *chiringuito* refreshment stand
el *chocolate* chocolate
el *chorizo* Spanish sausage
los *churros* churros (doughnut strips)
el *ciclismo* cycling
el *cielo* sky
los *cielos despejados* clear skies
cien, ciento one hundred
la *ciencia ficción* science fiction
las *ciencias* science
las *ciencias económicas* economics
ciento uno (ciento una) one hundred and one
por *cierto* certainly
el *cigarrillo* cigarette
cinco five
cinco mil five thousand
cincuenta fifty
el *cine* cinema
el *cinturón* belt

la *cita* appointment
la *ciudad* city
la *clase* class
el *clima* climate
la *clínica* clinic
el *club de jóvenes* youth club
el *club taurino* bullfighting club
el / la *cobarde* coward
la *cobaya* guinea pig
cobrar to charge
la *cocaína* cocaine
el *coche* car
(la) *cocina* kitchen / food technology
la *cocina (de gas / eléctrica)* (gas / electric) cooker
cocinar to cook food
el / la *cocinero/a* chef
coger to pick / take
la *cola* queue
el *colegio* school
el *collar* necklace
el *combustible* fuel
la *comedia* comedy
el *comedor* dining room
el *comentario* comment
comenzar to begin
comer to eat (lunch)
el / la *comerciante* trader / shopkeeper
el *comercio* commerce / shop / business studies
cometer to commit
cómico/a funny
la *comida* food
la *comida basura* junk food
la *comida rápida* fast food
la *comisaría* police station
como I eat
la *comodidad* comfort
cómodo/a comfortable
compaginar to combine
el / la *compañero/a* companion / friend
la *compañía* company
comparar to compare
compartir to share
competente competent
el *complejo (vacacional)* resort
el *comportamiento* behaviour
comportarse to behave
comprar to buy
ir de *compras* to go shopping
comprender to understand
la *comprensión*

understanding
comprensivo/a understanding
el *compromiso* commitment
común common
comunicando engaged (phone)
la *comunidad* community
las *comunidades indígenas* indigenous communities
el *concierto* concert
concurrido/a busy
la *condición* condition
las *condiciones de trabajo* working conditions
conducir to drive
la *conducta* behaviour
el / la *conductor(a)* driver
conectarse to connect
el *conejo* rabbit
confesar to confess
la *confianza* trust
confiar to trust somebody
el *conflicto* conflict / problem
conocer to meet / get to know
los *conocimientos* knowledge
ser *consciente de* to be aware of
la *consecuencia* consequence
conseguir to get / achieve
el *consejo* advice
considerar to consider
la *consigna* left-luggage office
construir to build
el *consumidor* consumer
consumir to consume
el *consumo* consumption
el / la *contable* accountant
contactar to contact
la *contaminación* pollution
contaminar to contaminate
contar to tell
el *contenedor* container
contener to contain
contento/a happy
contestar to answer
contratar to take on / hire
el *contrato* contract
contribuir to contribute
convencer to convince
conversar to talk
la *copa* cup / trophy
la *copia* copy
el *corazón* heart

la corbata   tie
el correo   mail
el correo basura   junk mail
el correo electrónico   email
correr   to run
la correspondencia   mail / post
la corrida de toros   bullfight
corro   I run
las cortinas   curtains
corto/a   short (hair)
la cosa   thing
la costa   the coast
costar   to cost
la costumbre   custom / tradition
crecer   to grow
creer   to believe
el crimen   crime
el cristal   glass
criticar   to criticise
el cruce   junction / crossroad
el cuaderno   exercise book
en cuanto sea posible   as soon as possible
cuarenta   forty
el cuarto de baño   bathroom
el cuarto de huéspedes   guest room
cuatro   four
cuatrocientos   four hundred
el cubo de la basura   rubbish bin
cubrir   to cover
la cuchara   spoon
el cuchillo   knife
el cuello   neck
el cuero   leather
el cuerpo   body
cuidar   to look after
cultivar   to grow
el cumpleaños   birthday
cumplir   to reach (a certain age)
el curso   course / school year
cuyo   whose

D

dañar   to damage / spoil
el daño   damage / harm
dar   to give
dar a   to have a view of
dar una vuelta   to go for a stroll
debajo de   under
deber   must / to owe

los deberes   homework
debido a   because of / owing to
decepcionado/a   disappointed
decepcionante   disappointing
decepcionar   to disappoint
los dedos   fingers / toes
dejar (el hogar)   to leave (home)
dejar de (fumar)   to stop (smoking)
delante de   in front of
delgado/a   thin
delicioso/a   delicious
demasiado/a   too much / too many
democrático/a   democratic
demostrar   to show / demonstrate
el / la dentista   dentist
por dentro   inside
la denuncia   complaint
el / la dependiente   shop assistant
el deporte   sport
los deportes acuáticos   water sports
los deportes de invierno   winter sports
deportista   sporty
la depresión   depression
la derecha   right
los derechos   rights
desagradable   unpleasant
desaparecer   to disappear
el desarrollo   development
desastroso/a   disastrous
desayunar   to eat breakfast
el desayuno   breakfast
descansar   to rest / have a break
el descanso   break / half-time / interval
descargar   to download
el descuento   discount
desde … a …   from … to …
el desempleo   unemployment
la desigualdad   inequality
desobediente   disobedient
el despacho   office
despejado/a   clear
despertarse   to wake up
me despierto   I wake up
después   after(wards)
destacar   to emphasise
el destino   destination

la destreza   skill
destruir   to destroy
el desván   loft
la desventaja   disadvantage
el detalle   detail
detestar   to hate
detrás de   behind
la deuda   debt
devolver   to give back
el día festivo   holiday / bank holiday
diariamente   daily / every day
la diarrea   diarrhoea
dibujar   to draw
el dibujo   art
los dibujos animados   cartoons
el diccionario   dictionary
diciembre   December
diecinueve   nineteen
dieciocho   eighteen
dieciséis   sixteen
diecisiete   seventeen
la dieta   diet
diez   ten
diez mil   ten thousand
la diferencia   difference
difícil   difficult
la dificultad   difficulty
el dinero   money
en directo   live
el / la director(a)   head teacher
el disco compacto   CD
la discoteca   night club
la discriminación   discrimination
la discusión   argument
discutir   to argue
diseñar   to design
disfrutar   to enjoy
disponer de   to have available
la distancia   distance
distinto/a   different
la diversión   entertainment
divertido/a   fun
divertirse   to have fun
divorciado/a   divorced
doblar   to bend
doce   twelve
el documental   documentary
domingo   Sunday
dormir   to sleep
dormirse   to go to sleep
el dormitorio   bedroom
dos   two
doscientos (doscientas)   two

hundred
dos mil two thousand
dos millones two million
la droga drug
el drogadicto drug addict
drogarse to take drugs
las drogas blandas soft drugs
las drogas duras hard drugs
la ducha shower
ducharse to have a shower
me ducho I shower
me duermo I go to sleep
el dulce sweet
durante during
durar to last
duro/a hard

E

la economía economy
la edad age
el edificio building
el edredón nórdico quilt
la educación education
la educación física PE
educar to educate
en efectivo in cash
el efecto invernadero greenhouse effect
egoísta selfish
el ejecutivo executive
el ejercicio exercise
el ejército army
la electricidad electricity
el / la electricista electrician
el electrodoméstico household appliance
elegir to choose
embarazada pregnant
emborracharse to get drunk
las emisiones (de CO₂) (CO_2) emissions
emocionante exciting
empezar to begin
el / la empleado/a employee
el empleo job
empotrado/a fitted
emprendedor enterprising
la empresa company / firm
enamorado/a in love
enamorarse to fall in love
me encanta(n) I love
encargado/a de in charge of
encargarse de to be in charge of
encontrar to find / meet

la encuesta survey
la energía energy
enero January
enfadar to anger
enfadarse to get angry
la enfermedad illness / disease
la enfermedad cardíaca heart disease
el / la enfermero/a nurse
el / la enfermo/a sick person
enfriar to get cold
la ensalada salad
la enseñanza education
la enseñanza secundaria secondary education
enseñar to learn / teach
entender to understand
la entrada ticket / entry
la entrada gratis free entry
entrar to come in / enter
entregar to hand in
entretenido/a entertaining
la entrevista interview
el entusiasmo enthusiasm
entusiasta enthusiastic
el envase container
enviar to send
enviar (mensajes) to text
equilibrado/a balanced
el equilibrio balance
el equipaje luggage
el equipo team
el equipo de música music system
equivocado/a wrong
es is
la escalera stairs
el escaparate shop window
la escasez scarcity
Escocia Scotland
escoger to choose
escribir to write
el / la escritor(a) writer
el escritorio desk
escuchar to listen (to)
escuchar música to listen to music
la escuela school
el esfuerzo effort
el espacio space
la espalda back
el español Spanish (language)
especial special
la especialidad speciality
el espectáculo performance /

show
el espectáculo de flamenco flamenco show
el espejo mirror
la esperanza hope
esperar to wait
espiar to spy
la esposa wife
el esposo husband
esquiar to ski / go skiing
estable stable
la estación station
la estación de autobuses / trenes bus / railway station
la estación de esquí ski resort
el estadio stadium
el estado civil marital status
los Estados Unidos the United States
las estanterías shelves
estar a favor to be in favour
estar bien de salud to be healthy
estar cerrado/a to be closed
estar de acuerdo to agree
estar de moda to be fashionable
estar en contra to be against
estar en forma to be fit
estar en huelga to be on strike
estar estresado/a to be stressed
estar harto de to be fed up of
estar ocupado/a to be occupied
estar pintado/a to be painted
estar seguro to be sure
la Estatua de la Libertad Statue of Liberty
el este east
el estereotipo stereotype
estrecho/a narrow
el estrés stress
estresante stressful
estricto/a strict
el estuche pencil case
el / la estudiante student
estudiar to study
los estudios studies
estupendo/a great
la evaluación assessment
evitar to avoid
el examen exam

excesivo/a excessive / too much
la excursión trip
el éxito success
las expectativas expectations
la experiencia laboral experience of work
la explicación explanation
explicar to explain
el éxtasis ecstasy
la extinción extinction
extrañamente strangely
el extranjero foreigner / abroad
extrovertido/a extrovert / outgoing

F

la fábrica factory
fácil easy
la falda skirt
faltar to lack / be absent
la familia family
fantástico/a fantastic
fascinante fascinating
fascinar to fascinate
me fastidia it annoys me
fastidiar to annoy
fatal awful
favorito/a favourite
febrero February
la fecha date
las felicidades congratulations
feliz happy
¡Feliz Navidad! Happy Christmas!
femenino/a girls'
fenomenal great
feo/a ugly
el ferrocarril railway / train
fiable trustworthy
la ficha form
la ficha de trabajo worksheet
la fiesta party / festival
la fiesta de cumpleaños birthday party
la filología language degree
el fin de semana weekend
el finde weekend (colloquial)
firmar to sign
la física physics
físico/a physical
la flor flower
la formación training
al fondo at the back
formal polite
fracasar to fail

el fracaso failure
el francés French (language)
el fregadero sink
fregar to wash (dishes)
fresco/a fresh
hacer frío to be cold
el / la friolero/a person who feels the cold
la fruta fruit
el fuego artificial firework
fuera away / outside
fuerte strong
fui I went
fumador smoking
el / la fumador(a) smoker
fumar to smoke
el fumar pasivo passive smoking
funcionar to work
el futuro the future

G

las gafas glasses
la galería de arte art gallery
la galleta biscuit
ganar to earn / win
tener ganas de to want to
la gaseosa fizzy drink
la gasolina petrol
gastar to spend
los gastos expenses
el gato cat
el / la gemelo/a twin
generalmente usually
la gente people
la geografía geography
el gerente manager
la gimnasia gymnastics
el gimnasio gym
el / la gitano/a gypsy
glotón / glotona greedy
el gobierno government
golpear to hit
la goma eraser
gordo/a fat
la gorra cap / hat
gracioso/a funny
el grado degree
el Gran Hermano Big Brother
los grandes almacenes department stores
la granja farm
el / la granjero/a farmer
la grasa fat
grave serious
Grecia Greece

gris grey
grueso/a thick
los guantes gloves
guapo/a good-looking
guardar to keep / save
el guía guide
la guía guidebook
el guión bajo underscore
los guisantes beans
la guitarra guitar
me gusta(n) I like

H

la habitación room
el / la habitante inhabitant
el hábito habit
hablador(a) chatty / talkative
hablo I talk
hace (un mes) (one month) ago
hace (dos semanas) (two weeks) ago
hacer to do
hacer falta to need / be needed
hacer la cama to make the bed
hacer la compra to do the shopping
hacer los deberes to do homework
hacer piragüismo to go canoeing
hacer prácticas to do work experience
hacer turnos to work shifts
hacia towards
el hambre hunger
la hamburguesa hamburger
la hamburguesería hamburger joint
hasta up to / until
hay there is / there are
hay que you have to
hecho made from
la heladería ice-cream parlour
el helado ice cream
la herida injury
la hermana sister
la hermanastra stepsister
el hermanastro stepbrother
el hermano brother
la heroína heroin
hice I did / made
el hielo ice

el *hígado* liver
la *hija* daughter
el *hijo* son
los *hijos* children
la *historia* history
el *hogar* home
la *hoja de papel* sheet of paper
el *hombre de negocios* businessman
honesto/a honest
honrado/a honest / honourable
a la *hora de* when it comes to
el *horario de trabajo* working hours
las *horas de trabajo flexibles* flexible working hours
horroroso/a horrific
el *hotel* hotel
el *huésped* guest
el *huevo* egg
el *huracán* hurricane

I

de *ida* single (ticket)
de *ida y vuelta* return ticket
el *idioma* language
el *iftar* evening meal during Ramadan
la *iglesia* church
igual same
la *igualdad* equality
la *imagen* image
imaginar to imagine
imitar to imitate
impaciente impatient
impedir to impede / prevent
imprescindible indispensable
impresionante impressive
el *impuesto* tax
el *incendio* fire
incluso even
incómodo/a uncomfortable
increíble incredible
independiente independent
industria industry
la *influencia* influence
la *información* information
la *informática* ICT
el / la *ingeniero/a* engineer
el *inglés* English (language)
la *injusticia* injustice
injusto/a unfair

el / la *inmigrante* immigrant
la *insolación* sunstroke
insolente insolent / cheeky
la *instalación* facility
las *instalaciones* facilities
el *instituto* school
insultar to insult
la *integración* integration
la *intención* intention
intentar to try
el *intercambio* exchange
interesante interesting
el / la *intérprete* interpreter
intimidar to intimidate / threaten
la *inundación* flood
el *invierno* winter
el / la *invitado/a* guest
invitar to invite
la *inyección* injection
ir to go
ir de camping to go camping
ir de compras to go shopping
ir de excursión to go on a trip
Irlanda Ireland
el / la *irlandés / irlandesa* Irishman/woman
irreversible irreversible
irse bien to fit / suit (of clothes, etc.)
la *isla* island
el *IVA* VAT
izquierdo/a left

J

el *jamón* ham
el *jardín* garden
el / la *jardinero/a* gardener
el / la *jefe/a* boss
el *jersey* jumper
joven young
los *jóvenes* young people
jubilado/a retired
jubilarse to retire
el *juego* game
jueves Thursday
el *jugador juvenil* youth team player
jugar to play
jugar a las cartas to play cards
el *juguete* toy
a mi *juicio* in my opinion

julio July
junio June

L

el *laboratorio* laboratory
el *ladrillo* brick
el *lago* lake
la *lámpara* lamp
la *lana* wool
los *lápices de colores* coloured pencils
el *lápiz* pencil
largo/a long
la *lata* tin
el *lavabo* handbasin
el *lavaplatos* dishwasher
me *lavo los dientes* I brush my teeth
la *lección* lesson
la *leche* milk
leer to read
las *legumbres* vegetables
lejos (de) far (from)
la *lengua* language
lentamente slowly
lento/a slow
la *letra* letter
levantar to lift
levantarse to get up
levantar la mano to put your hand up
me *levanto* I get up
la *ley* law
la *libertad* freedom
libre free
la *librería* bookshop
el *libro* book
el / la *líder* leader
ligero/a light
limitado/a limited
limpiar el cuarto de baño to clean the bathroom
limpio/a clean
la *línea* line
liso/a straight
la *literatura* literature
la *llamada* call
llamar (por teléfono) to call / telephone
llamarse (me llamo …) to be called (my name is …)
la *llave* key
la *llegada* arrival
llegar to arrive / get to
llegar a ser to become
lleno/a full

llevar   to wear / take
llevar una vida (sana)   to lead a (healthy) life
llevarse bien / mal con   to get on (well / badly) with
llorar   to cry
llover   to rain
loco/a   mad
luchar   to fight
luego   then
el lugar   place
en lugar de   instead of
los lugares públicos   public places
lujoso/a   luxurious
lunes   Monday
la luz   light

M

la madre   mother
la madre soltera   single mother
la madrugada   very early in the morning
maduro/a   mature
el magisterio   degree for becoming a primary school teacher
mal   badly
mal diseñado/a   badly designed
hacer mal tiempo   to be bad weather
maleducado/a   rude
la maleta   suitcase
malo/a   bad
lo malo   the bad thing
maltratar   to abuse
el maltrato   abuse
mandar (un texto)   to send (a text message)
la manera   way
las manos   hands
mantener   to keep
mantenerse en forma   to keep fit
la mantequilla   butter
la manzana   apple
el mapa   map
el maquillaje   make-up
la máquina   machine
maravillosamente   wonderfully
maravilloso/a   marvellous
la marca (la ropa de marca)   make (designer clothes)
de marca   branded

marcar un número   to dial a number
el marido   husband
los mariscos   seafood
martes   Tuesday
marzo   March
el masaje   massage
más   more
más de   more than
más que nada   more than anything
la mascota   pet
masculino   boys'
matar   to kill
las matemáticas   maths
el matrimonio   marriage
máximo/a   maximum
mayo   May
mayor   older
la mayoría   the majority
el / la mecánico/a   mechanic
la medianoche   midnight
media pensión   half board
las medias   stockings / tights
el / la médico/a   doctor
la medida   measure
medio/a   average
el medio ambiente   environment
en medio de   in the middle of
por medio   through the middle
el / la mejor   the best
a lo mejor   probably
lo mejor   the best
mejor   better
mejorar   to improve
menos   less
el mensaje   message
el mensajero instantáneo   Instant Messenger
a menudo   often
el mercado   market
la merienda   snack / picnic
la merluza   hake
la mermelada   jam
el mes   month
el metro   underground train system
la mezquita   mosque
el microondas   microwave (oven)
mientras   while
mientras que   while
miércoles   Wednesday
mil   thousand
mil dos   one thousand and two

el militar   soldier
un millón   million
mínimo/a   minimum
mirar   to look at / watch
la Misa de Gallo   Midnight Mass
mismo/a   same
al mismo tiempo   at the same time
la mitad   half
mixto/a   mixed
la mochila   rucksack / school bag
la moda   fashion
moderno/a   modern
mojarse   to get wet
me molesta   it bothers me
molestar   to annoy
de momento   at the moment
el monedero   purse
la montaña   mountain
la montaña rusa   roller coaster (theme park ride)
montar   to ride / go on a ride (at a theme park)
montar a caballo   to go horse riding
montar en bici   to ride a bike
el monumento   monument
la moqueta   fitted carpet
morado/a   purple
moreno/a   (dark) brown
morir   to die
mostrar   to show
motivar   to motivate
el motivo   reason
una moto(cicleta)   motorbike
el móvil (teléfono móvil)   mobile (mobile phone)
muchos/as   many
mudarse   to move house
el mueble   furniture
la muerte   death
muerto/a   dead
la mujer   woman
la multa   fine
el mundo   world
el mundo laboral   the world of work
el museo   museum
la música   music
muy   very

N

el nacimiento   birth
la nacionalidad   nationality
nada   nothing
nadar   to swim
nadie   no one
(la) naranja   orange
la nariz   nose
la natación   swimming
la naturaleza   nature
navegar la red   to surf the internet
navegar por Internet   to surf the internet
la Navidad   Christmas
necesario/a   necessary
necesitar   to need
negativo/a   negative
el negocio   business
negro/a   black
nervioso/a   nervous
nevar   to snow
la nevera / el frigorífico   fridge
la nieta   granddaughter
el nieto   grandson
la nieve   snow
la niñera   nanny
el / la niño/a   child
el nivel   level
el nivel del mar   sea level
la noche   night
la Nochebuena   Christmas Eve
la Nochevieja   New Year's Eve
nocivo/a   harmful
no fumador   no smoking
no hacer nada   to do nothing
el nombre   (first) name
el noreste   north-east
normalmente   normally
el noroeste   north-west
el norte   north
la nota   mark
notable   very good
las notas   marks
las noticias   news
novecientos   nine hundred
noventa   ninety
la novia   girlfriend
noviembre   November
el novio   boyfriend
estar nublado   to be cloudy
el nuestro / la nuestra   ours
nueve   nine

una nueva construcción   new development (housing)
nuevo/a   new
numeroso/a   large / numerous
nunca   never

O

obediente   obedient
el objetivo   aim / objective
obligatorio/a   compulsory
la obra benéfica   charitable work
las obras   building work
el /la obrero/a   worker
observar   to observe
obtener   to get / obtain
ochenta   eighty
ocho   eight
ochocientos   eight hundred
el ocio   leisure
octubre   October
odiar   to hate
el oeste   west
ofender   to offend
la oferta (especial)   (special) offer
la oficina (de correos)   (post) office
ofrecer   to offer
los ojos   eyes
el olor   smell
olvidar   to forget
olvidarse   to forget
once   eleven
la ONG (Organización No Gubernamental)   NGO (non-governmental organisation)
la opción   option
opinar   to give your opinion
la oportunidad   opportunity / chance
optar   to choose / opt
(de color) oro   gold
optativo/a   optional
el ordenador   computer
el ordenador portátil (el portátil)   laptop computer (laptop)
las orejas   ears
la organización benéfica   charity
orgulloso/a   proud
el otoño   autumn
el oxígeno   oxygen

P

paciente   patient
el padrastro   stepfather
el padre   father
la paga (semanal)   pocket money
pagar   to pay
pagar bien   to pay well
pagar mal   to pay badly
la página   page
el país   country
el pájaro   bird
la palabra   word
el palacio   palace
las palomitas   popcorn
el pan   bread
el / la panadero/a   baker
la pantalla   screen
los pantalones   trousers
Papá Noel   Father Christmas
el papel   paper
el papel higiénico   toilet paper
el paquete   parcel / packet
la parada   stop
el parador   state-run hotel
el paraguas   umbrella
parecer   to seem
parecido/a   similar
la pared   all
la pareja   couple
los parientes   relatives
el paro   unemployment
en el paro   unemployed
el parque acuático   water park
el parque de atracciones   theme park
el parque infantil   playground
el parque temático   theme park
la participación   participation
participar   to participate
el partido   game / match
pasado/a (de moda)   old-fashioned
el pasaporte   passport
pasar   to spend (time)
pasar la aspiradora   to hoover
pasar lista   to take the register
pasarlo bien / mal   to have a good / bad time

el pasatiempo hobby
    pasearse to walk / stroll
el paseo
    marítimo promenade
el pasillo hallway
el (un) paso (a) step
el pastel cake
la patata potato
las patatas fritas chips / crisps
el patio patio
las pecas freckles
    pedir to ask for
    pedir permiso to ask for permission
el peinado hairstyle
    pelearse to fight
la película film
la película de acción action film / thriller
la película de horror horror film
la película romántica romantic film
el peligro danger
    peligroso/a dangerous
    pelirrojo/a red-haired
el pelo hair
la peluquería hairdresser's
el / la peluquero/a hairdresser
los pendientes earrings
    pensar to think
la pensión guesthouse
    pensión completa full board
    peor worse / worst
    pequeño/a small
    perder to lose / miss
    perderse to get lost
    perezoso/a lazy
el periódico newspaper
el periodismo journalism
el / la periodista journalist
el periquito parakeet
el permiso permission
el permiso de conducir driving licence
se permite (fumar) (smoking) is allowed
    pero but
el perrito caliente hot dog
la persiana blind
la pesadilla nightmare
el pescado fish
    pesimista pessimistic
el petróleo oil
    picante spicy
a pie on foot

la piedra stone
la pierna leg
los pies feet
el ping-pong table tennis
las pintadas graffiti
el / la pintor(a) painter
la piscina swimming pool
el piso flat (housing)
la pista ski slope / runway
la pizarra board
las placas solares solar panels
    planchar to do the ironing
los planes plans
el planeta planet
la planta floor / storey / plant
(de color) plata silver
el plátano banana
el plato dish
la playa beach
la plaza square
la plaza mayor main square
la plaza de toros bullring
la población population
    pobre poor
los pobres poor people
la pobreza poverty
un poco a little
    poco/a little / few
    poder to be able to
el / la policía police officer
el polideportivo sports centre
el / la político/a politician
el pollo chicken
el polo norte north pole
    poner de los nervios to get on one's nerves
    poner el lavaplatos to put the dishwasher on
    poner la mesa to set the table
    ponerse to put on (clothes)
    ponerse a to begin to
    ponerse de pie to stand up
    por eso therefore
    por lo tanto therefore
    por otro lado on the other hand
    porque because
el porro joint / spliff
el portátil laptop
    positivo/a positive
la postal postcard
    practicar to do
    practicar deporte to play sport
    practicar la pesca to go fishing

    practicar la vela to go sailing
las prácticas laborales work experience
el precio price
    precioso/a beautiful
    preferir to prefer
la pregunta question
    preguntar to ask
el prejuicio prejudice
la preocupación worry
    preocupado/a worried
    preocupante worrying
    preocupar(se) to worry
    preparar to prepare
la presentación (oral) (oral) presentation
    presente present
la presión pressure
el préstamo lending
la prima female cousin
    primario/a primary
la primavera spring
    primera clase first class
en primera línea de mar right on the seafront
los primeros auxilios first aid
el primo male cousin
al principio at first
    privado/a private
    probar to have a go / try
    probarse to try on
el problema problem
    producir to produce
el producto product
el / la profesor(a) teacher
el programa programme
la prohibición ban
    prohibido/a banned
    prohibir to prohibit / forbid
    prometer to promise
    pronto soon / ready
la propina tip
    proporcionar to provide
el propósito aim
    proteger to protect
la proteína protein
    provocar to cause / provoke
la prueba test
la publicidad advertising
    público/a public ('state' when referring to schools)
el pueblo village / small town
    puedo I can
el puerto port
los pulmones lungs
la pulsera bracelet

punto dot
puntocom .com
el *punto de vista* point of view
puro/a pure / clean
púrpura purple

Q

¡qué asco! how disgusting
quedarse to stay
la *queja* complaint
quejarse to complain
quemar to burn
querer to want / love
querer decir to mean
el *queso* cheese
quiero I want
la *química* chemistry
quince fifteen
la *quinceañera* party for a girl's 15th birthday
quinientos five hundred
quitar la mesa to clear the table

R

el *racismo* racism
racista racist
el *Ramadán* Ramadan
rápidamente quickly
raramente rarely
raro/a strange
el (un) *rato* (short) time / a little while
el *ratón* mouse
la *reacción* reaction
realista realistic
el / la *recepcionista* receptionist
recibir to receive
reciclable recyclable
reciclar to recycle
recomendar to recommend
reconocer to recognise
el *recreo* break (time)
el *recuerdo* memory
el *recurso* resource
la *red* network
reducir to reduce
regalar to give (as a present)
el *regalo* present
la *región* region
la *regla* ruler / rule
regresar to return
la *rehabilitación* rehabilitation

rehabilitar to rehabilitate
reír to laugh
la *relación* relationship
relacionarse to relate to / get to know
relajarse to relax
la *religión* religion
rellenar to fill in
RENFE State railway in Spain
renovable renewable
repartir to share / give out
repasar to revise
el *reproductor de MP3* MP3 player
la *residencia para ancianos* retirement home
residencial residential
el *residuo* waste
los *residuos químicos* chemical waste
respetar to respect
el *respeto* respect
respirar to breathe
respiratorio/a breathing / respiratory
la *responsabilidad* responsibility
responsable responsible
la *respuesta* reply / answer
el *resultado* result
el *resumen* summary
el *retraso* delay
reunirse to meet / get together
reutilizar to reuse
la *revista* magazine
los *Reyes Magos* the Three Kings / Three Wise Men
rico/a tasty / rich
riguroso/a strict / tough
el *riesgo* risk
el *río* river
rizado/a curly
robar to steal
las *rodillas* knees
rojo/a red
la *ropa* clothes
(de color) *rosa* pink
rubio/a blond
el *ruido* noise
ruidosamente noisily
ruidoso/a noisy
la *rutina* routine

S

sábado Saturday
saber to know
sabroso/a tasty
el *sacapuntas* pencil sharpener
sacar buenas notas to get good marks
sacar malas notas to get bad marks
sacar (dinero) to raise money
sacar fotos to take pictures
sacar la basura to take out the rubbish
el *saco de dormir* sleeping bag
la *sala de espera* waiting room
la *sala de profesores* staff room
el *salario* salary
el *salchichón* salami-style sausage
salgo I leave / go out
la *salida* exit
salir to go out
salir con los amigos to go out with friends
salir de marcha to go out (drinking)
el *salón* lounge
el *salón de actos* assembly hall
la *salud* health
saludable healthy
la *sangría* Sangria (mixture of fruit and wine)
sanitario/a sanitary / health
sano/a healthy
el *santo* saint's day
sé I know how to
el / la *secretario/a* secretary
secundario/a secondary
seguir (+ -ando / -iendo) to carry on
según according to
de *segunda mano* second hand
la *seguridad* safety
seguro/a safe / secure / sure
el *seguro (del coche)* (car) insurance
seis six

seiscientos (seiscientas) six hundred
el sello stamp
la selva jungle
las selvas tropicales tropical forests
los semáforos traffic lights
la semana week
la semana pasada last week
la Semana Santa Easter Holidays / Holy Week
sencillo/a simple
el senderismo hiking
la sensación sensation
sensible sensitive
sentarse to sit
el sentimiento feeling
sentir(se) to feel
separado/a separated
separar to separate
septiembre September
la sequía drought
la serie policíaca crime series
seropositivo/a HIV positive
sesenta sixty
setecientos (setecientas) seven hundred
setenta seventy
severo/a strict
si if
la sidra cider
siempre always
la sierra mountain range
siete seven
el silencio silence
el sillón armchair
simpático/a nice
sin duda without a doubt
sin embargo nevertheless / however
los sin hogar homeless people
sin techo homeless
el síndrome de abstinencia withdrawal symptoms
el sitio place
el sitio web website
la situación situation
el sobre envelope
la sobrepoblación overpopulation
sobresaliente excellent
la sociedad society
el / la socorrista lifeguard
hacer sol to be sunny
solamente only
el soldado soldier

solicitar to apply
la solicitud application
solo/a alone
sólo only
soltar to release
soltero/a single
la solución solution
solucionar to solve
el sombrero hat
la sombrilla sunshade
son are
el sondeo survey
la sopa soup
el sótano cellar / basement
suave gentle
subir to go up / rise
la suciedad dirt
sucio/a dirty
el sudeste south-east
el sudoeste south-west
el sueldo salary
el suelo the floor
el sueño sleep / dream
sufrir to suffer
la sugerencia suggestion
el suhoor breakfast during Ramadan
el supermercado supermarket
el suplemento supplement
el sur south
suspender to fail
la sustancia química chemical substance

T

el tabaco smoking / tobacco
el tabaquismo smoking
la talla size (clothes, shoes, etc.)
el taller workshop
los talones heels
tal vez perhaps
el tamaño size
el tamaño de la letra font size
también also
tampoco nor
(ni) tampoco neither
tan so
tanto/a so much
las tapas snacks
la taquilla ticket office
tardar to take (time)
tarde late
por la tarde in the afternoon
la tarea task

la tarjeta card
la tarjeta de crédito credit card
la tarta cake / tart
la tasa rate
el té tea
el teatro theatre
el tebeo comic
el techo roof
el teclado keyboard
la tecnología technology
la telenovela soap opera
el teletrabajo working from home
la televisión plana flatscreen television
el tema theme / topic
temprano early
las tendencias trends
el tenedor fork
tener to have
tener derecho a to have the right to
tener dolor de (cabeza) to have a (head)ache
tener hambre to be hungry
tener miedo to be afraid
tener nervios to be nervous
tener que to have to
tener razón to be right
tener sed to be thirsty
tener sueño to be tired
tener suerte to be lucky
tengo I have
tengo que I have to
el tenis tennis
terminar to finish
la terraza terrace
el terreno land
el terrorismo terrorism
el texto text
la tía aunt
el tiempo weather
a tiempo completo full time
el tiempo libre free time
a tiempo parcial part time
la tienda tent / shop
la tienda de ropa clothes shop
las tijeras scissors
tímido/a shy
el tío uncle
típico/a typical
el tipo type
tirar to throw / throw away
el título university degree
la toalla towel

el *tobillo*   ankle
te *toca a ti*   it's up to you / it's your turn
tocar   to play (a musical instrument)
todavía   still
todo/a   all
todo recto   straight ahead
la *tolerancia*   tolerance
tolerante   tolerant
tomar   to have (breakfast / food / drink) / to take
tomar el sol   to sunbathe
tomar la primera / segunda / tercera calle   to take the first / second / third street
tomar un año libre / sabático   to have a gap year
torear   to fight bulls
hay *tormenta*   it's stormy
torpe   clumsy
una *torre / un bloque*   tower block
la *tortilla*   omelette
la *tortuga*   tortoise
la *tostada*   toast
tóxico/a   poisonous / toxic
el / la *trabajador(a)*   worker
trabajador(a)   hardworking
trabajar   to work
el *trabajo*   work
los *trabajos manuales*   craft subjects
traducir   to translate
el / la *traductor(a)*   translator
el *tráfico*   traffic
el *traje*   costume / outfit
el *traje de luces*   bullfighter's suit
tranquilo/a   quiet / calm
el *transporte público*   public transport
el *tranvía*   tram
el *tratamiento*   treatment
tratar   to treat
tratar de   to try to
travieso/a   naughty
trece   thirteen
treinta   thirty
treinta y uno (treinta y una)   thirty-one
el *tren*   train
el *tren de cercanías*   local train
tres   three
trescientos (trescientas)   three hundred

el *trimestre*   term
triste   sad
el *triunfo*   triumph / success
el / la *tutor(a)*   tutor

U

único/a   only
el *uniforme*   uniform
la *universidad*   university
uno   one
usar   to use
útil   useful
utilizar   to use
la *uva*   grape

V

vago/a   lazy
vale la pena   it's worth it
valer   to be worth
el *valle*   valley
los *vaqueros*   jeans
variado/a   varied
a *veces*   sometimes
el / la *vecino/a*   neighbour
vegetariano/a   vegetarian
veinte   twenty
veintiuno (veintiuna)   twenty-one
la *velocidad*   speed
vender   to sell
la *ventaja*   advantage
la *ventana*   window
ver   to see / watch (a film / television)
veranear   to spend your summer holidays
el *verano*   summer
verde   green
las *verduras*   green vegetables
el *vertedero*   rubbish tip
el *vertido*   spillage
el *vestido*   dress
vestirse   to get dressed
los *vestuarios*   changing rooms
el / la *veterinario/a*   vet
una *vez*   once
de *vez en cuando*   from time to time
vi   I saw / watched
la *vía*   track
viajar   to travel
el *viaje*   journey / travel
la *víctima*   victim
la *vida*   life
la *vida campesina*   country life

la *vida familiar*   family life
la *vida nocturna*   nightlife
la *videoconsola*   video console
el *videojuego*   video game
el *vidrio*   glass
viejo/a   old
el *viento*   wind
hacer *viento*   to be windy
viernes   Friday
el *vino*   wine
la *violencia*   violence
la *violencia doméstica*   domestic violence
violento/a   violent
visitar   to visit
la *víspera*   eve
la *vista*   view
me *visto*   I get dressed
la *vitamina*   vitamin
la *viuda*   widow
el *viudo*   widower
vivir   to live
en *vivo*   live (music)
el *vocabulario*   vocabulary
volar   to fly
el / la *voluntario/a*   volunteer
volver   to return
el *voto*   vote
la *voz*   voice
el *vuelo*   flight
vuelvo   I return

Y

y   and
ya no   no longer
ya que   because
el *yogur*   yogurt

Z

la *zapatería*   shoe shop
las *zapatillas de deporte*   trainers
los *zapatos*   shoes
la *zona*   zone / area
una *zona céntrica*   central area
la *zona peatonal*   pedestrian zone
el *zumo (de naranja)*   (orange) juice

Acknowledgements

The author and the publisher would also like to thank the following for permission to reproduce material:

Illustrations
Kathy Baxendale pp11, 13, 16, 19, 57, 65, 72, 98, 101, 104, 116, 120, 135; Mark Draisey pp58, 96, 112; Dylan Gibson p12; Celia Hart pp10, 12, 84, 101, 153, 155; Abel Ippolito p155; Dave Russell pp10, 74, 75, 97

Images
p7, students chatting: © Design Pics Inc. / Alamy; p9, boy at computer: Shutterstock; p10, A: BigStockPhoto.com, B: iStockphoto, C: Shutterstock, D: BigStockPhoto.com, E and F: 123rf.com
p16, topic banner: iStockphoto, Eli, Marga, Ángel and Javier: all iStockphoto, Fátima: Fotolia; p18, Elena: iStockphoto, Antonio: BigStockPhoto.com, Javier: I love images / Alamy, Luisa: Agencja FREE / Alamy; p20, Gabriela: iStockphoto, Juan: 123rf.com, Marta: Fotolia; p22, spa room: iStockphoto; p24, all iStockphoto; p25, man with alcohol: iStockphoto; p26, girl with hand on chin: BigStockPhoto.com, wine at table: 123rf.com; p32, topic banner: iStockphoto, A: Fotolia, B and C: iStockphoto, D: BigStockPhoto.com, E: Fotolia, F: iStockphoto; p34, two boys: John Birdsall / Alamy, woman and teen girl: Design Pics Inc./ Alamy, couple: iStockphoto; p36, Lucía: Shutterstock, Hugo: iStockphoto, Mariela and Yolanda: Shutterstock, Ramón and the Menéndez family: iStockphoto; p38, family photo: 123rf.com, family in traditional costume: 123rf.com, boy in stripy top: Fotolia; p40, smiling women and businesswoman: BigStockPhoto.com, woman ironing: Fotolia; p42, slum dwelling: iStockphoto, Peruvians sitting outside house: Thomas Cockrem / Alamy, boy holding water bucket: Jacques Jangoux / Alamy; p48, girl: Fotolia; p56, topic banner: Fotolia, cinema: Jeffery Blackler / Alamy, rock concert and footballer: Shutterstock, teenager doing homework and beach: iStockphoto; p58, girls with popcorn: iStockphoto; p59, Laura: 123rf.com, Pablo: Fotolia, Noelia: BigStockPhoto.com, Raúl: iStockphoto; p60, Mateo and Juan: iStockphoto, Alba: Fotolia, Nicolá: 123rf.com; p62, group of teenagers: Fotolia, teenage girls in restaurant: Media Minds / Alamy; p64, Luisa: iStockphoto; p66, Sara: Fotolia, Isabel: BigStockPhoto, Jorge:

iStockphoto; p72, topic banner: iStockphoto; p74, A: Greg Balfour Evans / Alamy, B: PhotoAlto / Ale Ventura / Getty Images, C and D: Fotolia; p76, A: Shutterstock, B and C: iStockphoto, D: kevin wheal spain / Alamy; p78, Centauro car hire office: Life File Photo Library Ltd / Alamy, AVE trains: Atlanpic / Alamy; p80, skier: Fotolia, snowboarder: 123rf.com, L. American dancing and scuba divers: iStockphoto; p82, London hackney carriage: Tony French / Alamy, London Oxford Street: iStockphoto; p88, Mexican crafts: iStockphoto, Day of the Dead shrine: Charles O. Cecil / Alamy, tacos: Fotolia, beach and Aztec pyramid: iStockphoto; p96, topic banner: Fotolia; p99, white farm buildings, block of flats and white villa: iStockphoto, red-brick terraced houses: BigStockPhoto; p100, village in forest: Fotolia, white village and green mountain range: BigStockPhoto.com; p102, shopping centre: mpworks / Alamy, Spanish village: iStockphoto; p106, clock and grapes and table food: iStockphoto, Christmas procession: AFP / Getty Images, nativity scene: BigStockPhoto; p112, topic banner: iStockphoto, wall of graffiti: 123rf.com; p118, cycle track and pedestrian zone: Ukman / Alamy, nautical petrol tanker: AFP / Getty Images; p119, carbon footprint: iStockphoto; p124, Fuente Vaqueros: Fotolia; p132, topic banner: iStockphoto, modern building: Fotolia; p134, students facing blackboard: Fotolia; p136, group of students: iStockphoto; p138, teenagers together: iStockphoto; p140, Ana and Pedro: iStockphoto; p142, girl with hands on face: Fotolia; p148, topic banner: Shutterstock, Laura: Shutterstock, Ramón: Antenna / Getty Images, Sara: iStockphoto; p150, girl in black bow tie and waistcoat: Fotolia; p152, beach: Fotolia, blond boy: 123rf.com, black boy: BigStockPhoto.com, brunette girl: Fotolia, boy in sunglasses: iStockphoto; p154, skyscraper office block: iStockphoto; p156, Luisa: 123rf.com, Susana: iStockphoto, José: BigStockPhoto.com; p158, teenagers studying: iStockphoto; p159, bullfighter: iStockphoto; p164, using microscopes: 123rf.com.

Every effort has been made to trace the copyright holders but if any have been inadvertently overlooked the publisher will be pleased to make the necessary arrangements at the first opportunity.